WALKING THE LAKE DISTRICT FELLS
BORROWDALE
SCAFELL PIKE, CATBELLS, GREAT GABLE AND THE DERWENTWATER FELLS

MARK RICHARDS

CICERONE

© Mark Richards 2021
Second edition 2021
Reprinted in 2025 (with updates)
ISBN: 978 1 78631 038 5
eISBN: 978 1 78362 846 9

Originally published as *Lakeland Fellranger*, 2008
ISBN: 978 1 85284 540 7

Printed in China on responsibly sourced paper on behalf of Latitude Press Ltd.

A catalogue record for this book is available from the British Library.
All photographs are by the author unless otherwise stated.
All artwork is by the author.

Maps are reproduced with permission from HARVEY Maps, www.harveymaps.co.uk

Cicerone's EU representative for GPSR compliance is Easy Access System Europe, Mustamäe tee 50, 10621 Tallinn, Estonia. Email gpsr.requests@easproject.com.

Updates to this Guide

While every effort is made by our authors to ensure the accuracy of guidebooks as they go to print, changes can occur during the lifetime of an edition. Any updates that we know of for this guide will be on the Cicerone website (www.cicerone.co.uk/1038/updates), so please check before planning your trip. We also advise that you check information about such things as transport, accommodation and shops locally. Even rights of way can be altered over time. We are always grateful for information about any discrepancies between a guidebook and the facts on the ground, sent by email to updates@cicerone.co.uk.

Register your book: To sign up to receive free updates, special offers and GPX files where available, register your book at www.cicerone.co.uk.

Front cover: Gully view into the upper Newlands Beck valley from High Spy
Title page: Skew Gill from the path south of Styhead Tarn

CONTENTS

Map key 5
Volumes in the series 6
Author preface 7
Starting points 8

INTRODUCTION 13
Valley bases 13
Fix the Fells 14
Using this guide 15
Safety and access 17
Additional online resources 18

FELLS 19
1 Allen Crags 19
2 Armboth Fell 26
3 Base Brown 32
4 Bell Crags 38
5 Bleaberry Fell 45
6 Brandreth 54
7 Castle Crag 63
8 Catbells 72
9 Eagle Crag 82
10 Glaramara 87
11 Grange Fell 98
12 Great Crag 112
13 Great End 119
14 Great Gable 127
15 Green Gable 142
16 Grey Knotts 150
17 High Rigg 158
18 High Seat 166
19 High Spy 175
20 High Tove 185
21 Maiden Moor 191

22	Raven Crag	198
23	Rosthwaite Fell	203
24	Scafell Pike	212
25	Seathwaite Fell	226
26	Sergeant's Crag	231
27	Ullscarf	237
28	Walla Crag	248

RIDGE ROUTES 256
1 The High Spy ridge 256
2 Around the Jaws of Borrowdale 259
3 The Gillercomb Skyline 263
4 Glaramara ridge walk 267

More to explore 271
Useful contacts 272
A fellranger's glossary 273
The Lake District Fells 277

MAP KEY

Key to route maps and topos

 Route on a defined path

12 **Starting point**

 Route on an intermittent or undefined path

4 **Route number** (on topos)

▲ **Fell summit featured in this guide** (on maps)

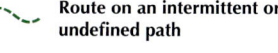 **Fell summit featured in this guide** (on maps)

3 **Route number** (on maps)

N

0 ____ 500
_____ m
1:40,000

Harvey map legend

 Lake, small tarn, pond
 River, footbridge
Wide stream
Narrow stream
 Peat hags
 Marshy ground

Contours change from brown to grey where the ground is predominantly rocky outcrops, small crags and other bare rock.

Improved pasture
Rough pasture
Fell or moorland
Open forest or woodland
Dense forest or woodland
Felled or new plantation
Forest ride or firebreak
Settlement

 Boundary, maintained
Boundary, remains

On moorland, walls, ruined walls and fences are shown. For farmland, only the outer boundary wall or fence is shown.

Contour (15m interval)
Index contour (75m interval)
Auxiliary contour
Scree, spoil heap
Boulder field
Scattered rock and boulders
Predominantly rocky ground
Major crag, large boulder
O.S. trig pillar, large cairn
Spot height (from air survey)

Dual carriageway
Main road (fenced)
Minor road (unfenced)
Track or forest road
Footpath or old track
Intermittent path
Long distance path
Powerline, pipeline
Building, ruin or sheepfold, shaft

The representation of a road, track or footpath is no evidence of the existence of a right of way.

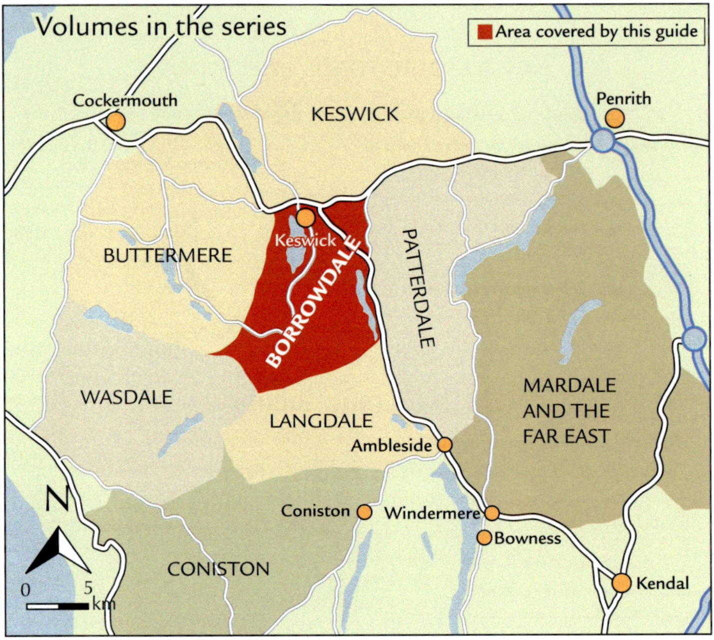

WALKING THE LAKE DISTRICT FELLS – BORROWDALE

Bird's-eye view of Borrowdale from Rosthwaite Fell (photo: Maggie Allan)

AUTHOR PREFACE

This land of living dreams we call the Lake District is a cherished blessing to know, love and share. As we go about our daily routines, we may take a fleeting moment to reflect that someone, somewhere, will be tramping up a lonely gill or along an airy ridge, peering from a lofty summit or gazing across a wind-blown tarn and taking lingering solace from its timeless beauty. The trappings of modern life thrust carpet and concrete under our feet, and it is always wonderful to walk the region's sheep trods and rough trails and to imprint our soles upon the fells. This series sets out to give you the impetus and inspiration to make space in your schedule to explore them time and again, in myriad different ways.

However, the regular paths of long tradition deserve our care. Progressively many of the main paths are being re-set with cobbles and pitching by organisations such as Fix the Fells, to whose work you have contributed by buying this guide. But in many instances, the best consideration we can give these pathways is rest. The modern fellwanderer should show a new 'green' awareness by choosing to tread lightly on the land and to find new ways around the hills. One of the underlying impulses of this guide is to protect these beloved fells by presenting a diversity of route options for each and every fell – and also, in this new edition, recommending 'fell-friendly' routes to each summit which are less susceptible to erosion.

Another feature of this latest incarnation of Fellranger, apart from the smaller size to slip in your pocket or pack, is the addition of a selection of inspiring ridge routes at the end of each volume for those of you who like to spend a little longer with your head and feet in the heavenly realms, relishing the summit views and the connections between the felltops, as well as some accompanying online resources for readers with a digital bent.

Mark Richards

STARTING POINTS

	Location	Description	GR	Access	Ascents described from here
1	Rosthwaite	Car park in centre of village	257 148	NT, B	Castle Crag, Grange Fell, Great Crag, High Spy
2	Quayfoot	NT car park in woods off road bend	253 168	NT, B	Grange Fell
3	Grange-in-Borrowdale	Sizeable parking area beside B5289 N of village	256 176	FP, B	Castle Crag, Catbells, Grange Fell, High Spy, Maiden Moor
4	High Brandelhow Jetty	Jetty served by the Keswick Launch	252 197	L	Catbells, Maiden Moor
5	Hawse End Jetty	Jetty served by the Keswick Launch	251 213	L	Catbells
6	Uzzicar	Large layby S of farm access-track junction	232 217	FP	Catbells
7	Chapel Bridge, Little Town	Sizeable layby beside bridge (fills quickly at peak times) or nearby field at Little Town	231 193	FP	Catbells, High Spy, Maiden Moor
8	Black Sail Youth Hostel	Walk/bike-in youth hostel at the head of Ennerdale	195 123	F	Brandreth, Great Gable, Green Gable
9	Gatesgarth	Farmer-owned car park with overflow in yard behind buildings	195 150	PP, B	Brandreth, Great Gable, Grey Knotts
10	Honister Pass	Large visitor-centre parking area on the pass (plus NT car park beside YHA hostel)	225 135	PP, NT, B	Brandreth, Great Gable, Green Gable, Grey Knotts
11	Little Gatesgarthdale	Generous layby on road bend beside beck	230 136	FP, B	Grey Knotts
12	Seathwaite	Verge parking S of Seathwaite Bridge and in allocated field at Seathwaite Farm	235 123	FP	Allen Crags, Base Brown, Brandreth, Glaramara, Great End, Great Gable, Green Gable, Grey Knotts, Scafell Pike, Seathwaite Fell

	Location	Description	GR	Access	Ascents described from here
13	Seatoller	Car park next to bus turning area	245 137	NT, B	Castle Crag, Glaramara, Grey Knotts, High Spy, Rosthwaite Fell
14	Stonethwaite	Copious verge parking beside road to hamlet; fills quickly at peak times	261 138	FP	Allen Crags, Eagle Crag, Glaramara, Great Crag, Rosthwaite Fell, Sergeant's Crag, Ullscarf
15	Watendlath	NT car park in hamlet	276 163	NT	Bell Crags, Grange Fell, Great Crag, High Seat, High Tove, Ullscarf
16	Surprise View	Two generous parking areas in woods beside road	268 189	FP	Grange Fell, High Seat
17	Ashness Bridge	Large car park S of bridge	269 196	FP	Bleaberry Fell, Grange Fell, High Seat, Walla Crag
18	Kettlewell	Popular car park beside B5289	267 195	NT, B	Grange Fell
19	Great Wood	Large car park in woodland E of B5289	272 214	NT, B	Bleaberry Fell, Walla Crag
20	Keswick (Lake Road)	Large town-centre car park	265 233	PP, B	Bleaberry Fell, Walla Crag
21	Tewet Tarn verge	Very limited verge parking on road bend	306 239	FP	High Rigg
22	St John's in the Vale Church	Parking area by church (give preference to churchgoers)	306 225	FP	High Rigg
23	Causeway Foot, Naddle valley	Layby opposite Causeway Foot Farm	293 218	FP, B	Bleaberry Fell, High Seat
24	Rough How Bridge	Verge parking along old road parallel to A591	300 206	FP, B	Bleaberry Fell, High Seat, Raven Crag
25	Legburthwaite (A591 layby)	Verge/layby parking at junction	316 194	FP, B	High Rigg
26	Thirlmere Dam	Small parking area on W side of dam	307 189	FP	Raven Crag

STARTING POINTS *continued*

	Location	Description	GR	Access	Ascents described from here
27	Armboth	Large United Utilities car park with toilets	305 172	PP	Armboth Fell, High Tove, Raven Crag
28	Dob Gill	Large United Utilities car park with toilets	316 140	PP	Armboth Fell, Bell Crags, Ullscarf
29	Steel End	Small United Utilities car park	320 130	PP	Ullscarf
30	Old Dungeon Ghyll, Great Langdale	NT car park	286 061	NT, B	Allen Crags, Scafell Pike
31	Brotherilkeld	Generous layby W of phonebox at the foot of Hardknott Pass	210 011	FP	Scafell Pike
32	Wha House	Small car park N of Wha House Farm	200 009	FP	Scafell Pike
33	Wasdale Head	NT car park	182 075	NT	Scafell Pike
34	Wasdale Green	Lots of rough parking (but fills quickly in season)	186 085	FP	Great End, Great Gable, Scafell Pike

FP – free parking

PP – pay parking

NT – National Trust (free to members)

B – on a bus route (in season)

L – served by the Keswick Launch (in season)

F – only accessible by foot or bike

Scots pine on Castle Crag

Looking to the distant Blencathra from the main walkers' highway from Honister to Green Gable

INTRODUCTION

Valley bases

No valley better epitomises the romance of mountain Lakeland than Borrowdale. From Keswick, venture past Derwentwater and through the dramatic Jaws of Borrowdale to the traditional settlements of Rosthwaite, Seatoller and Seathwaite or to Stonethwaite, the entry-point for the wild glen of Langstrath. To the west the Newlands valley holds further allure, and to the east lies the Thirlmere valley, offering quiet ascents onto the unfrequented central ridge from Bleaberry Fell to Ullscarf. In between hides the upland sanctuary of Watendlath.

Trees lend so much to the early charm, but with altitude you will find raw scrawny fell country – domain of stocky Herdwick sheep – and mighty crags: serious mountain terrain demanding the utmost respect and preparation. Many ascend the Scafell massif and Great Gable from Seathwaite-in-Borrowdale, with such ascents requiring smart choices in regard to route, timing and weather. This guide will help you make these choices, but sound navigation and the proper use of a map are also essential skills.

Facilities

Keswick is known far and wide as the capital of Lakeland adventure. Easily accessed, it has hotels, guest houses, B&Bs and humbler pitches to serve all manner of preferences and budgets. Hotels, pubs and tearooms abound, reflecting the special place the region holds in people's hearts.

Getting around

Until the early 1970s Keswick was served by a train from Penrith, but now the car and bus are supreme. Throughout the year the 555, X5/X4 and Borrowdale Rambler bus services operate regularly along the primary valley roads, propelling you to and from the wondrous fells.

Parking is not to be taken for granted anywhere in this popular park. Always allow time to find an alternative parking place, if not to switch to a different plan for your day or just set out directly from your door – perfectly possible if you find accommodation within any of the main valleys. Always take care to park safely and only in laybys and car parks, not on the side of the narrow country roads. Consult the 'Starting points' table to find out where the best parking places (and bus stops) are to be found. Note that although, in general, one preferred starting point is specified for each route, there may be alternative starting points nearby should you arrive and find your chosen spot taken.

Fix the Fells

The Fellranger series has always highlighted the hugely important work of the Fix the Fells project in repairing the most seriously damaged fell paths. The mighty challenge has been a great learning curve and the more recent work, including complex guttering, is quite superb. It ensures a flat foot-fall where possible, is easy to use in ascent and descent, and excess water escapes efficiently, minimising future damage.

The original National Trust and National Park Authority partnership came into being in 2001 and expanded with the arrival of Natural England, with additional financial support from the Friends of the Lake District and now the Lake District Foundation (www.lakedistrictfoundation.org). But – and it's a big but – the whole endeavour needs to raise £500,000 a year to function. This enormous figure is needed to keep pace with the challenges caused by the joint tyranny of boots and brutal weather. The dedicated and highly skilled team, including volunteers, deserve our sincerest gratitude for making our hill paths secure and sympathetic to their setting. It is a task without end, including pre-emptive repair to stop paths from washing out in the first place.

Bearing in mind that a metre of path costs upwards of £200, there is every good reason to cultivate the involvement of fellwalkers in a cause that must be dear to our hearts… indeed our soles! Please make a beeline for www.fixthefells.co.uk to make a donation, however modest. Your commitment will, to quote John Muir, 'make the mountains glad'.

Using this guide

Unlike other guidebooks which show a single or limited number of routes up the Lakeland fells, the purpose of the Fellranger series has always been to offer the independent fellwalker the full range of approaches and paths available and invite them to combine them to create their own unique experiences. A valuable by-product of this approach has been to spread effects of walkers' footfall more evenly over the path network.

This guide is divided into two parts: 'Fells' describes ascents of each of the 28 fells covered by this volume, arranged in alphabetical order; 'Ridge routes' describes a small selection of popular routes linking these summits.

Lane to Rosthwaite (photo: Maggie Allan)

Fells

In the first part, each fell chapter begins with an information panel outlining the character of the fell and potential starting points (numbered in blue on the guide overview map and the accompanying 1:40,000 HARVEY fell map, and listed – with grid refs – in 'Starting points' in the introduction). The panel also suggests neighbouring fells to tackle at the same time, including any classic ridge routes. The 'fell-friendly route' – one which has been reinforced by the national park or is less vulnerable to erosion – is also identified for those particularly keen to minimise their environmental impact.

After a fuller introduction to the fell, summarising the main approaches and expanding on its unique character and features, come the route descriptions. Paths on the fell are divided into numbered sections. Ascent routes are grouped according to starting point and described as combinations of (the red-numbered) path sections. The opportunities for exploration are endless. For each ascent route, the ascent and distance involved are given, along with a walking time that should be achievable in most conditions by a reasonably fit group of walkers keen to soak up the views rather than just tick off the summit. (Over time, you will be able to gauge your own likely timings against these figures.)

In many instances a topo diagram is provided alongside the main fell map to help with visualisation and route planning. When features shown on the maps or diagrams appear in the route descriptions for the first time (or the most significant time for navigational purposes), they are highlighted in **bold**, to help you trace the routes as easily as possible.

As a good guide should also be a revelation, panoramas are provided for a small number of key summits, and panoramas for every fell in this guide can be downloaded free from www.cicerone.co.uk (see 'Additional online resources' below). These name the principal fells and key features in the direction of view.

Advice is also given at the end of each fell chapter on routes to neighbouring fells and safe lines of descent should the weather close in. In fellwalking, as in any mountain activity, retreat is often the greater part of valour.

Ridge routes

The second part of this guide describes some classic ridge routes in the Borrowdale area. Beginning with an information panel giving the start and finish points, the summits included and a very brief overview, each ridge

Raven Crag from Fisher Crag

route is described step by step, from start to finish, with the summits and key features highlighted in **bold** in the text to help you orientate yourself with the HARVEY route map provided. Some final suggestions are included for expeditions which you can piece together yourself from the comprehensive route descriptions in 'Fells'.

Appendices

For more information about facilities and services in the Lake District, some useful phone numbers and websites are listed in 'Useful contacts'. 'A fellranger's glossary' offers a glossary to help newcomers decode the language of the fells, as well as explanations of some of the most intriguing place names you might come across in this area. The 'Alphabetical list of fells in the Fellranger series' is a comprehensive list of all the fells included in this eight-volume series, to help you decide which volume you need to buy next!

Safety and access

Always take a map and compass with you; make a habit of regularly looking at your map and take pride in learning how to take bearings from it. In mist this will be a time-saver and potentially a life-saver. The map can enhance your day by showing additional landscape features and setting your walk in its wider context. That said, beware of the green dashed lines on Ordnance Survey® maps. They are public rights of way but no guarantee of an actual route on the ground. Take care to study the maps and diagrams provided carefully and plan your route according to your own capabilities and the prevailing conditions.

Please do not rely solely on your mobile phone or other electronic device for navigation. Local mountain rescue teams report that this is increasingly the main factor in many of the incidents they attend.

The author has taken care to follow time-honoured routes and keep within bounds of access, yet access and rights of way can change and are not guaranteed. Any updates that we know of to the routes in this guide will be made available on the Cicerone website, www.cicerone.co.uk/1038, and we are always grateful for information about discrepancies between a guidebook and the facts on the ground, sent by email to updates@cicerone.co.uk or by post to Cicerone Press, Juniper House, Murley Moss, Oxenholme Road, Kendal, Cumbria, LA9 7RL.

Additional online resources

Summit panoramas for all of the fells in this volume can be downloaded for free from the Cicerone website (www.cicerone.co.uk/fellranger), where you will also find a ticklist of the summits in the Walking the Lake District Fells series, should you wish to keep a log of your ascents, along with further information about the series.

1 ALLEN CRAGS 784M/2572FT

Climb it from	Seathwaite **12**, Stonethwaite **14** or Old Dungeon Ghyll (Great Langdale) **30**
Character	Rugged and remote, yet with handy access from the high point of the ancient pass between Great Langdale and Wasdale
Fell-friendly route	4
Summit grid ref	NY 236 085
Link it with	Glaramara or Great End
Part of	Glaramara ridge walk

Defined by deep valleys and sustaining the 2000ft contour for more than two miles, a ridge leads north from the saddle north of Esk Hause, with Glaramara at its mid-point. Allen Crags forms its southernmost high point, the first rise on a perennially popular fell-top trek. It's a modest bag when set against the likes of neighbouring Great End, but a good objective for those all-too-frequent days when the Scafells are obscured by mist.

The best route climbs from the Grains Gill valley (1–5), from which aspect the fell's rougher and more characterful qualities are foremost. In truth, only

↑ *Allen Crags from Great End*

from this side can the fell be considered a primary objective for a circular fell walk. The greater ridge walk, via Allen Crags, Glaramara and Rosthwaite Fell, goes north from the saddle below Esk Hause, having come up from Stonethwaite by way of lonely Langstrath (6) or by Grains Gill, or even from Seathwaite via Styhead Pass.

Ascent from Seathwaite 12 *off map N*

Adventurous options breaking pathless from the regular valley way

Via Allen Gill →*4.5km/2¾ miles* ↑*610m/2000ft* ⏱*2hr 25min*
1 Follow the valley bridleway through the farmyard via gates, advancing to **Stockley Bridge**, from where two handsome packhorse-bridge routes divide. After the hand-gate turn left, beside the wall, on a path up **Grains Gill**. There are several options from this point: Routes **2–5**.

2 Having followed Route **1**, shortly after the next hand-gate, with obvious path pitching, bear half-left down to a broad wooden footbridge and then head upstream. It is easier to remain at beck level initially. With the approach of the wooded gorge, bear left up the bank to enjoy a grandstand view of the waterfall in Ruddy Gill. Follow the moraine ridge. When you come to **Allen Gill** follow it on the right bank, climbing steeply, keeping to the grass until you reach the source, just below the ridge path from Glaramara. Go right and pass immediately to the right of **High House Tarn**, from whose northeastern edge you can get a great view of the Langdale Pikes with the tarn in the foreground. Even more photogenic is the tiny rock-girt Lincomb Tarn, set among the outcrops just a little further up (to the south). Follow the stony ridge path direct to the summit cairn.

Via Ruddy Gill →*4.7km/3 miles* ↑*610m/2000ft* ⏱*2hr 40min*
3 Having followed Route **1**, the less taxing option is to stay with the sheltered **Ruddy Gill** path, scene of considerable pitching work in recent years. This path advances over a footbridge where the gill begins to race dramatically down a gully and plunges into Allen

1 Allen Crags

Gill to form Grains Gill. Further upstream it is worth stepping aside to admire the cascades. Stay with the modern hard trail to the saddle.

If you prefer a grassy climb, take a short diversion after the footbridge, off to the left, on an old path. Bear half-left as you approach a second ford across a gill. A little-used grass path leads up the bank. Pass a small flat outcrop and bear half-left (without a path) onto the narrow grassy moraine rigg

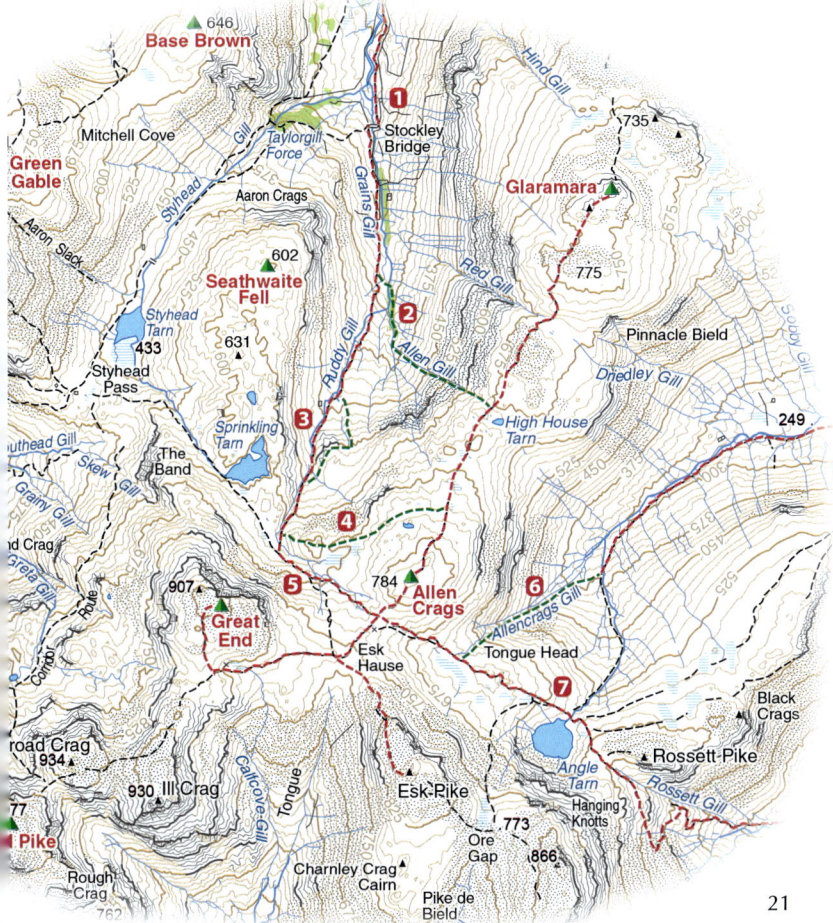

WALKING THE LAKE DISTRICT FELLS – BORROWDALE

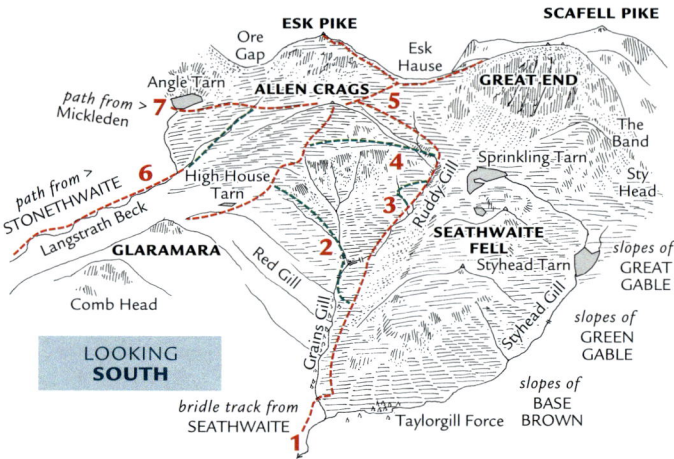

LOOKING **SOUTH**

(ridge). Then, rising easily to the skyline, bear right, crossing two tiny gills. Mount the boiler-plate slab above the prominent outcrop to gain a broad marshy shelf. Skirt this to the right (west), passing a small cairn. Cross a further gill then bear right, passing a small cairn, to regain the modern path.

4 Just as the gill turns sharp left (east) at the end of Route **3** you can climb off the main path onto an attractive, undulating spine-of-rock ridge (no path). With the craggy slope of Allen Crags ahead, bear half-left up the prominent grass ramp,

Bridle path by Ruddy Gill

1 ALLEN CRAGS

traversing wet ground between outcrops to gain the ridge path north of the fell-top. Join the path and turn back south to the summit.

5 The normal course, having set out on the Grains Gill/Ruddy Gill approach with Routes **1** and **3**, is to ford **Ruddy Gill** as it bends left and keep beside the red-soiled ravine, ignoring the right-hand branch path leading directly to Esk Hause. At the shallow saddle cross-paths go left (north) up the loose trail to the summit.

Ascent from Stonethwaite **14** *off map NE*

Via Langstrath →*9km/5½ miles* ↑*685m/2245ft* ⏲*3hr*

A 'sneaking up' process among scenery that encourages the mind to wander too, allowing you to get away from it all

6 Follow the main track from the hamlet. As you turn into the Langstrath valley choose between the bridleway (east side), reached over the footbridge, and the footpath (west side); the former is better underfoot. All the really good scenery – of which there is plenty – is exhausted by the time you reach the footbridge at the foot of Stake Beck. Cross the bridge and ignore the rising bridleway, which takes the Cumbria Way into Great Langdale. Continue on the narrow trod running along the base of Rossett Pike. The path copes well with the inevitable marsh. Where **Allencrags Gill** and the stream from Angle Tarn meet, ford and follow Allencrags Gill on an intermittent path, climbing to **Tongue Head**. Turn right towards the saddle, where, setting its sights on Allen Crags, the path winds northeast to the top.

Ascent from Old Dungeon Ghyll, Great Langdale 30 *off map E*

Via Rossett Gill →*6.7km/4¼ miles* ↑*690m/2265ft* ⊕*2hr 45min*

A long valley walk-in connects you with the main thoroughfare up to the hause.

7 From the Old Dungeon Ghyll car park advance with the valley bridleway along Mickleden to the footbridge, where the Stake Pass and Rossett Gill paths fork. Go left. The old pony route is currently being enhanced with sturdy pitching on the zig-zag beneath Bowfell's high buttresses. The path dips by the outflow of Angle Tarn and climbs Tongue Head to the Allen Crags hause. A cross-wall wind-shelter just south of the hause (marked with a cross on the HARVEY map) is a key landmark to locate. Turn right for the summit.

The summit

A single cairn on a small rock base marks this delightful top. The view is special. The Langdale Pikes, Bowfell, Esk Pike, Great End and Great Gable all feature large – a scene fit for a majestic fresco.

Safe descents

In deteriorating conditions aim to reach the saddle on the connecting ridge (with a cross-wall wind-shelter some 60 metres further S). It is SW of the summit, a matter of eight minutes' descent on a loose but obvious trail. Turn left (E) for Langstrath (**6**) or – far better – Great Langdale (**7**) in 6.4km, or right (W) for Borrowdale, following Ruddy Gill (**5**, **3**, **1**) for just over 4.8km or continuing via Styhead Pass for Wasdale Head in 6.4km (not mapped).

Ridge routes

Glaramara →*2.7km/1¾ miles* ↓*160m/525ft* ↑*130m/425ft* ⊕*1hr 10min*
Head N on the ridge path. This is one of those uncomplicated paths that never seems to get going, never clear of rock long enough to really allow you to stride out. The mid-point depression, with its cluster of pools around High House Tarn, is a place to dawdle. Beyond, the ridge bulks further and

1 ALLEN CRAGS

Allen Crags from Sprinkling Tarn

you cross two intermediate tops separated by the depression at the head of Red Gill. Cairns may lure you left from the trail for the fine westward view en route to the cairnless rock summit, with its snug wind-shelter.

Great End →*2km/1¼ miles* ↓*60m/195ft* ↑*195m/640ft* ⏲*1hr*
Descend SW to the saddle and follow the clear path SW, passing the wind-shelter and rising to the multi-cairned Esk Hause. Bear right (W). The popular trail leads up into the shallow hollow of Calf Cove. On gaining the brow bear right (N), crossing the stone-free mid-ridge to either of the cairned tops.

2 ARMBOTH FELL 479M/1572FT

Climb it from	Armboth **27** or Dob Gill **28**
Character	Gaiters are of distinct advantage when venturing to this lonely tump-top!
Fell-friendly route	1
Summit grid ref	NY 296 159
Link it with	Bell Crags or High Tove

Fells do not get more pudding-like than this squidgy squadgy lump. You are never far from water when strolling on this moor, especially around the peaty, sphagnum-encroached hollow where Launchy and Fisher Gills have a common sluggish birth. Needless to say, summit-baggers are the more likely visitors to this outpost. Thankfully there are a few outcrops to distract from its otherwise nondescript demeanour, and evidence of Celtic rock art has been spotted on rocks west of the summit, though is difficult to find. You may be lucky enough to spot the small herd of shy red deer which roams this quiet area.

Routes follow the watercourses flanking the fell, Fisher Gill (1) and Launchy Gill (4), with other options weaving up the undulating eastern (2) and southeastern (3) slopes. The Launchy Ghyll Nature Trail (5) offers a short attractive loop beside the cascading gill.

↑ *Armboth Fell's summit rocks (photo: Maggie Allan)*

Ascent from Armboth 27

Direct →*3.2km/2 miles* ↑*285m/935ft* ⏲*1hr 40min*

1 Start from the United Utilities car park. Facing out from the point of entry, go right then first left at the kissing-gate to the start of the fell path destined for Watendlath, which traverses the intervening ridge via High Tove. A clear path crosses a stout little bridge spanning **Middlesteads Gill**. Pass through a wall gap and the hurdles in a wooden sheep pen to ascend, past a group of large rocks, on a partly repaired and stepped path rising beside the forestry fence shielding **Fisher Gill**. The path switches right and enjoys a fine view across the reservoir to the Helvellyn range. Passing under a sycamore and skirting juniper, climb to a wall-gap beside the plantation fence. Keep to the footpath for a matter of 200 metres then fork half-left just after entering bracken, on a

WALKING THE LAKE DISTRICT FELLS – BORROWDALE

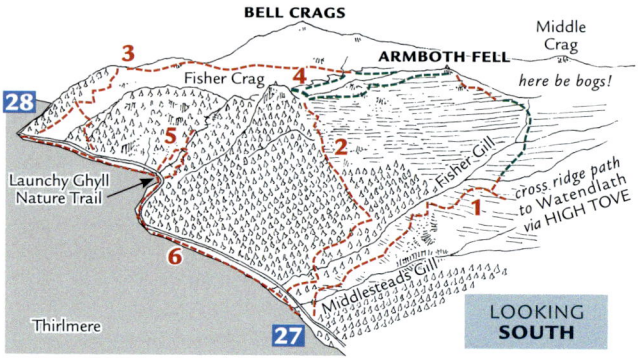

strong sheep trod, to ford a feeder-gill. Accompany the righthand rim of the shallow upper ravine of Fisher Gill, shaded by birch and rowan. As the gill winds on with ever-decreasing gradient aim half-left through sickly looking heather towards the prominent outcrop, and if you are lucky you might find the one path that leads to that very evident summit outcrop. Only the latter stages of the route can be said to be free of excitement – that is, unless you set yourself the challenge of finding the rock art!

Via Fisher Crag →*3.5km/2¼ miles* ↑*285m/935ft* ⏱*1hr 50min*

A venturesome route revelling in the prime viewpoint over Thirlmere

2 Go left along the reservoir's west-shore road to the forestry parking area and gate/stile on the right, just before the road crosses **Fisher Gill**. A forest track winds uphill, crossing Fisher Gill. Note, to the left, the old Armboth Hall summer-house perched among the trees on a knoll, finding contemporary use as a lunch shelter for forest workers. The track continues more steeply and drifts away from the gill at a left-hand bend, with plantation fencing on the right. Climb to a ladder-stile with a stone sheepfold and ruined bothy close at hand. The path wends up beside the old wall and fence to crest the moor. Carefully climb over the locked gate in the fence and climb (no path) onto the immediate top of **Fisher Crag**, where a cairn nestles among the heather. Return to the gate and head basically southwest, initially over marshy ground, to work a way up the rocky fell to the summit.

Thirlmere from Fisher Crag (photo: Maggie Allan)

Ascent from Dob Gill 28

Via Stone Hause →4.2km/2½ miles ↑285m/935ft ⏱1hr 50min

An exaggerated southerly sweep traversing the infrequently visited higher banks of Bell Crags

3 Start at the United Utilities Dob Gill car park. Exit and follow the road left (north) to where a path begins at a stile on the left and leads through a wall gateway and up the northern edge of the plantation, passing a curious empty metal tree cage, to reach the open track as it exits the forestry. Go right then quickly left to a hand-gate in the wall corner. An old shepherds' path winds steeply up the bracken-dogged fellside. As the ground eventually eases on Brown Rigg, pass a couple of old sheepfolds tucked into nooks in the outcrops. Deer-management quad vehicles exit at the top forest gate and have provided a line to follow, via Stone Hause, out across the bowl-shaped gathering grounds of **Launchy Gill**, to a ford above Launchy Tarn – actually rather a shallow lazy meander. Beyond, the tracks are soon lost. Cross the wire fence and climb the rough though gently angled slope to the summit.

Via Launchy Gill ➔ *4.7km/3 miles* ⏲ *2hr 20min*

Turn this excursion into a round trip and include the Launchy Ghyll Nature Trail (Route 5), using the lakeside road to link things together.

4 Fellwalkers with a wanderlust can make a swiping route that ignores the summit altogether. Start out with Route **3** and, having forded the upper course of Launchy Gill, amble downstream, via Launchy Tarn and the old wall beside the cascade section, and find a fence-stile where the wall resumes, approaching the forest edge. From here follow the forest-top wall and gradually rise to Fisher Crag, from where you can descend to the road via Route **2**.

Launchy Ghyll Nature Trail ➔ *0.4km/¼ mile* ⏲ *30min*

The best series of cataracts falling into Thirlmere, tumbling through the forestry, issues from the lonely wastes between Bell Crags and Armboth Fell: this is Launchy Gill.

5 The waymarked forest trail offers a relaxing stroll for casual visitors as it climbs from laybys either side of the road bridge situated midway between the Armboth and Dob Gill car parks. Halfway up a footbridge crosses the ravine. Above this point the gorge narrows and steepens; not surprisingly, the secure trail smartly turns tail, switching back down to the road. As you may suspect, the best falls lie out of sight, higher up. From the top of the steps on the southern side half-a-dozen steps signify the beginning of an old unsecured path up through the conifers to two impromptu viewing points. The top fall is supremely elegant and luxuriant. There is no access to the open fell above as the forest-bounding fence is walker-tight!

The summit

A slender rib of ice-worn rock, like the inverted hull of a boat, forms the summit, which has a small cairn precariously perched on the very top. The only evidence of visitation is a narrow trod approaching from the direction of Fisher Gill. Perhaps this lack of obvious human 'damage' is one of the fell's understated virtues. A damp plateau extends south and a solitary erratic acts as a target for otherwise aimless strolls. The southern slopes of the fell,

Summit outcrop

approaching the wide hollow of Launchy Gill, are defined by a tight, fortunately barbless fence, erected to restrict red deer.

Safe descent

The simplest course is N across a largely pathless moor. Ford Fisher Gill and join the footpath coming down from High Tove, which leads by the forest fence (**1**) to the security of the Thirlmere shore road at Armboth. The nearest habitation is to the left, beyond the dam, at Bridgend Farm (camp site), 2.4km, and the nearest phone kiosk is at Legburthwaite, a further 800 metres away.

Ridge routes

Bell Crags →*1.6km/1 mile* ↓*75m/245ft* ↑*165m/540ft* ⏲*50min*
There is no path from start to finish, but it is a far sweeter route than the spinal ridge track beside the fence from High Tove to Bell Crags! Walk S to the lone erratic (boulder) then descend, with the shapely peak of Bell Crags ahead. Carefully cross the plain wire fence and ford Launchy Gill, passing another solitary erratic before mounting above the actual Bell Crags outcrop and climbing past the large sheepfold to the peaked summit.

High Tove →*1.3km/¾ mile* ↓*45m/150ft* ↑*75m/245ft* ⏲*30min*
To minimise time travailing through the marsh head N, descending to ford Fisher Gill and join the old footpath linking Armboth with Watendlath. The westward-trending path is never very convincing and even has the audacity to almost 'dissolve' on the wet rise to the summit cairn on the skyline.

3 BASE BROWN 646M/2119FT

Climb it from	Seathwaite **12**
Character	A steep-sided ridge invariably side-stepped by walkers heading for headier heights out of Gillercomb
Fell-friendly route	3
Summit grid ref	NY 225 114
Link it with	Green Gable
Part of	The Gillercomb Skyline

Travellers approaching Seathwaite from Seatoller will have this fell strikingly in view. The lower ridge extension of Green Gable, it forms a strong eastern shoulder, embracing Gillercomb. Steep and abrupt, it deters timorous walkers, whose habit will be to stick resolutely to the paths. Hence it has become the prized trophy of the discerning few.

Two major waterfalls come within the fell's shadow: the flamboyant cascades of Sour Milk Gill and Taylorgill Force, with walkers who choose to follow the rough path on the west bank of the Derwent (4) from Seathwaite getting the best view of the latter. There are two common lines of ascent, both springing from the Sour Milk Gill path climbing into Gillercomb (1). The impressive north ridge (2)

↑ *Base Brown from Seathwaite Bridge*

3 BASE BROWN

is infinitely more enjoyable than the back-door route up Gillercomb (3), **which is best reserved as an efficient means of descent. A third climb, rarely undertaken, comes round the eastern side with Styhead Gill (4) to gain the ridge on grass.** However, if it's a round trip you are seeking then the complete skyline circuit of Gillercomb itself is the bees' knees.

Ascent from Seathwaite 12

There are but two natural lines of ascent for this stern little fell. Head on up the northern prow or, more circumspectly, hold to the path leading to the southern head of Gillercomb. Both routes share a common start and the early-phase climb into Gillercomb.

Via Sour Milk Gill →*2.4km/1½ miles* ↑*520m/1705ft* ⏱*1hr 30min*
The pitched path, developed over recent years to improve direct ascents to Great Gable from the Borrowdale valley, provides the primary springboard for ascent. The pitching is not consistently of the best order, but hopefully in due course improvements can be made to this popular staircase.

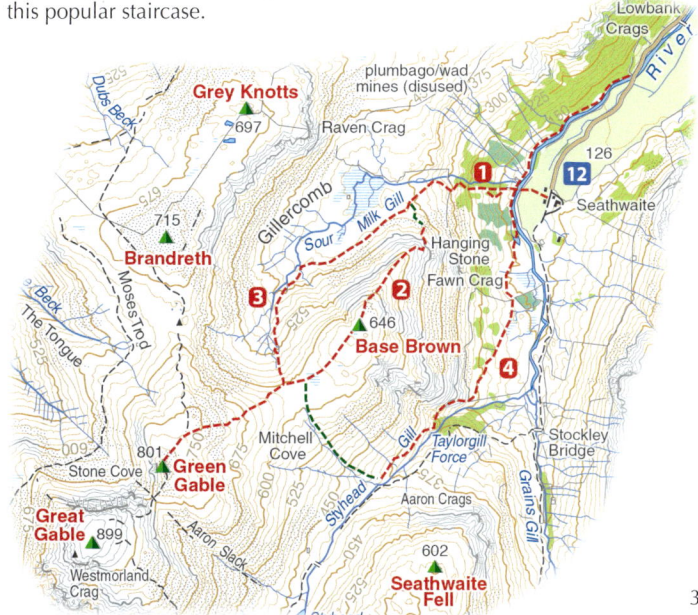

WALKING THE LAKE DISTRICT FELLS – BORROWDALE

Sour Milk Gill

1 You can embark on the gated riverbank path from Seathwaite Bridge or, from the road-end, go through the middle of the barn on the right, opposite the farmhouse, to cross the new **Derwent** footbridge. By either means join the pitched path, climbing beside a wall (left) to a novel low-slung ladder-stile, the like of which you might not have encountered. Climbing on, an early diversion left offers a chance to inspect

3 BASE BROWN

Seathwaite Slabs, partially obscured since they face away from the path; the angle of the rock wall lends confidence to climbers of all standards. You can climb straight up to regain the pitched path, with a fine ice-smoothed rock to stand on at the top.

Sour Milk Gill soon makes a dynamic entrance into proceedings, and it is possible to venture close at two points – the great fall and cascade section a thrilling moment after any period of wet weather. The path tackles a tree-sheltered rock gully, a fun moment which comes as a rude surprise on the steady pitched way. The pitching resumes and draws up to a rock shelf beside a wall, then trends left to a gate. Enthralling outlooks are a consistent feature of this ascent but are especially good from the rock shelf, showing off Seathwaite's impressive dale-and-fell setting beautifully. Look north to see the spoil banks of the famous Seathwaite wad mines, the origin of the Keswick pencil industry. The path arrives at the highest fall and readily allows a close inspection, enjoying a fine view both of the fall and down the beck into delightful Borrowdale. The path duly enters **Gillercomb** by a large rock, from behind which the beck's thunder emits. Attention is inevitably drawn to the impressive facing cliff of Raven Crag, otherwise (and more widely) known as Gillercomb Buttress. From here you have a choice of Routes **2** and **3**.

2 The first route variant takes leave of the stone-pitched trail on the level section – you can use the small bowed, grooved outcrop on the left as your cue to depart. There is no hint of a path in the early stages up the grass-and-rock slope but aim to the right of the huge fallen rock. At this point find hints of the passage of walkers close up by the rock, which nestles in a chaotic bed of splintered rock debris. All eyes will look up towards the **Hanging Stone**, a comparatively small, perilously perched rock which looks set to join its great compatriot at any moment. The path winds up left, ever more evident on the ground, and runs under the Hanging Stone cliff to round the corner. The sheep path splits, with the direct path veering up onto the crest and keeping above the Hanging Stone; a lower path roughly contours until easier ground is found and a pathless ascent can be made up the bilberry bank to a shallow depression on the ridge. Somehow it feels as if the climb should be over, but no such luck, as the ridge seems to step on for quite some distance until the summit is reached. Take your time, for it is a lovely route, far easier to accomplish than first impressions might suggest.

Boulder below the Hanging Stone

Via upper Gillercomb →*3.2km/2 miles* ↑*520m/1705ft* ⏱*1hr 45min*

3 Alternatively, keep company with the pitched path, which leads south and rises into the innermost quarter of **Gillercomb**, climbing beneath Base Brown's steep and uninviting western slopes. There is a stoic pull to the ridge, where the path veers right as a gravelly trail towards Green Gable. At this point turn left onto the grassy path leading easily northeast, stepping over the marshy Blackmoor Pots to reach the summit cairn.

Via Mitchell Cove →*3.2km/2 miles* ↑*520m/1705ft* ⏱*2hr 20min*

This side-door approach, like Route 2, is best reserved for ascent, specifically because of the hands-on rock scramble as you draw near to Taylorgill Force.

4 From the **Derwent** footbridge – accessed from Seathwaite Farm – turn left through the gate and follow the footpath upstream. The path drifts up from the stony river via a kissing-gate, with stony passages unavoidable. Cross a ladder-stile beside a sheep-creep and a pine tree, passing below an old fold and a wall and by large boulders, with Hind Crag prominent across the valley, shielding the western flanks of Glaramara. The path draws towards **Taylorgill Force** and mounts rocks to a hand-gate tight beside a cliff, after which more

3 Base Brown

earnest scrambling ensues – simple stuff when dry. It is reminiscent of a minor Jack's Rake and thus daunting for walkers unused to such adventures. Fear not: the journey soon eases and the path scoops on with handsome views of the graceful waterfall. The stony gully up to the right should be quickly dismissed as a means of ascent. Continue upstream with the path, following **Styhead Gill**. Soon after, the beautiful water-chute cascades of Mitchell Gill flow into the beck. At this point leave the path and follow the right-hand gill up the pasture slope without incident to the ridge top, where the summit cairn is swiftly reached by heading right.

The summit

A small rock plinth gives the cairn – as well as the limbs of the inevitably chuffed and puffed walker – a happy resting place. The top of the fell is surprisingly open and belies the tiered craggy defences.

Safe descents

Do not drift laterally from this summit: the NW and E slopes are particularly nasty and perilous traps for stray walkers in mist, although you can cautiously follow the NE ridge down. The sure-footed way is to head SW on the ridge path, crossing the peaty dip, from where you then have two options. Bear right into Gillercomb on the popular part-pitched path from Green Gable (**3**), bound for Sour Milk Gill (**1**), or – simpler still, yet seldom trod – bear left, descending pathless beside Mitchell Gill (**4**) to ford Styhead Gill to join the pitched trail from Styhead, via Stockley Bridge. These two routes are navigable in mist; brook no other way in uncertain conditions.

Ridge route

Green Gable →*1.6km/1 miles* ↓*40m/130ft* ↑*190m/625ft* ⏲*45min*
Follow the one clear ridge path SW, with just a small peaty patch to negotiate on the gentle slope down to the depression where the Gillercomb path breaks onto the ridge. A loose gravelly trail ensues, maintaining direction, rising via one tiny rock-step to join the Brandreth ridge path at cairns. This heavily used, excessively cairned path climbs steadily, with rising anticipation, to the summit cairn and wind-shelter.

4 BELL CRAGS 558M/1831FT

Climb it from	Dob Gill **28** or Watendlath **15**
Character	A great viewpoint above low crags and the morass of Launchy Gill
Fell-friendly route	5
Summit grid ref	NY 298 143
Link it with	Armboth Fell, High Tove or Ullscarf

By curious convention, Bell Crags, the wedge of rough country rising west from the shores of Thirlmere between Launchy and Dob Gills, initially as craggy afforestation but later as a wonderfully wild fell, is not recognised as a separate fell. Yet nearby High Tove and Armboth Fell – 'official' fells – are poor contenders beside the far more striking height of Bell Crags. The fell stands smartly to attention above Launchy Gill, master of all it surveys.

The old bridle path from Wythburn to Watendlath via Harrop and Blea Tarns might be said to prove the point, effectively annexing the fell from the greater mass of Ullscarf. The fell-top can be reached via the long tendril-like path that leads acutely southeast from Watendlath (9), but more efficient and scenic are the routes from the southwest shore of Thirlmere at Dob Gill (1–8).

↑ *Bell Crags from Tarn Crags*

4 Bell Crags

Ascent from Dob Gill 28

Three paths climb from the vicinity of the United Utilities Dob Gill car park.

Via Harrop Tarn →*3.2km/2 miles* ↑*395m/1295ft* ⏲*1hr 45min*
1 An engineered path climbs directly from the signboard and winds up through the mature forestry to the outflow of Harrop Tarn. Here join Route **4**.
   2 Alternatively, the old bridle route begins from the road on the south side of the beck, a hand-gate with signpost giving access. Note the Binka Stone, a distinctive ice-smoothed outcrop, to the left. Rise, passing through a second hand-gate after 40 metres; the stony stair climbs through dense juniper to a ladder-stile crossing the tall deer fence. The path leads through the forest and over a section of duckboards to the footbridge and ford at the outflow of Harrop Tarn.
   3 From the road south of where Route **2** breaks off, a somewhat circuitous route can be followed that climbs the eastern slope through juniper to the cairn on top of Birk Crag before descending northwest to Harrop Tarn via a deer gate.

Bell Crags from Harrop Tarn (photo: Maggie Allan)

4 Having reached Harrop Tarn via Route **1**, **2** or **3**, the old bridle route follows the clear forest track by a small grove of beech. After crossing a footbridge over a shallow feeder-gill the track swings right, but the path heads straight on to quickly link up with a further forest track. As this track bears right again a signpost indicates the bridle path, which leads straight on up to a double deer-door gate by an old fold. Exiting the forestry, the bridle path winds purposefully on up the open slope to the broad damp depression. Standing Crag is the notable feature to the south and Blea Tarn is in view to the west. Do not go through the hand-gate in the ridge-top fence. Instead tip-toe, as best you can, across an uncomfortable marsh to the right (north) to firm ground, on course for the summit.

5 Alternatively, on exiting the forestry with Route **4**, follow the forest fence immediately right, branching off at will to climb the fell and finding your own way, small outcrops being the only minor hindrance to an easy pathless ascent. The summit lies at the northern tip of the slightly undulating ridge.

Via Mosshause or Stone Hause →3km/1¾ miles ↑355m/1165ft ⏲1hr 30min

6 Leave the road a few metres north of the car park at a stile. A path leads up through a gateway in a wall bounding the northern edge of the forest to a track, where you can join either Route **7** or **8**.

7 From the end of Route **6**, pass through the hand-gate into the plantation and, at the first fork in the forest track, either go straight ahead or bear up right. Both tracks unite with the bridle path, and waymarking guides you to the right up to a double deer-door gate by an old fold to leave the forestry as per Route **4**.

8 From the end of Route **6** go right then quickly left to a hand-gate in the wall corner. An old shepherds' path winds steeply up the grooved fellside, and fine views back over the head of Thirlmere give excuse for a breather or two. As the ground eases pass a couple of old folds tucked into nooks in the outcrops. Bell Crags comes into view once the forestry corner is passed. Evade bracken patches while crossing Stone Hause and mount the ramped slope of the upper fell to the prominent summit.

4 Bell Crags

Ascent from Watendlath 15

The 5 miles from the shores of Derwentwater to Bell Crags via Watendlath is equally split between single-track road and fell path (rising via Ashness Bridge, the path section described in Routes 9–10). An excellent idea is to contemplate a range-crossing traverse, linking bus stops at Rosthwaite in Borrowdale and Wythburn road-end at the southern end of Thirlmere, accessed by means of the Borrowdale Rambler route and the half-hourly 555 Lakeslink bus services (both out of Keswick).

Via Blea Tarn →4km/2½ miles ↑290m/950ft ⏲1hr 50min

9 Most walkers will start from the National Trust car park (pay and display). Exit either over the ladder-stile or right from the point of entry to a gate. The waymarked footpath fords **Raise Gill** and soon begins the zig-zag ascent of the steep bank, following centuries-old sled trails used for conveying peat from High Tove for domestic heating. The point of departure from the Armboth path is marked on a slate at the wall corner, 'to Wythburn'. The green path contours around the hillside, initially with an intake wall for company, though the wall is replaced as a guide by strategic cairns on the long gradual rise southeast. The path clips the brow, missing the fence corner, and dips to the outflow of **Blea Tarn**, a wind-whipped sheet of water. The damp path proceeds up the tough tussocky herbage to the watershed fence and hand-gate. Pass through the gate, bearing left, and negotiate the marsh to reach firm ground, rising to the short north–south summit ridge.

Via High Tove →4.5km/2¾ miles ↑320m/1050ft ⏲2hr

This is not a route upon which one can heap much praise, being reminiscent of a Pennine bog-hopping yomp, with the presence of red grouse only increasing the similarity!

10 An option when the ground is either bone dry or gripped in frost is to complete the ascent to High Tove with the sled trails (see Route **9**) then turn south to follow the east side of the ridge fence to Bell Crags.

Fold above Launchy Gill (photo: Maggie Allan)

The summit

Well, yes, it's true: the summit is innominate on all maps. But the name has been bestowed in this guide, elevating it from being a mere outcrop set low on the northern slope. A small cairn rests on the southern top, while a larger outcrop makes a more convincing summit at the northern tip of the ridge. The fell offers the most marvellous northern prospect, looking to Blencathra.

On the high shelf directly beneath the summit to the north stands possibly the neatest sheepfold in Lakeland; it certainly deserves close inspection. The small compartment appears to have had a roof. Nearby is a further small roofless bothy, next to modest evidence of quarrying in the flaky rock.

Safe descents

Join the old bridle path traversing the depression immediately S of the summit. The easiest option is E (**4**), and the improving path leads down into the plantation surrounding Harrop Tarn, though Dob Gill, on the shore of Thirlmere, has no services for the wet and weary. Better then the westward line (**9**) to Watendlath – and Borrowdale beyond – though you may have to suffer facing into the prevailing wind and no doubt the worst the elements can throw at you!

Ridge routes

Armboth Fell →*1.6km/1 mile* ↓*165m/540ft* ↑*75m/245ft* ⏲*35min*
Descend via the grand sheepfold due N, watching for the outcrops. As the slope levels pass an old cairn and an erratic before fording the feeder-gill to Launchy Gill, then cross the wire fence. Pass through the old wall and proceed up the rough easier-angled slope to the prominent erratic on the brow. The summit outcrop lies across marshy ground ahead.

High Tove →*3.2km/2 miles* ↓*50m/165ft* ↑*10m/35ft* ⏲*1hr 10min*
The many energetic souls who innocently set their sights on an end-to-end ridge walk from Great Langdale to Keswick should be under no illusion: the terrain N of Bell Crags is as wet as it gets on any ridge walk in Lakeland. The only saving grace is the presence of the fence, to which one either clings or bounces. The final rise to High Tove is at least on improving ground.

Ullscarf →*2.8km/1¾ miles* ↓*30m/100ft* ↑*210m/690ft* ⏲*1hr 30min*
Aim SW to the fence. Ignoring the hand-gate, continue on a clear path which passes a large pool, sliced through by the fence, and head directly for the foot of Standing Crag. The path takes a leftward slant in climbing up through a weakness to the top of the crag. The fence resumes from the very top, a spot worth visiting for the fine view. The path keeps close company with the fence to the acute corner, where you bear S across the grassy plateau, following the line of old fence stumps, and proceed to the summit cairn.

5 BLEABERRY FELL 589M/1932FT

Climb it from	Keswick **20**, Great Wood **19**, Ashness Bridge **17**, Causeway Foot (Naddle valley) **23** or Rough How Bridge **24**
Character	Shielded by crags to east and west, the delightful upper slopes are grass and heather.
Fell-friendly route	1
Summit grid ref	NY 285 195
Link it with	High Seat or Walla Crag

Bleaberry Fell forms a convincing northern culmination to a range of admittedly modest and marshy tops stemming from the central plateau of High Raise. To east and west stirring crags command valley views. The two-tiered competitive climbing walls of Falcon Crag, facing over Derwentwater and warmed by late afternoon sunshine, have long attracted climbers. When seen from across the Naddle valley or from Castlerigg stone circle, Bleaberry Fell projects a striking headland, strengthened by Dodd Crag and the shy cliffs of Shoulthwaite Gill. Walkers lured to explore this eastern aspect (5–8) are seldom disappointed, especially as the climb to the summit is rewarded with a rapturous panorama of famous fells. From the east, Route 2 follows steep Cat Gill to gain the higher ground and Route 3 rises from Ashness Bridge on a lovely contouring path above Falcon Crag. There is one more option (1), from the north, tracing a pathless ascent across the marshy hollow of Low Moss.

↑ *Looking to Blencathra from Bleaberry Fell's summit cairn*

WALKING THE LAKE DISTRICT FELLS – BORROWDALE

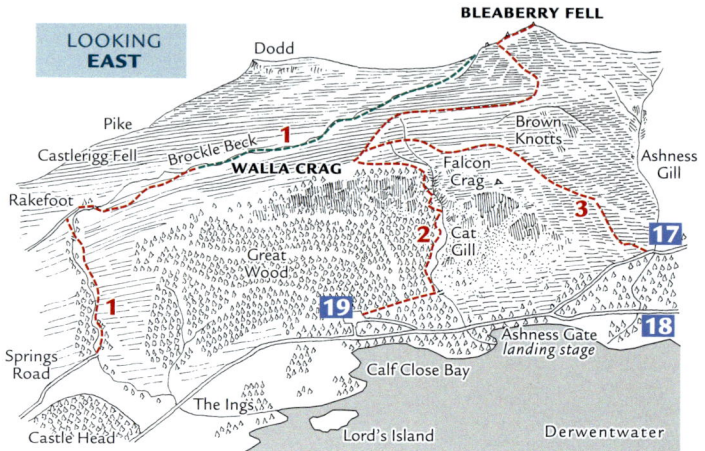

Ascent from Keswick 20 off map NW

Via Springs Road and Brockle Beck →5.7km/3½ miles ↑510m/1675ft
⏱2hr 30min

A rewarding – if latterly off beat – direct way from the centre of Keswick

1 From the Moot Hall leave the town centre via St John's Road, which becomes Old Ambleside Road. Just before this road pitches uphill fork right into **Springs Road**. Continue by Springs Farm, keeping close company with the wooded ravine, the path in its later stages running beside pasture fencing. Note that the fenced path bearing right can be used to access Great Wood and gain a more direct ascent of Walla Crag. The easier course continues uphill, passes through a kissing-gate, dips into the dell again then crosses a footbridge to join the minor road at a hand-gate. Go right, forking right at the approach to **Rakefoot farm**. Cross the footbridge and rise to a stile (and padlocked field-gate).

A clear track ascends and forks, the path by the wall being the direct way to Walla Crag. However, as a purist intent on Bleaberry Fell, keep to the less well-trodden track leading straight on and, as this bears up right again, continue on the grass path (little more than a sheep trod), which advances to

5 BLEABERRY FELL

the fenced sheepfold and ruined shepherds' dwelling, destroyed when used for tank firing practice in World War II. From this damp hollow on **Low Moss** traipse through quite dense heather, tracing the diminishing **Brockle Beck**. With increasing vagueness, the path leads on by a fold into a

Old fold beside Brockle Beck

shallow combe. Angle up to the right onto the natural scarp shelf, now with evidence of a path, and continue to reach the large cairn at the top of the steep section of the popular path from Walla Crag. The worn trail trends up left, via an intermediate cairn, to the summit.

Ascent from Great Wood 19

Walkers frequently choose to include Walla Crag in their adventure. The reasoning is flawless: it offers two exceptional viewpoints, on a rising tide of visual delight.

Via Cat Gill →3.2km/2 miles ↑510m/1675ft ⏱2hr 20min

2 From the National Trust car park (pay and display) follow the woodland path south to the footbridge spanning **Cat Gill**. However, do not cross, but instead pass up through the hand-gate and climb steeply beside the confined gill. A further hand-gate is encountered on the beautifully engineered and stepped path climbing to the scarp-top. You can cross the first wall-stile on the left into the wooded scarp-edge enclosure or continue more easily on the green sward to a stile much closer to the top. The summit cairn of **Walla Crag** stands back from the edge on a bare rock plinth. From the brink enjoy quite the best view of Derwentwater, backed by Keswick and Skiddaw.

Backtrack over the stile and join the obvious path shaping to contour above Cat Gill. Be sure to take the left fork, then ford two headstreams on course to round the shoulder of **Brown Knotts**. Skirting a marsh, climb the newly secured path and rise onto the summit bluff.

Ascent from Ashness Bridge 17

Via Falcon Crag →3.2km/2 miles ↑430m/1410ft ⏱2hr

The early scarp-slope views over Derwentwater make this route extra special.

3 The top of Cat Gill (see Route **2**) can be reached on converging paths climbing from Ashness Bridge. Either follow Ashness Gill's north-bank path, traversing to the hand-gate on the left, or take the lower path directly from the bridge, branch right after the stile and climb via the higher fence-stile to join the upper path, which rises above **Falcon Crag**. A spur diversion to the

5 BLEABERRY FELL

left allows you to visit the handsomely sited cairn on top of the crag, with its fine view of Walla Crag in profile and across the island-dotted lake towards Bassenthwaite and the distant Solway Firth. The continuing path above the deep re-entrant of **Cat Gill** provides another notable scenic moment before merging with paths from Walla Crag and Cat Gill and turning right, with Route **2**, bound for the summit.

Ascent from Causeway Foot in the Naddle valley 23

4 A secretive backstairs approach can begin from the layby at Dale Bottom, opposite Causeway Foot Farm, though this involves a roadside out-leg, passing beyond the old Vicarage to the ladder-stile on the right, then joining the contouring footpath behind **Brackenrigg**, which connects into the valley for Routes **5–8**.

Looking across the Naddle valley to Dodd Crag from Piper House

WALKING THE LAKE DISTRICT FELLS – BORROWDALE

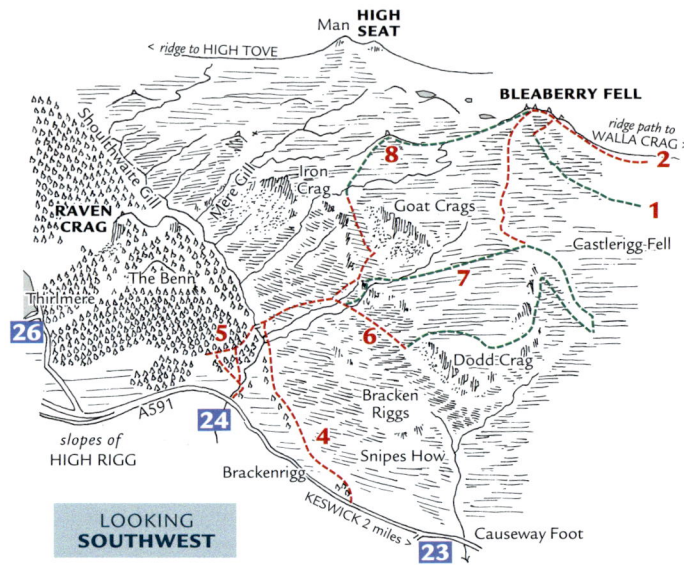

Ascent from Rough How Bridge 24

A trio of intriguing routes climb above the stern facade to attain an inspiring summit panorama.

Via Dodd Crag →*3.2km/2 miles* ↑*445m/1460ft* ⏲ *1hr 40min*
5 Follow the approach lane (footpath) to **Shoulthwaite farm** (Caravan Club site). Pass through to the kissing-gate entrance into the woodland. Branch immediately right, up by the internal forest fence, to join the forest track and go right. As the track forks go right, to the tall deer-balking kissing-gate, and cross the **Shoulthwaite Gill** bridge, with an old weir on the upstream side. Follow the winding path up the facing fellside, with the wall to the right, and cross a gill. As you come level with the large erratic over the wall the three routes (**6–8**) fan their separate ways.

6 From the end of Route **5**, go through the hand-gate and follow the drove-way, which contrives to beat back the bracken. It fords the gill then

5 BLEABERRY FELL

starts to climb. On reaching the brow leave the obvious path and climb the steep slope to the skyline on the left, short of the outcrop. On the face of it this is an apparent folly, but essential, as the primary path disappears under Dodd Crag and the way beyond is rough and confused. Steep though the climb may appear, your way is only hampered by bracken.

The grassy fell-top is a blessed relief. Wander to the right to the leading edge of **Dodd Crag**, a superb viewpoint over High Rigg to Clough Head and Blencathra. Follow the scarp edge southwest towards Bleaberry Fell, but as the working wall has only one wall-stile, this must be sought and climbed. To locate it descend and follow the wall north. As the slope levels encounter the rushy headstream of a gill and look intently for the through-stones in the wall. Cross this old shepherds' stile with due care. Turn back south, following the wall up and over the ridge to the junction with a fence. Now go right, all the way to the summit. While not attractive in itself, the resultant summit view definitely compensates.

Dodd Crag

Via Goat Crags →2.7km/1¾ miles ↑435m/1425ft ⏱1hr 30min

This is the most direct and the easiest route from the Shoulthwaite valley.

7 From the end of Route **5** go straight up the open bracken-inhibited gill, skirting to the left of the outcrop. Weave up and through a ravine, keeping the rising wall to the right, and continue to the junction with a fence. Pass to the west-side stile/gate and follow the fence left (south) to the summit.

The more interesting option

8 From the end of Route **5** bear up half-left. Climb, with several guiding cairns, onto the high shelf under **Goat Crags** via an easy cleft. The rocky edge angles up to pass above a waterfall, better appreciated from the valley floor – though if you already know it from below this moment is all the more impressive. The route turns up the gill and wanders onto the prominent cairned knoll to the south before traversing northwest across the damp hollow to the fence corner and stile immediately below the summit.

The summit

The highest ground is clothed in a ragged mix of heather, bilberry and tough fell grass. Various cairns identify viewpoints on the rise to the wind-shelter and tumbled heap at the top. There is no doubting its merits as a major viewpoint, and this and Walla Crag are a peerless pair from which to admire the greater Derwentwater arena of fells and lakes.

Safe descents

Follow the main path descending NW from the summit (**2**) – this is the assured way. The fell is lined with serious crags at the lower level, making the course of Brockle Beck to Rakefoot (**1**) a sure release from potential woes, though it is better to keep to the popular turf trail the whole way.

Summit wind-shelter

Ridge routes

High Seat →*2km/1¼ miles* ↓*50m/165ft* ↑*30m/100ft* ⏲*30min*
The ridge path is dubious, dreary and damp. The fence gives some guidance but is actually better ignored altogether. The usual route leaves the summit, passing a cairn, and weaves a course due S, well to the W of the fence and avoiding excessively wet hollows as best it can. Cross a stile, where raw peat gives dry boots their final challenge, short of the climb to the summit knoll and old Ordnance Survey pillar.

Walla Crag →*2km/1¼ miles* ↓*255m/835ft* ↑*45m/150ft* ⏲*50min*
Follow the popular path NW; the steep slope is loose so take your time. Skirt around a marsh and pass a sheepfold sheltering on the eastern slope of Brown Knotts. The clear path runs downhill, fording two gills above the deep combe of Cat Gill, to reach a stile entry into the wooded scarp enclosure. The summit cairn stands back from the edge on a bare rock plinth.

6 BRANDRETH 715M/2346FT

Climb it from	Seathwaite **12**, Honister Pass **10**, Gatesgarth **9** or Black Sail Youth Hostel **8**
Character	A fine threshold viewpoint, easily attained except from the east
Fell-friendly route	2
Summit grid ref	NY 215 119
Link it with	Green Gable or Grey Knotts
Part of	The Gillercomb Skyline

Merging with Grey Knotts to form the headwall of Gillercomb, Brandreth is exclusive neither to Borrowdale nor Ennerdale but a high threshold to both, drawing together the body of fell from the Northwestern and High Stile ranges towards the Gables. A flaw in this 'betweenness' is its almost total lack of distinguishing shape. However, as the former site of a beacon the fell-top once held focal importance, lying at the boundary junction of three manors, and it commands an extensive view.

The routes from the surrounding valleys – Seathwaite to the east (1), Warnscale to the northwest (3) and Ennerdale to the west (4–5) – all include a steep ascent. Perhaps unsurprisingly, the popular route (2) takes advantage of the high start offered by Honister Pass, following the Old Tramway then breaking south across the flanks of Grey Knotts to tackle the summit from the west.

↑ *Brandreth from Base Brown*

6 BRANDRETH

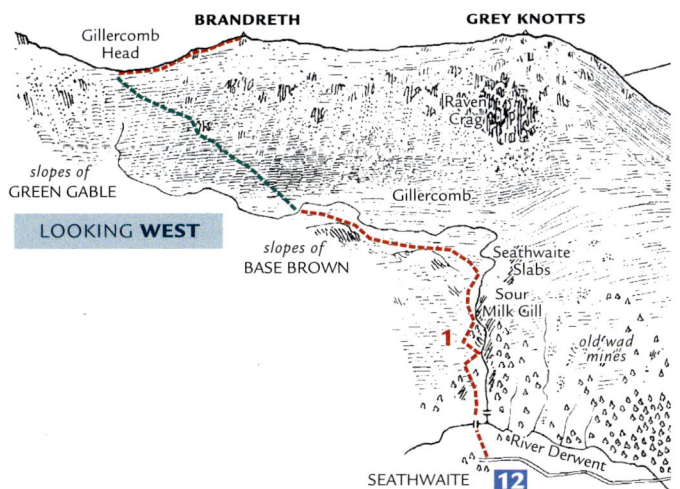

Ascent from Seathwaite 12

Direct →*3.2km/2 miles* ↑*610m/2000ft* ⏲*2hr 10min*

Suited to the free-spirited walker, once the conventional path is left in Gillercomb the route climbs steep and pathless out of the hanging valley.

1 You can embark along the gated riverbank path from Seathwaite Bridge or, from the road-end, go through the middle of the barn on the right, opposite the farmhouse, to cross the new **Derwent** footbridge. By either means join the pitched path, climbing with a wall (left) to a novel low-slung ladder-stile, the like of which you might not have encountered. Climbing on, an early diversion left offers a chance to inspect Seathwaite Slabs, partially obscured since they face away from the path; the angle of the rock wall lends confidence to climbers of all standards. You can climb straight up to regain the pitched path, with a fine ice-smoothed rock to stand on at the top.

Sour Milk Gill soon makes a dynamic entrance into proceedings and it is possible to venture close at two points, the great fall and cascade section a thrilling sight after any period of wet weather. The path tackles a tree-sheltered rock gully, a fun moment which comes as a rude surprise on the steady pitched way. The pitching resumes and draws up to a rock shelf beside a wall then trends left to a gate. Enthralling outlooks are a consistent feature of this ascent but are especially good from the rock shelf, showing off Seathwaite's impressive dale-and-fell setting

6 BRANDRETH

Pool at Gillercomb Head

beautifully. Look north to see the spoil banks of the famous Seathwaite wad mines, the origin of the Keswick pencil industry. The path arrives at the highest fall and readily allows a close inspection, enjoying a fine view both of the fall and down the beck into delightful Borrowdale.

Enter the great corrie of **Gillercomb**, with handsome slabs beyond the wall to the right and the mighty Raven Crag ahead. Follow on with the part-pitched path, skirting the western base of **Base Brown**. As this popular path begins to rise, with a craggy shoulder of Base Brown ushering the path right, come above cascades and here leave the regular way. Ford the stream and take a pathless, diagonal half-left, rising line, aiming towards the saddle in the ridge. En route aim for a small rounded outcrop, passing up left from its base, then weave through further modest outcropping, with good turf to be found all the way to the top. Once on the ridge, with the tarns at hand, turn right over the broken ground. It takes some 5 minutes from here to complete the climb to the summit.

Ascent from Honister Pass 10

The more regular route takes advantage of Honister Pass's elevation: almost 300m of ascent is quite some saving on the conventional valley start.

Direct →3.2km/2 miles ↑350m/1150ft ⏱1hr 50min

2 From the car park follow the regular path off the quarry track, heading west. The track, initially rerouted from the Old Tramway, climbs to the lost Drum House engine stance on the skyline. Here turn left (south). The popular path to Great Gable, inevitably over-burdened with cairns, leads across the easy western slopes of Grey Knotts. Take the left-hand option where the path forks, the right-hand path leading to Loft Beck, carrying Coast-to-Coast traffic. Reach and cross a fence-stile then bear up left to reach the summit unerringly.

Ascent from Gatesgarth 9

Direct →4.8km/3 miles ↑610m/2000ft ⏱3hr

This route might prove of particular value as a return from a round that also gathers in Fleetwith Pike and Grey Knotts. But taken in ascent it is a fine direct line, in tremendous surroundings for most of the way.

3 Follow the open track leading off the road and curve naturally into the great combe of Warnscale Bottom, with the shadowed crags of Haystacks brooding ahead. Watch for the right-hand branch path, leading to a broad footbridge, and ford Black Beck. (Anticipating problems) the path draws sharp right as Warnscale Beck tumbles over mounting rock-steps ahead. The part-pitched path rises up the rough slope, intimate with the dark cliffs of Haystacks and Green Crag. It keeps its distance from the Warnscale Hut bothy but should you pay a visit to this old slaters' working abode (maintained by the Mountain Bothies Association), please show it due respect. Continue with the path, which winds up to a large ice-etched slab on the brow. Swing right on the popular path and at the next fork bear left, rising to the right of the great bulk of Great Round How to cross a fence-stile at the angle of the fence, then following the fence direct to the summit.

6 Brandreth

Ascent from Black Sail Youth Hostel 8

There are two routes from Black Sail Youth Hostel.

Direct →*2.8km/1¾ miles* ↑*425m/1395ft* ⏲*2hr*

4 Follow in the footsteps of through-walkers engaged in the Coast to Coast Walk, heading southeast along the lower slopes of **Haystacks** and skirting above the moraine. Arrive at **Loft Beck**, ford the beck and, from the cairn, begin the steep pitched trod up the enclosed valley. As this eases follow on, and as you near the fence bear up right, the fence being a sure guide southeast to the summit.

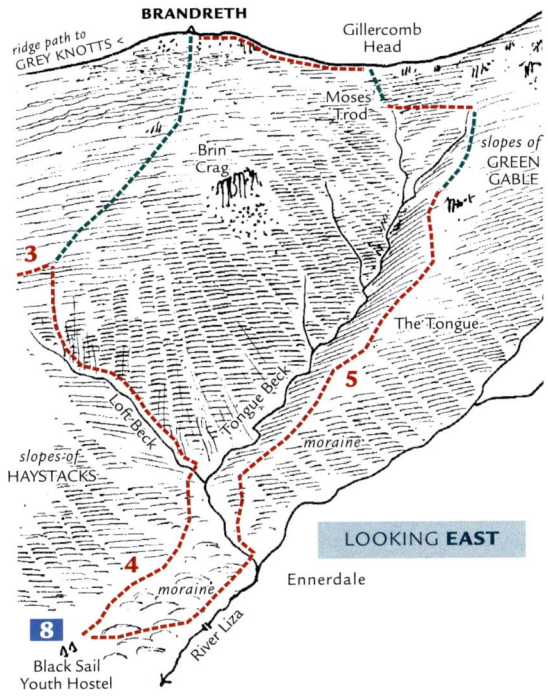

Buttermere Vale from Moses Trod

5 From the foot of **Loft Beck** (see Route **4**) it is possible to drop down from the cairn and ford **Tongue Beck** to embark on **the Tongue** ridge climb.

You can also reach this spot, if the becks are low, by following the path from the hostel towards the footbridge spanning the **Liza**. Short of the bridge follow the base of the moraine on a path that fords **Loft Beck** at its confluence with the infant Liza. Follow the obvious path by the old fold, weaving up the nearly conical moraine ridge to reach the **Tongue Beck/Loft Beck watersmeet**. Do not cross, but bear up right on the evident path, which duly draws onto the ridge, draped in grassy moraine deposit.

Ahead you will see a handsome waterfall in the steep upper realms of Tongue Beck: this is well worth visiting although there is no path and the ground is steep. The ridge path skirts to the left of ridge-top outcrops and then strides onto a pathless prairie to meet up with the heavily used **Moses' Trod**. Turn left and, coming by an old fold, veer right on grass, easing up to the tarn-adorned saddle of **Gillercomb Head**, from where the summit is swiftly gained, due north.

6 Brandreth

The summit

The broad summit is littered with minor rock outposts. The accepted top seems to be fixed at the end of a line of three metal posts, around which a few stones have been gathered. However, the ground might swell still further some 80 metres to the south, where a cairn rests amid a clutter of rock. The all-round view is extensive, if not exactly breathtaking. Most of the big players are visible – Pillar, Grasmoor, Skiddaw, Helvellyn, Glaramara, Bowfell, Great Gable – but none is thrilling. The Gables are the biggest presence and together they do a pretty good job of hiding the Scafells – although, not to be denied, Great End, Ill Crag and the ultimate ground of Broad Crag peer over the shoulder of Green Gable.

Safe descents

First, be aware that the eastern slope holds all the cliff dangers. The three metal stakes give a valuable clue in mist, useful for three destinations. Take their lead and head W, quickly coming alongside the new fence. At the first stile cross and follow the heavily cairned path, which leads first to a junction

Looking north along the ridge to Grey Knotts

with Moses' Trod and thereafter easily down to the Drum House site (**2**). Turn right with the incline path for Honister or left for Warnscale and Gatesgarth in the Buttermere valley. For Ennerdale ignore the initial stile and continue down by the fence (**4**). This naturally leads into Loft Beck, joining the Coast to Coast path. For Seathwaite head S to the depression of Gillercomb Head (**1**), with its cluster of tarns. Choose your moment to leave the edge, left, into Gillercomb, weaving your way down to ford the beck and join the part-pitched path running across the western slope of Base Brown. Go left for Sour Milk Gill.

Ridge routes

Green Gable →*1.6km/1 miles ↓55m/180ft ↑145m/475ft ⊕40min*
Head S – the minor outcropping is easily negotiated – down to the saddle of Gillercomb Head, which is attractively decorated with tarns. The ridge path, converging with the Honister path, is very evident, rising on S. As the path from Gillercomb merges from the left, the path swings SW and is over-embellished with cairns on its route to the summit.

Grey Knotts →*0.8km/½ miles ↓30m/100ft ↑15m/50ft ⊕20min*
Take a northerly course and cross the light fence-stile, advancing on grass a short distance to the left of the ridge fence, thus avoiding the tarns, to reach the summit outcrop.

7 CASTLE CRAG 290M/951FT

Climb it from	Grange-in-Borrowdale 3, Rosthwaite 1 or Seatoller 13
Character	Borrowdale in miniature: a mighty dwarf, its sheer slate cliffs, clothed in trees, culminate in a tiny table-top viewing station.
Fell-friendly route	3
Summit grid ref	NY 249 159
Part of	Around the Jaws of Borrowdale

The unsullied beauty of Borrowdale is most special in the transition towards Derwentwater. Here stands Castle Crag, barbican defender of the Jaws of Borrowdale, rising as a rock-jewel amid a tangle of slate and trees. The hard slate is a handsome building stone, once greatly prized – as evidenced by the architecturally fascinating quarries on the fell's slopes.

Families will love Castle Crag: the exuberant mini-mountain peak requires so little effort and offers so much reward. The short stiff climb, largely beneath a canopy of conifers and native trees, culminates on a neat rock plinth, where the walker is treated to the most thrilling bonanza of lake and mountain vistas, the sudden drop being a real wow factor.

↑ *Castle Crag from High Doat*

WALKING THE LAKE DISTRICT FELLS – BORROWDALE

While the fell is commonly climbed from Grange or Rosthwaite (1–4), a grand way to experience it is to walk that extra few kilometres from Seatoller and include the diminutive High Doat (6), which is endowed with its own remarkable outlook into upper Borrowdale and picturesque Stonethwaite.

Ascent from Grange-in-Borrowdale 3

Via Broadslack Gill →*2.4km/1½ miles* ↑*215m/705ft* ⏲*1hr*

An enchanting walk, especially when autumn gold tints the leaves, most of this route is beneath a canopy of trees – quite a rare circumstance for a Lakeland fell walk.

1 A lane leaves the main street by the mid-town café, almost opposite the Victorian church which is attractively constructed from Castle Crag slate. After passing an ever-open gate the metalled lane forks and you keep left on the track, passing between two camping fields. At the first small footbridge you might opt to bear right on the path leading to **Dalt Quarry** and its attractive reflective pool. However, most walkers will stay put on the more regular way, soaking up the glorious scene of pebbles and trees at the great sweeping bend of the crystal-clear **Derwent**. After the second footbridge bear right, rising on a track to a gate. The track continues as a part-pitched way up the

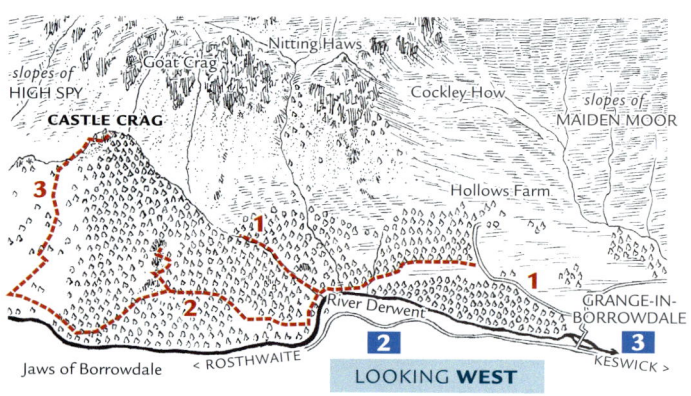

7 Castle Crag

secret valley drained by Broadslack Gill, to the east of Castle Crag. After the old sheepfold on the left watch for a path breaking up the slope to a wall-stile. It continues to a fence-stile at the base of the slate tip, with a handsome view towards Goat Crag. Follow the fence to meet and join the main (heavily used) path winding up the spoil bank. The upper quarried hollow has so much loose slate that on occasion visitors are tempted to creatively play; currently a multitude of slates stand on edge as open-air art. The summit is reached by keeping right and mounting through the larches.

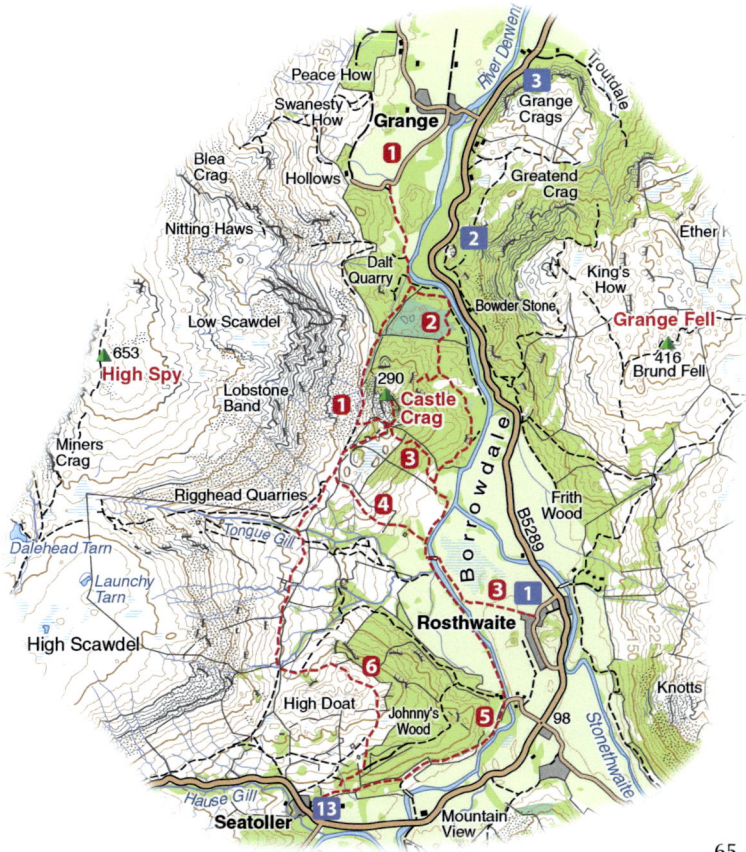

Goat Crag

Via the Jaws of Borrowdale →*3.2km/2 miles* ↑*230m/755ft* ⏲*1hr 15min*
2 After the second footbridge (see Route **1**) at the great bend in the river – where many visitors are understandably lured to pause and gaze – bear left up the short hollow-way to a gate/stile. The path heads on beside the bright waters of the Derwent before drifting away from the river, in the process softening some of the unwelcome traffic noise. It then leads through a clearing and comes, via steps, to a wall-gap, where it re-enters the woodland.

Coming through a shallow rock-cutting, you might reasonably be tempted to bear right on a spur route to visit two notable caverns. The top cave is the more famous, being associated with the local character Millican Dalton, who died in 1947 at the age of 80, and who used to use this cave's upper inner portion as living and sleeping accommodation. A word of advice: walkers have been tempted to wander on from the upper cavern, since an obvious path does lead right to cross the wooded ridge, and there is even evidence of intrepid scramblers completing the ascent on the north side. Please treat these apparent paths with disdain. While you can venture onto the wooded ridge for the views – which are indeed good – you should retrace your steps back down to the regular path at the eastern foot of the quarries to continue.

Passing on below the lower cavern, which is fashioned into an impressive arch, the path wends pleasantly through the much-extolled Jaws of Borrowdale

Millican Dalton's cave (photo: Maggie Allan)

woodland to emerge at a kissing-gate into pasture. The continuing track (Route **3**) heads for Rosthwaite, but attend to the adjacent fence as the track shapes to curve left, and find here a stile/gate giving access to the bank pasture. A clear path climbs to a proper wall-gap (gate missing) and continues through the bracken to a ladder-stile, crossing the wall beside a group of mature pines. This gives access to the foot of the discarded slate, where you join the steep twisting passageway to the top, through the spilling shards.

Ascent from Rosthwaite **1**

Via the Derwent →*2.4km/1½ miles* ↑*230m/755ft* ⏲*1hr*
3 Follow the lane by Yew Tree Farm and its understandably popular Flock-In tearoom. The lane leads to the banks of the Derwent and follows the river downstream to cross the cobbled New Bridge. Bear right and, coming to a pair of gates, keep right along the riverside track. The track swings left and you branch left, crossing the stile/gate to ascend the bank into the trees, with handsome views back to the Stonethwaite valley. Slip through a gateway and complete the initial phase of the climb by crossing a wall via a ladder-stile. Pass the stately pines and embark on the slate trail, winding to the old quarry, then complete the ascent by means of the path on the right-hand side.

Via the old road →*2.8km/1¾ miles* ↑*240m/785ft* ⏲*1hr 10min*

An interesting variation, often used as the return on a circular expedition

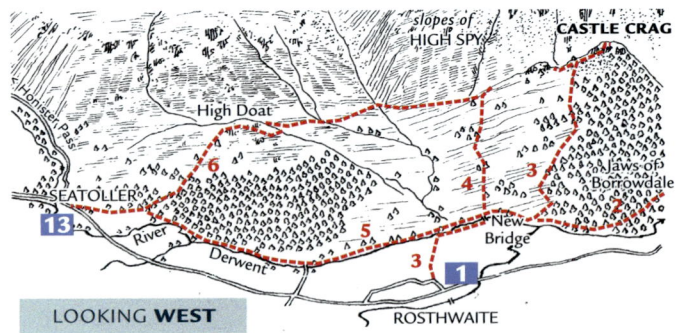

7 CASTLE CRAG

4 Follow Route **3** to cross **New Bridge** then take the left-hand gate. The footpath leads up the open pasture via a fence-stile in an adapted wall-gateway. Clear on the ground, the path winds up the pasture to a hand-gate in the bounding wall and quickly steps onto the old road, an old miners' track, by the fence sheep-handling pens on the pass. Follow on down for only a matter of 50 metres before bearing off right, keeping to the path beside the wall as it rises below the small crag. Ignore the first fence-stile and continue with the fence close right until confronted by a wall. Here cross the stile and then, immediately after, the ladder-stile over the wall, and ascend the slate trail to the summit.

Ascent from Seatoller 13

Via the Derwent →*4km/2½ miles* ↑*225m/740ft* ⏲*1hr 25min*

A joyous riverside approach

Chain via ferrata approaching Longthwaite

5 Leave the National Trust car park via the short lane at the eastern end. Cross the stile and keep the wall to your right, advancing to a kissing-gate where you switch sides, behind Glaramara outdoor centre. Now in woodland, slip through the left-hand wall at a gap in open ground, and after the next kissing-gate re-enter woodland, with a wall close right, and descend to a hand-gate. The **Derwent** makes an excited entrance and the path becomes an adventure, with a fixed chain aiding progress over the grooved bedrock. Pass through the grounds of Borrowdale Youth Hostel (Longthwaite) and follow the road to pass (not cross) the road bridge. Follow the river downstream, via stiles, to join Route **3** or **4** at **New Bridge**.

Via High Doat →*4.4km/2¾ miles* ↑*320m/1050ft* ⏲*1hr 40min*

The upper gallery route

6 Take leave of the car park as per the previous route, but after the stile fork left. Keep forward on the green path, advancing to a gate, then rise through light woodland, with a fence on the right, to a gateway giving access to the open slope of **High Doat**. A clear way exists through the bracken via a second gateway (gate off its hinges), passing over the top. Make a point of seeking the summit as few walkers seem to give this grand little top due regard. The path sweeps over to a wall-stile and winds down and across the pasture to another wall-stile to join the bridleway linking Little Gatesgarthdale with Grange. Turn right to advance along this age-old trade and quarrymen's trod, en route crossing two footbridges, to unite with Route **4** just on the saddle before the track descends from a fence-fold.

The summit

A knob of bedrock slate forms a conclusive summit. To this is attached a slate Great War roll of honour to the men of Borrowdale. Hence, on Remembrance Sunday, when the weather is too bad for the normal Great Gable service, people gather here to reflect. A wind-shelter, perched on the summit like a bird's nest, is useful but awkward to enter.

The Jaws of Borrowdale is indeed an exquisite place to be and to reflect on life. The situation is at once thrilling and enthralling. Larch trees hamper the view to east and west but north and south the walker is treated to sumptuous scenes. Northwards views extend over the sylvan vale and gracious Grange to Derwentwater and the sleek peaks of the Skiddaw massif, with the wooded bulk of King's How close at hand half-right. To the south lies the land-locked heart of Borrowdale, centred on the wooded slopes of High Doat and Rosthwaite, backed by Eagle Crag, Rosthwaite Fell, Glaramara and the more remote Great End and Scafell Pike.

Summit outcrop – a popular perch

This place of beauty was, in ancient times, a temporary last refuge during times of local clan warfare, being the site of an Iron Age encampment – hence the fell-name.

Safe descents

Descend S, taking the utmost care in skirting the E side of the quarry rim through the larches, and keep faithfully to the old quarrymen's paths that zig-zag down to the foot of the slate spoil. A ladder-stile over the wall sets you on course for Rosthwaite (**3–4**) or Grange (**2**), while the fence-stile to the right leads into the wild pass on the W side of the craggy fellside, where you can join the old Rigghead track; head N for Grange (**1**) and S for Seatoller (**6**).

8 CATBELLS 451M/1480FT

Climb it from	Hawse End Jetty 5, High Brandelhow Jetty 4, Grange-in-Borrowdale 3, Uzzicar 6 or Chapel Bridge (Little Town) 7
Character	A steep, bracken-skirted ridge with a rocky culmination to remind novice walkers that this is a real mountain to be respected
Fell-friendly route	6
Summit grid ref	NY 244 198
Link it with	Maiden Moor
Part of	The High Spy ridge

Seekers of solitude must choose carefully when to visit Catbells as it is rightly popular. If ever there was a fell gifted with Lakeland views, then it is this little gem. Loved by all, it's where you bring children to ignite their thrill in mountain scenery – the name itself sounds charming and playful.

The fell was exploited for lead from the late 18th century, with the Brandelhow Mine, evidenced by the spoil debris seen in Yewthwaite Comb, worked in shafts and levels, while the Old Brandley Mine, seen from the ridge-top of Skelgill Bank, was open-cast.

↑ *Catbells from Skelgill Bank*

8 CATBELLS

Catbells terminates the northward arm of the great ridge stemming from High Spy via Maiden Moor which divides Borrowdale from the Newlands valley. This simple ridge allows several options for ascent, and proximity to Derwentwater, which is serviced by the most delightful round-lake Keswick Launch, enables you to indulge in the lovely combination of lake cruise and fell climb.

By far the most popular ascent route (1) follows the northern ridge; however, it is possible to reach the summit from all points of the compass. Routes lead up from the neighbouring valleys of Derwentwater (2–3) and Newlands (4–6) to saddles on Skelgill Bank (2, 4) and at Hause Gate (3, 5–6), where the main ridge path can be easily joined. Route 7 offers a pleasing circular walk via the fell foot and lake shore.

Ascent from Hawse End Jetty 5

Many walkers will content themselves with parking (for a fee) in the field opposite Gutherscale Lodge (when available) or will stride from Portinscale with the Cumbria Way, but the Keswick Launch is the more exhilarating option.

Via Skelgill Bank →*2.4km/1½ miles* ↑*380m/1245ft* ⏱*1hr 30min*

The way of the many

1 A path leads directly up from the jetty, through the woodland fringe, to the double hairpin bend with a cattle grid in its midst. At the top hairpin

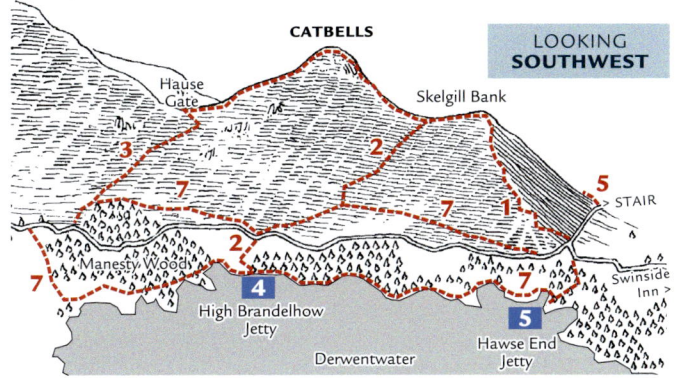

bear right, and almost at once step onto the rising part-pitched path from the National Trust collection box. This switches left by the rails and leads up onto the first nose of the bracken-clad ridge, where a further path is met coming from the opposite side. Set to work climbing the ridge, with some pitching and inevitable loose gravelly debris on the over-subscribed path. Near the top of **Skelgill Bank** find a small plaque to Thomas Arthur Leonard, who died in Conwy in 1943, a prime mover in the open-air movement which aimed to create opportunities for working people to gain access to these wonderful places. Coming onto the crest of Skelgill Bank is a moment of quite some elation. The parade along its undulating grassy 'roof-top' gives wonderful views on either side, although fell-lovers will get the greatest thrill from the Newlands fell array, with Causey Pike impressively on show. The final bare rock path to the summit is most comfortably handled in ascent.

Ascent from High Brandelhow Jetty 4

Via Brandelhow Mine →*2km/1¼ miles* ↑*380m/1245ft* ⊕*1hr 25min*
2 Head up, half-left, in the woodland to exit via a hand-gate. Bear uphill, amid evidence of mining spoil, on a path which is shielded from the old Brandelhow mine workings by fencing, en route to the open road. Step onto and straight over this road, bearing up the right-hand path. Follow this on its steady rise until, at its highest point, a clear path steps purposefully up left, through the bracken, heading steeply up to the saddle on **Skelgill Bank**. Join the ridge path and turn left to engage in the final pull to the top.

Ascent from Grange-in-Borrowdale 3

Via Hause Gate →*3.2km/2 miles* ↑*380m/1245ft* ⊕*1hr 35min*
3 Follow the road from Grange until, just after **Manesty house** and before woodland, you find a path ushered off the road, left, around a large stone. This leads to a gate. There follows an area of spot-pitching, which remedies a patch of sorely worn path. Keep up left at the path fork, zig-zagging to **Hause Gate** (where 'gate' refers to a natural gap rather than an actual gate). Here turn right to complete the ascent.

The pinnacle of Catbells, east of the summit and little more than a metre high

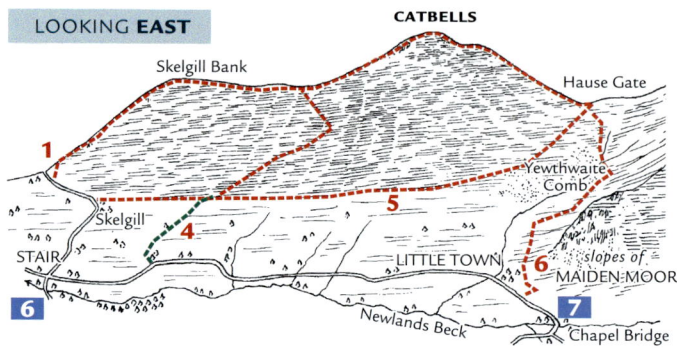

Ascent from Uzzicar 6

Via Stair and the Conservation Walk →*3.2km/2 miles* ↑*365m/1200ft*
⏲*1hr 30min*

A stairway to a heavenly height

4 Stair has little capacity for casual parking; walkers may opt to use the generous verge parking above Uzzicar Farm and wander down with the field-path, past the remnants of the old Barrow lead mine, to Stair Bridge. Cross and, after passing the Newlands Adventure Centre, turn right by the community hall and the Ramblers' Gordon Walker Chalet to follow the minor road south. After some 450 metres seek a gate on the left at a bend, with a permissive path notice. This Conservation Walk is one of the wider benefits of an agricultural land-management scheme. Entering rushy fields, follow the open track to a new field-gate/stile in a fence/hedge. Ascend the next field to cross a fence-stile, continue up the ensuing pasture and cross an open ditch to reach the top right-hand corner of the field. Ignore the first stile/gate on the right, head up through the recessed stile/gate and ascend the field to a hand-gate in the intake wall. Now at the foot of the open fell-slope, step over the lateral drove-way and follow the inviting ascending path through the bracken as it hairpins en route to the skyline saddle. Join the ridge path to complete the climb up the steepening ridge of Catbells, with some awkward bedrock to negotiate.

Via Yewthwaite Comb →4km/2½ miles ↑380m/1245ft ⏲1hr 30min

The quiet side of the fell, on reassuringly stable and well-graded paths

5 You can start at Stair (see Route **4**), following the byroad up to Skelgill farm. Turn immediately right, after the road-gate, to the gate giving access to the lateral drove-way running south above the intake wall. Alternatively, you can reach this gate via the minor road leading southwest from Gutherscale Lodge. Both routes then follow the drove-way for about 1km, passing beyond the summit. Then, seek a track forking half-left, which climbs steadily across some scree, above the untidy legacy of the Yewthwaite Mine, with a minor rock-step hampering speedy progress. On reaching the open saddle of Hause Gate join the ridge path leading left (north) to the summit.

Ascent from Chapel Bridge, Little Town **7**

Via Yewthwaite Comb →2km/1¼ miles ↑335m/1100ft ⏲1hr 10min

6 Follow the road up from Chapel Bridge to go through the gate immediately prior to the first house. This leads onto a track, which hairpins, keeping up left as it comes alongside the wall. As the wall shapes to curve left bear right at the path fork. The clear path duly rises to a double ford of Yewthwaite Gill (nice waterfall here) and ascends by a fold and the remains of mine structures up a loose trail. It eventually comes onto grass as it climbs to the broad Hause Gate saddle. Bear left, following the simple ridge path to the summit.

Lower-level walk from Hawse End Jetty **5**

Circular walk from the Keswick Launch →5.2km/3¼ miles ↑120m/395ft ⏲2hr

This route shares the low-level pleasures of the lapping lake with a slightly elevated made-way (suitable for wheelchairs) along the lower slopes of Catbells and offers marvellous views over the fringing trees to Derwentwater's grand surround of fells.

7 Step off the launch and follow the shore path south, a walk full of charm and many scenic moments. En route to High Brandelhow Jetty pass the cupped-hand carving, an amazing feature installed by the National Trust to

WALKING THE LAKE DISTRICT FELLS – BORROWDALE

Walkers boarding the Keswick Launch at Hawse End Jetty

mark their centenary, set amid the first property they acquired in the Lake District in 1902, Brandelhow Park. Pass on by the jetty, keeping to the shore and skirting round a bay, the boathouse and dwelling on Brandelhow Point attracting most admiration. After a hand-gate pass a timber garage to reach another gate, following the roadway. Ignore the leftward access to Abbot's Bay and come by the Warren. Turn left off the metalled roadway, following the footpath beside the fence; this leads to a lovely view across Abbot's Bay.

The newly engineered trail leads on by a wall-gate onto a winding passage across low marsh, with serpentine boardwalks constructed from recycled plastic. Shortly after the 's'-shaped boardwalk, close to **Great Bay**, take the slightly less-than-obvious path half-right, which leads via a gate at a woodland corner and on across pasture, via further gates, to the road. Turn right, passing **Manesty house**, to leave the road on the bridleway. After gaining height, by a gate take the first fork right to come above the woodland, tight by a wall. Above Brackenburn, pass a scenic seat and tablet in memory of the writer Sir Hugh Walpole on a small outcrop. The path, an easily graded grand parade, comes down to meet the road at a small quarry only to take off again immediately beyond. Deemed suitable for wheelchair users, the path rises and then drifts gently down again to rejoin the road. At the road bend keep right with the path down to a kissing-gate, where it regains the road briefly at its second hairpin before heading right, down by the wall, to cross a metalled road and regain Hawse End Jetty… and your journey back to Keswick.

The summit

The summit is bare rock, with no scope for a cairn to survive a zillion kicking feet. The view is everything. Come prepared to idle and be amazed. Admire Derwentwater and survey the Northwestern Fells, with the ridges of Knott End, Scope End and Robinson a brilliant composition.

Safe descents

The easiest footing on the ridge is to be found to the S. Head back to Hause Gate and choose between descent left (**3**), down to the Manesty road, or right (**6**), to Little Town via Yewthwaite, or even the drove-way N (**5**) to Skelgill and Gutherscale.

Ridge route

Maiden Moor →2.4km/1½ miles ↓90m/295ft ↑215m/705ft ⏱50min
Follow the ridge path S, with just the one minor rock obstacle on Mart Bield, down to Hause Gate. Pass on through on the worn trail, which leaves no room for doubt on the rise onto Maiden Moor – that is, unless you fail to take the slightly less prominent path, half-right, as the scarp edge is reached. This leads attractively round the brink to crest Bull Crag and reach the modest summit cairn.

Catbells backed by Skiddaw from Maiden Moor

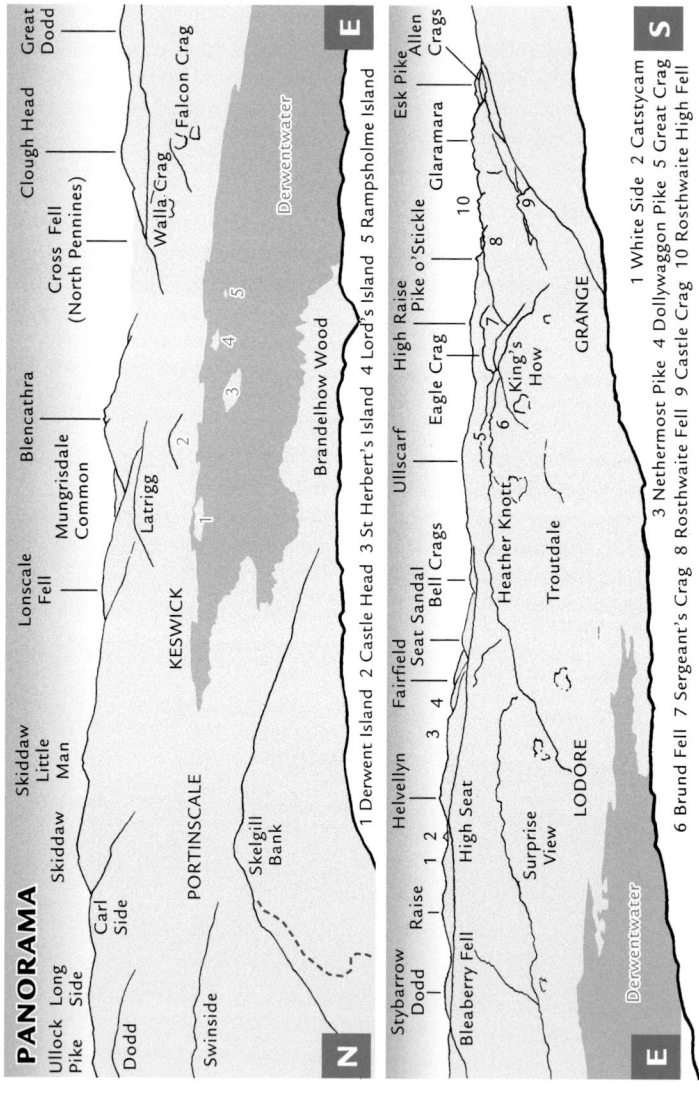

8 CATBELLS

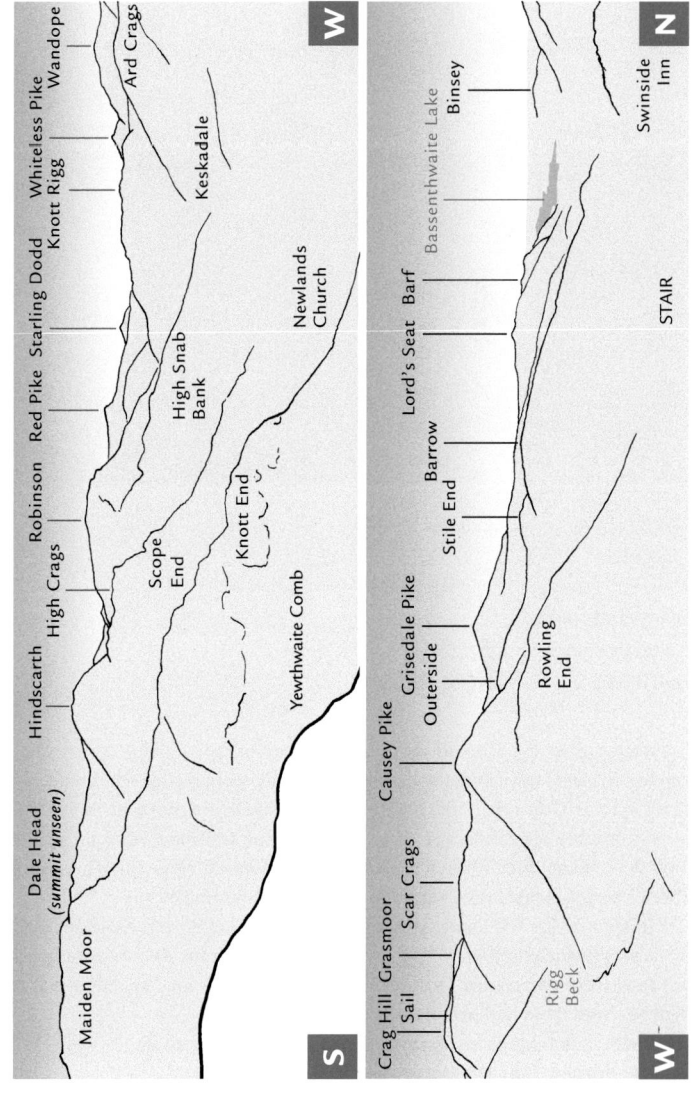

9 EAGLE CRAG 520M/1706FT

Climb it from	Stonethwaite **14**
Character	Every inch a tough challenge for the walker – though the airy crag-top view is ample reward
Fell-friendly route	2
Summit grid ref	NY 275 120
Link it with	Sergeant's Crag

Eagle Crag gives the Stonethwaite valley a stunning focal point, a real camera-catcher. Walkers traversing the central range via Greenup Edge see it much in the same light as Grasmere folk consider Helm Crag: it is a much-loved ingredient in an adorable fell landscape. The fell marks the termination of an extended limb descending directly from High Raise, a featureless ridge smartly coming to attention upon Sergeant's Crag en route to this grand finale.

In spite of the fell name, your chances of spotting golden eagle are nigh on nil. It was documented in 1777 that 'here is every year an airy or nest of eagles', but they were persecuted to extinction, the valley folk mighty relieved at their demise. How times and perceptions change!

There is but one prime ascent (1) and one backdoor route (3) which is best kept for descent, foul weather or not.

↑ *The Stonethwaite valley, focused on Eagle Crag, from the Borrowdale road*

9 EAGLE CRAG

Ascent from Stonethwaite 14

Direct →*3.2km/2 miles* ↑*425m/1395ft* ⏱*2hr 10min*

An exhilarating, thoroughly pleasurable climb weaves up through the heather and rock bands.

1 From the centre of the hamlet follow the lane signposted 'Greenup Edge', which leads over the **Stonethwaite Beck** bridge. After the gate go right with the gated bridle-track. Cross the footbridge immediately above the

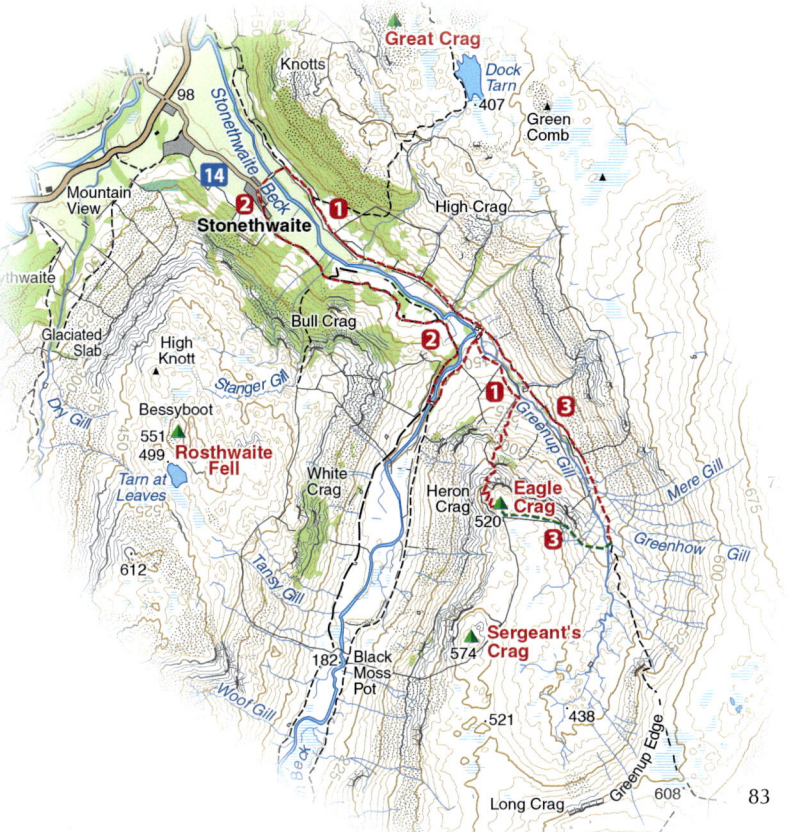

confluence of Greenup Gill and Langstrath Beck. Bear left and cross the fence-stile, taking care to keep to the low side of the flush marsh, which is abundant in delicate bog flora. The path brushes through bracken of potentially monster proportions; keep parallel with the Greenup Gill fence. Pass through a hand-gate in the down-wall, and while a path continues low beside the wall and gill, continue on the shepherds' path, angling gently up the slope to a wall-gap.

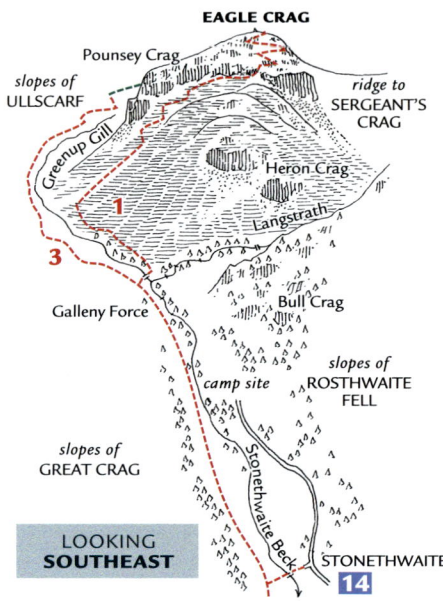

At this point the climb proper begins. Keep the partly broken wall to the right, and the path, confirmed by modest cairns of transitory existence, winds up to a fragile stile at the top of the rising wall hugging the undercliff.

If your temper has been tested by the sweaty work to this point, prepare for a fell-ecstasy lift-off. A narrow breach in the craggy defences permits a short stair climb. The way beyond suggests two options but in reality there is but one. The path leading up left ends abruptly but gives a handsome view of Pounsey Crag. Backtrack to continue – this is important, as there is no safe fellwalking ground further left. The prime route goes immediately right, along the ledge marked with ice-like fragments of quartz, and terminates with a fine full-height view of Sergeant's Crag. Now switch up, making several similar sharp turns to avoid rock bands, with much heather underfoot. Both the immediate and outward scenery is consistently exciting. Duly – and with no little sorrow for an end to the fun – the tilted summit slab is rounded.

The Stonethwaite valley from 50 paces north of the summit

2 Follow the lane through the hamlet (noting the Langstrath Hotel for end-of-walk refreshment). The gated track passes above the popular camping meadow, latterly passing Alisongrass Hoghouse (camping barn). As you near the beck listen to the roar of Galleny Force down in the tree cover, left. The track bends right, via a gate, to accompany the clear cascading waters of Langstrath Beck, passing through a gate to a footbridge. Cross and bear left to meet up with Route **1**.

Via Greenup Gill →*3.6km/2¼ miles* ↑*440m/1445ft* ⏱*2hr 15min*

The fell has only one other tenable line of ascent for the ordinary mortal, one that is more likely to be used for descent by walkers wisely avoiding the risk of trying to unlock the intricacies of the principal ascent.

3 From the Greenup Gill/Langstrath Beck confluence (see Route **1**) ignore the footbridge and continue up the Greenup Gill path via gates. The forbidding presence of Eagle and Pounsey Crags lends drama to the ascent along a bridle route made all the more popular by its inclusion in the Coast to Coast Walk. Just short of the moraine branch right, ford the gill and make a steady ascent left, thereby avoiding serious outcrops and quickly beating the bracken. There is no path but follow the natural line, which turns and contours to the base of the truncated wall above **Pounsey Crag**. Follow the wall to a ladder-stile crossing the ridge-top wall and go right to the small rock-step at the wall corner to complete the climb.

The summit

A broad, tilted rock outcrop, surmounted by a small cairn, forms the summit, and heather abounds. A second natural block lies prostrate a few metres to the north. This has the appearance of a fallen pillar, though of course it's nothing of the sort. The best view is northwest, looking back from whence you came, through the Stonethwaite valley. The best place from which to admire the valley lies some 50 metres north of the summit; a thin path leads to the spot – this must not be misconstrued as a line of descent!

Safe descent

Descend S from the summit (**2**), via the small rock-step in the wall corner, then cross the ladder-stile a matter of 30 metres along the ridge wall. Follow the descending wall E until the wall abruptly ends above a cliff. Contour right until easier slopes permit you to complete the descent via steep open fellside. There is no hint of a path after leaving the wall end. Ford Greenup Gill and join the bridle path leading down into the Stonethwaite valley.

Ridge route

Sergeant's Crag →*0.8km/½ mile* ↓*10m/35ft* ↑*60m/195ft* ⏲*30min*
Descend S, cross the stile to the right of the wall corner and follow the ridge wall. The path is clear enough and later it drifts half-right up to the summit. Be mindful that cliffs line the near western slopes.

10 GLARAMARA 783M/2569FT

Climb it from	Seatoller 13, Seathwaite 12 or Stonethwaite 14
Character	A central presence and great favourite, steep-sided, with a rocky crown
Fell-friendly route	1
Summit grid ref	NY 246 105
Link it with	Allen Crags or Rosthwaite Fell
Part of	Glaramara ridge walk

Cumbria is blessed with a generous helping of the most delightfully lyrical fell names, Glaramara being a favourite of many. The elevated central setting gives it further distinction over and above the charming name. Indeed, if any fell can be called the Borrowdale fell, then this is it, especially when coupled with its more prominent components, Thorneythwaite Fell and Combe Head.

The summit is also part of a greater mass of fell, the principal northern spur of the Scafell massif, and the mid-point of a ridge rising smartly from Stonethwaite, climbing in rough steps over Rosthwaite Fell and initially culminating above Combe Gill at Combe Head. This ridge is defined and thoroughly isolated by deep dales: the headstreams of Borrowdale to the west and lonely roadless Langstrath to the east.

↑ *Combe Head from the summit of Glaramara*

10 GLARAMARA

Glaramara makes a great objective from Stonethwaite (5), Seatoller (1–3) or Seathwaite (4). The quickest way to the top is by Hind Gill (4) but the best way, by far, is by the handsomely curved and craggy Thorneythwaite Fell ridge (1).

Ascent from Seatoller 13

Via Thorneythwaite Fell →4.2km/2½ miles ↑680m/2230ft ⏱2hr 15min

The royal road to the top, the Thorneythwaite Fell ridge obviates the need to climb Rosthwaite Fell.

1 Begin from the National Trust car park in Seatoller. Follow the verge past the appropriately named Glaramara holiday centre. At **Strands Bridge**, beside the terrace of gabled cottages known as **Mountain View**, go right with the Thorneythwaite farm access lane. Watch for the kissing-gate on the left after 70 metres. Pass through and follow the rough track, which becomes a grooved path, rising up the lightly wooded ridge to a further kissing-gate in the intake wall. Without wavering, keep to the obvious path climbing the north ridge,

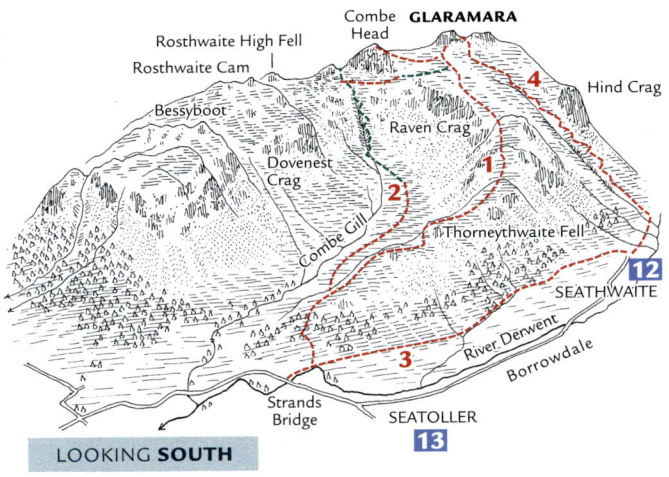

LOOKING **SOUTH**

making one pronounced switch up right onto a craggy step. There is a fine view into the inner recesses of the lost valley of Combe Gill to Dovenest and Raven Crags, facing each other across the dale-head. The climb gives ample opportunity to survey the handsome fell surround of Honister Pass, the growing majesty of Great Gable looming above Base Brown. As height is gained you can drift onto the edge above the Combe Gill valley for splendid views, then climb onto **Combe Head**. This is a handsome place to stand – better than Glaramara, in terms of the northern view. Alternatively, keep assiduously to the trail, which steps over marshy ground before coping with the headstream of **Hind Gill** to confront Glaramara proper. The fell path turns rock ramble in tackling a six-metre scramble; being prone to shadow, this can be slippery when wet or icy and for good measure the rocks are awkwardly rounded too! If this is a bit more than you are willing to take, then no worries; either skirt to the left or – easier still – to the right, rounding the main outcrop to complete the climb from the south or west.

Glaramara from King's How

10 GLARAMARA

Via Combe Gill →*4.2km/2½ miles* ↑*690m/2265ft* ⏲*2hr 30min*

The Combe Gill valley gives an entirely different perspective; the sturdy qualities of the fell constantly impress upon the route.

2 Branch from the Thorneythwaite Fell route (Route **1**) shortly after passing through the intake gate. A fine waterfall in Combe Gill holds attention short of the path fork, which is marked by a cairn. A clear trod leads by the curious remains of an oval fold, set on a slope. The path leads into the moraine-fringed hollow at the heart of the combe. This route is most commonly used by climbers heading for Raven Crag, on which the severity of the routes is intensified by the lack of sun; Dovenest Crag, on the opposing fellside beneath Rosthwaite Cam, is, by comparison, quite balmy. The caves, which make the lower portion of the crag a place for brave speleologists, may give you a reason to return another time. Departing from the path, aiming for the sheepfold, you must make your choice between Dovenest or **Combe Gill**. Keeping to Plan A, follow the gill due south; at the mouth of the ravine clamber onto the right-hand bank. The ground may be steep but an occasional cairn and the faint traces of a zig-zagging path, as height is gained, will embolden your stride. The ravine climbs straight out of the combe to a shelf directly below **Combe Door**. The regular ridge path from Rosthwaite Fell contours this shelf and can be followed to the right. Alternatively, clamber on up to Combe Door, the view back to Rosthwaite Fell, the Jaws of Borrowdale and Derwentwater providing ample justification. Passing through the gap, past the shaded tarn, take one of two paths mounting onto **Combe Head** up to the right, the second, furthest, climbing onto an all-too-brief slab then rising up the edge northwest to the Combe Head cairn. Glaramara lies across the damp hollow to the south.

Link route from Seatoller to Seathwaite →*3.2km/2 miles* ⏲*55min*

3 The 3.2km of valley path from **Strands Bridge** to Seathwaite have been adopted by the Allerdale Ramble. This lovely track gives walkers relief from the inevitable traffic on the Seatoller to Seathwaite road. Follow the farm-lane, guided left as it turns towards the farm, along a fenced passage to a hand-gate. Now with a wall on your right, advance on a basically level track below the rugged wooded slopes of **Thorneythwaite Fell**, via a couple of gates, the track latterly becoming a path, en route to **Seathwaite Farm**.

Ascent from Seathwaite 12

Via Hind Gill →2.5km/1½ miles ↑680m/2230ft ⏲2hr

Hind Gill is more often than not incorporated into route plans late as a quick retreat from the tops, though many will appreciate it as an equally nifty ascent. The steep section of this path certainly deserves attention and pitching work, if for no other reason than to heal the growing scar!

4 Follow the regulation valley path from the farm. After the second gate bear left via a gate, fording the several bouldery strands of Hind Gill. Ascend the pasture via a broken wall to a hand-gate in the intake wall. The path winds up the right-hand side of the gill. Dispel thoughts of following the gill itself. Hind Crag is not particularly obvious from the path. Cairns litter the path; several may be found on the spacious open fell above, leading to the summit. The best approach to the summit is from the south.

The Helvellyn range from Glaramara

10 GLARAMARA

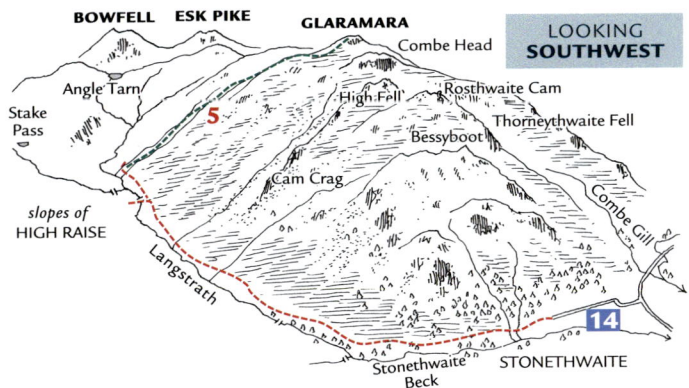

Ascent from Stonethwaite 14

Via Langstrath →*6.5km/4 miles* ↑*685m/2245ft* ⏲*3hr*

An ascent that combines the fullest enjoyment of the Langstrath valley with a sneaky line beside an attractive ravine

5 The route to Sobby Gill is straightforward. Keeping to the west-side track up Langstrath, ignore the Tray Dub footbridge. Keep the valley beck close left to minimise contact with the ubiquitous bracken, though the ground is quite marshy. With a broken wall and sheepfold in view some 150 metres ahead, take a bold turn right as a notable gill enters the beck. Hold to the left-hand gill where it forks; this is Sobby Gill. The bracken relents as the slope steepens. There is no evidence of a path but no matter; the going is easy enough and the views to Bowfell and Esk Pike offer ample compensation. A pinnacle is passed as the upper grains draw up to a rocky arête, beyond which the gill melts into the pasture to a red-scarred birth. Climb on either to ascend Combe Head or take the direct line to Glaramara.

Summit cairn

The summit

The name Glaramara strictly belongs to the summit. Which summit? The more northerly. The southern top has a more permanent cairn and a sumptuous prospect to Great End and Great Gable. A cairn seldom lasts long on the main top. A small wind-shelter lies tucked into the adjacent rocks on this splendid high platform.

Safe descents

There is a 'nasty' lurking close at hand, which has the potential for grief, especially in icy conditions, situated on the main path on the N side of the summit outcrop; the rocks are rounded and invariably wet as they catch little sun and the steps down long. The problem is no problem. Leave the summit, stepping down S into a shallow depression, and go right; this puts easy ground underfoot at a stroke. Wandering N, follow Hind Gill (**4**) then bear off NW; as a quickie descent to Seathwaite it's fine. But 'green' walkers will not wish to exacerbate its erosion, preferring to go down the Thorneythwaite Fell ridge (**1**), in which case continue N along a clear path that quickly materialises across the headstream of Hind Gill. The ridge path brings the walker down to Strands Bridge, a short stride from Seatoller... and that lovely little tearoom!

Ridge routes

Allen Crags →*2.7km/1¾ miles ↓130m/425 ft ↑160m/525ft ⏲55min*
Glaramara marks the point of transition on the greater ridge, as well as in the fortunes of walkers: the joyous roller-coaster journey S is uninterrupted by obstacles. The ridge path avoids the second summit, heading SSW across a stony plateau to a marshy depression. Further stony ground, peppered with tiny pools, ensues before the dip to High House Tarn. Make a point of drifting left at the next rise to find the exquisite Lincomb Tarn, spell-bindingly beautiful, held in the grip of outcrops. The ground gradually rises, with further small pools adding interest, until the summit cairn is at hand. All that ascent and still only a stride higher than Glaramara – one metre to be precise!

Rosthwaite Fell →*3.2km/2 miles ↓60m/195ft ↑85m/280ft ⏲1hr 20min*
Beware: Rosthwaite Fell is intricate and confusing in mist. There are two crucial early options: neither is preferable; both are entertaining given suitable weather. Follow the northern path heading for Thorneythwaite Fell – mindful of the rock-step off Glaramara. Curve right, under the scarp of Combe Head, along a terrace, the path only becoming apparent as the shelf narrows beneath Combe Door and above the deep cleft of Combe Gill. Contour to dip into the marshy bowl of Great Hollow. Traverse to cross a short length of wall then keep to the right of the crest of Rosthwaite High Fell (a viewpoint not to be ignored). The path holds to an eastern drift, avoiding Rosthwaite Cam, winding down towards Tarn at Leaves; keep up on the minor ridge to its W before climbing the final cone of Bessyboot.

    The alternative route slants right from the foot of the rock-step, across the marshy hollow, skirting around the eastern flank of Combe Head, then weaves along the eastern edge to the broken wall below Rosthwaite High Fell. A further route option slips through a breach in the Combe Head scarp, descending W through Combe Door to join up with the terrace path above Combe Gill.

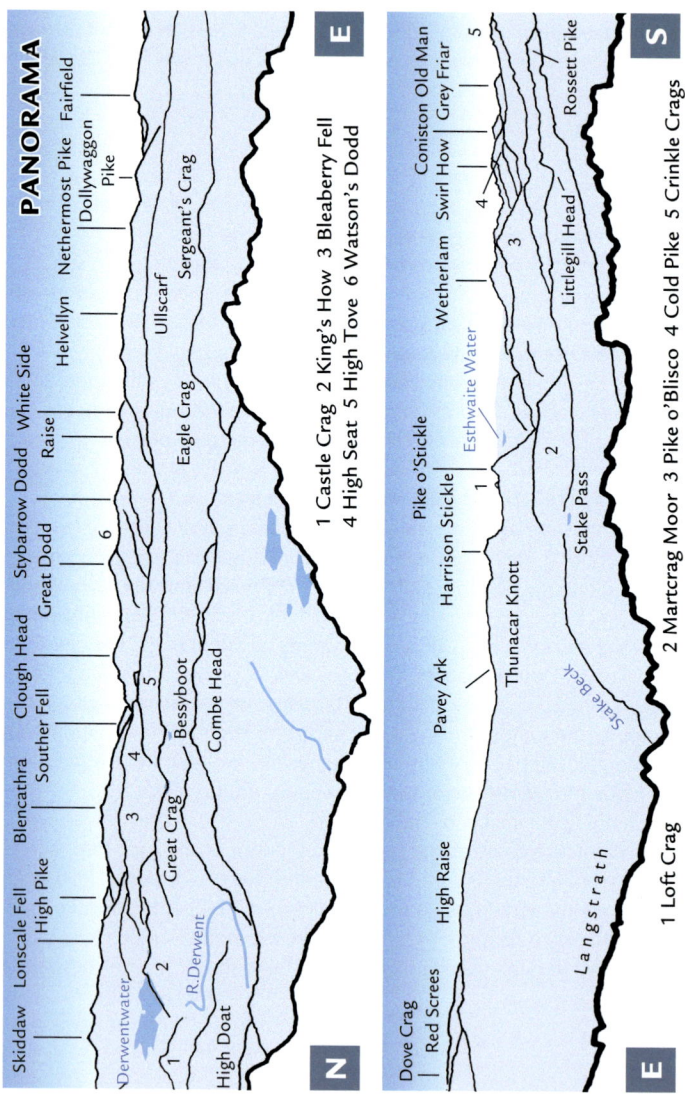

10 Glaramara

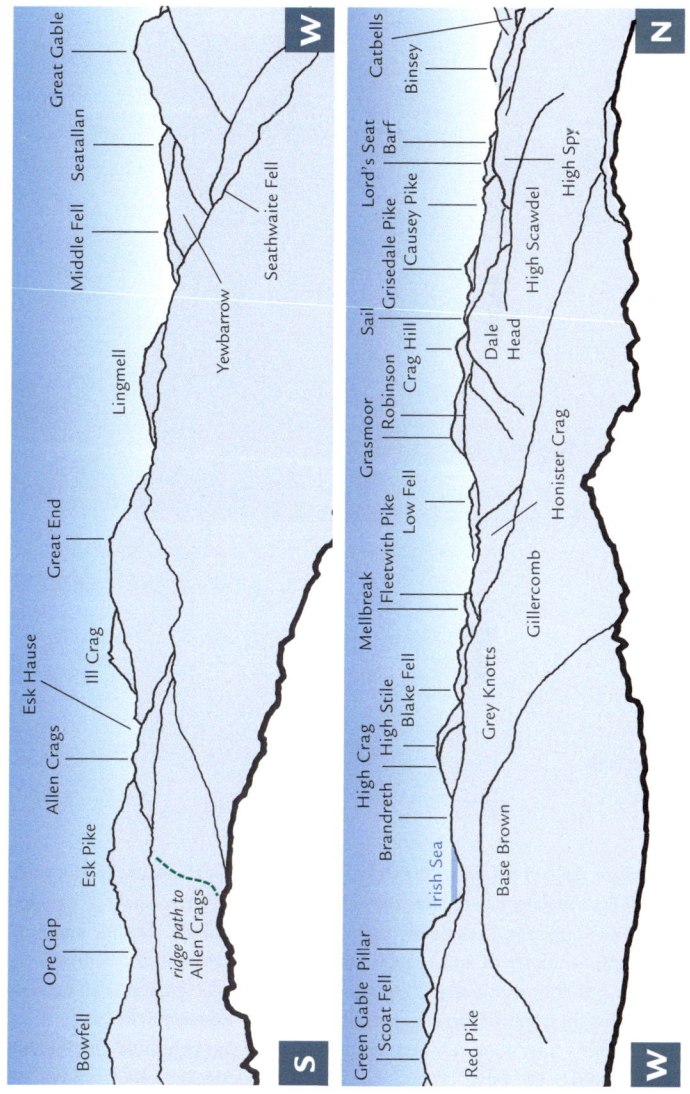

11 GRANGE FELL 416M/1365FT

Climb it from	Grange-in-Borrowdale **3**, Quayfoot **2**, Rosthwaite **1**, Watendlath **15**, Surprise View **16**, Ashness Bridge **17** or Kettlewell **18**
Character	Verdant, heather-clad, craggy-edged and fascinatingly complex
Fell-friendly route	8
Summit grid ref	NY 264 162
Link it with	Great Crag
Part of	Around the Jaws of Borrowdale

This rough tangled fell forms the steep, verdant eastern cheek of the much adored Jaws of Borrowdale, where Derwentwater gives way to Borrowdale proper. To new eyes it must appear a confusing rocky height, with birch, heather and bilberry clinging tenaciously to an irregular knobbly ridge, where three summits vie for individual attention. In terms of elevation this is a modest fell. But what Grange Fell lacks in height is more than compensated for by the infusion of the picturesque.

Climbers have long relished the accessibility and firm holds of Shepherd's, Black, Greatend, Bowder and Gowder Crags, while walkers have found

Brund Fell, the highest of Grange Fell's three summits, from King's How

11 GRANGE FELL

comparable pleasure in unlocking the fell's apparent labyrinth of paths, combining the sylvan with a wild heather-scape. Of the three summits, two are commonly visited, King's How (1–2, 5–6) and the actual top, Brund Fell (3, 7–11), while the third, Heather Knott (4, 12), set well to the north, remains little visited. But walkers who disregard it miss out, for the traverse of this northern limb of the ridge from Lodore is delectably intricate. The climb onto the northern top of Brown Dodd (12) deserves to be better known, though the going is tough over the ridge-top where the heather has not been heavily grazed.

Ascent from Grange-in-Borrowdale 3

Via Troutdale →*2.5km/1½ miles* ↑*365m/1200ft* ⏱*1hr 45min*

1 Embark either from the Grange Bridge bus stop or the small layby south of the Leathes Head Hotel. Walk beside the valley road to the bridle lane branching right from behind the hotel. This leads to Troutdale Cottages and through a gate into Troutdale. A clear path runs on towards Comb Gill. Do not ford the gill but keep right, rising into the woodland above it. The path rises to a hand-gate where you bear left, fording a gill to rise into the birchwood shrouding the looming Greatend Crag.

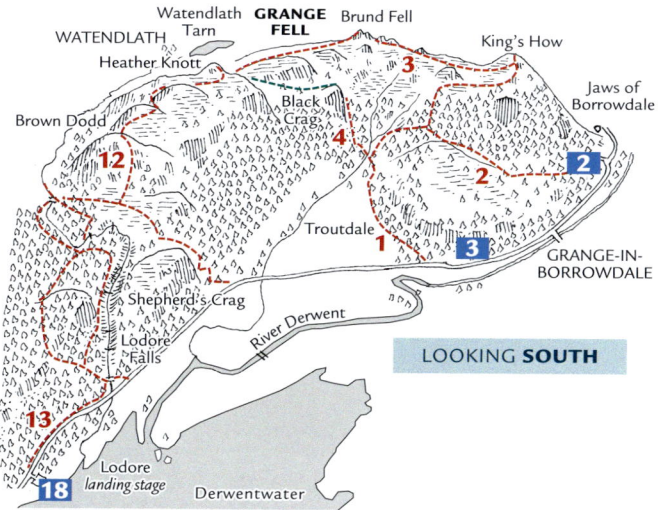

The path climbs purposefully on a stone-pitched staircase to heaven, winding up to a marshy hollow. Keep right, climbing under a yew tree, and ascend to the high-point of the cross-ridge wall; don't be tempted to follow this down as it ends precipitously above Bowder Crag. Go left, joining the narrowing heather ridge, winding up to the summit of **King's How**.

Ascent from Quayfoot National Trust car park 2

Via King's How direct →*2.5km/1½ miles* ↑*320m/1050ft* ⏱*1hr 25min*

There is a choice of two routes leading either north or south, the northerly line (Route 2) the more direct option.

2 A hand-gate in the bounding fence marks an exit to the car park at its upper end. A minor path crosses the gill depression, passes a large erratic and slips through an old slate quarry to join the green bridle path. This contours directly ahead, above a damp slope, before climbing onto the ridge to reach a hand-gate in the saddle. (A spur path can be followed on the left, just prior to the hand-gate. It crosses a ladder-stile, heading north to approach the birch-fringed brink of **Grange Crag**, a little-visited and quite enchanting viewpoint, especially notable for its bird's-eye view of Grange Bridge. Backtrack

Derwentwater from King's How

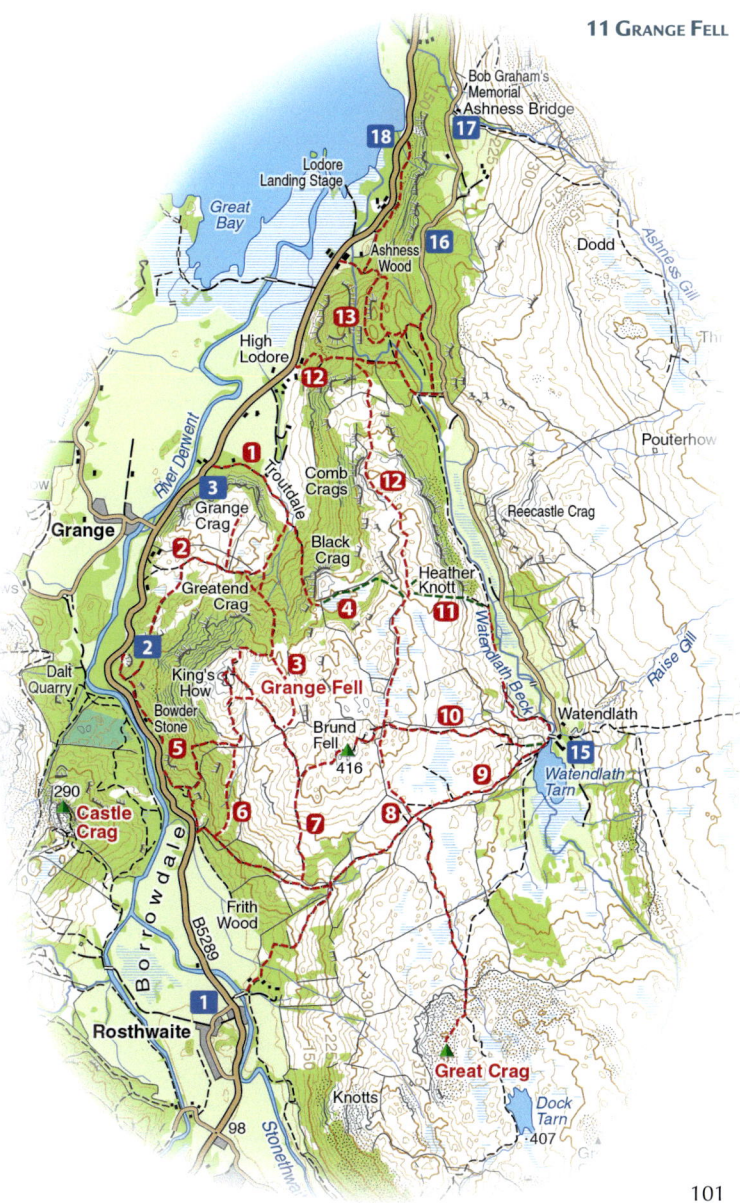

to continue.) Beyond the hand-gate in the saddle there is a handsome view of **Greatend Crag**, with an erratic in the foreground. Advance until a path is spotted forking right, short of the next hand-gate in a wall, and here join Route **1**.

Direct →*2.5km/1½ miles* ↑*340m/1115ft* ⏲*1hr 35min*

3 The 'stairway to heaven' from Troutdale outlined in Route **1** can side-step King's How and progress directly to Brund Fell. Having completed the major stepped ascent, cross the fence stile on the left. The path runs up a shallow side-valley with a wall on the left and, in its later reaches, curves right to join the direct path from King's How. Cross the ladder-stile to the left and rise to the next brow, where the path bears acutely left to climb to the top of **Brund Fell**.

Via Heather Knott →*1.5km/1 mile* ↑*350m/1150ft* ⏲*1hr 45min*

A beautiful approach to Heather Knott, based on the path established by climbers to reach Black Crag and the famous Troutdale Pinnacles

4 Follow the path from Troutdale Cottages as for Route **1**, only this time stride across Comb Gill, climbing purposefully into the natural woodland on a well-made path to the base of **Black Crag**. A loose trail works up beneath the towering pinnacles to a notch beside a gill. Cross the fence tight by the rock. You can clamber left over the adjacent outcrop to discover a superb – if perilous – view down into Troutdale. The primary way follows the wall, left, beside Bleacrag Moss, curving up the rough valley head to the hand-gate, where the ridge path below **Heather Knott** is joined. Don't miss the opportunity to visit this fabulous little summit.

Via the Jaws of Borrowdale →*2.5km/1½ miles* ↑*390m/1280ft* ⏲*1hr 45min*

The impressive Bowder Stone merits a visit before you embark on the climb.

5 Follow signs to the **Bowder Stone** and pass a fenced quarry, via a gate, on a popular surfaced pathway. Find the massive tilted boulder in a glade; the near side is sufficiently angled to give climbers scope for wet-weather bouldering practice. It lies here not because it tumbled from the crag above, like so much

11 GRANGE FELL

of the rock in the vicinity, but rather it was transported by the random haul of a glacier – an Ice Age erratic. A flight of wooden steps gives access to the naturally notched top.

The path, a former quarry extraction track, continues and declines to a hand-gate at the road. Follow the roadside verge path until a footpath sign and stile indicate the beginning of a path to the left. A clear path ascends through the bracken, first onto the low rigg on the right, then curving left up through the bracken to slip under a yew tree, climbing to go through a broken wall, then winding up the steep, lightly wooded fellside. The views improve as height is gained, particularly after you come above a wall, where they open to the south over the meadows of Borrowdale, backed by the highest hills in England. Proceed up the final open section to reach the summit of **King's How**.

6 This point can also be reached by means of an unusual and intriguing modern invention. It begins a little further along the valley road at Red Brow, identified by the recessed layby, just where the road opens out to the Borrowdale meadows. Go through the gate, ascend the bridle path and, a few metres short of a tiny gill ford, bear sharp left up the bank. An evident path leads uphill. Ignore the early footpath, right, since it quickly becomes consumed by bracken, having fallen from favour. Continue climbing the wooded

The Bowder Stone (photo: Maggie Allan)

WALKING THE LAKE DISTRICT FELLS – BORROWDALE

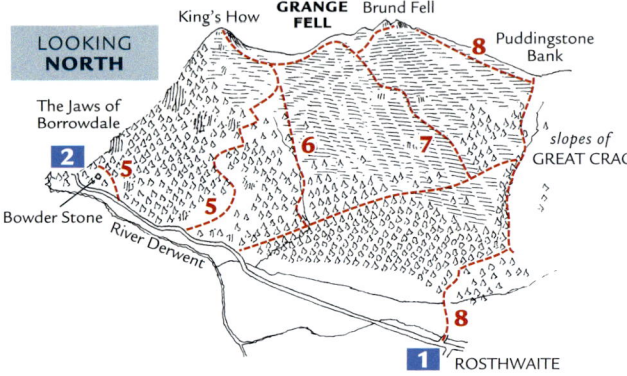

edge. The path persists to a gateway in a wall, where you link up with Route **5** to climb the final open section of the south ridge to the top of **King's How**.

7 Alternatively, having started out with Route **6**, continue up the bridle path on a delightful woodland way and ascend to a hand-gate. The path traverses a bracken fellside, passing the cluster of rocks known as the Resting Stones. From here there is a lovely view down to the green Rosthwaite vale. Watch for the ladder-stile, left, before the conifer copse. You can continue to a kissing-gate to join the Puddingstone Bank path (Route **8**) or cross this ladder-stile, climbing the slope beside the plantation, slanting left on a pronounced path. As King's How duly comes into view the path forks. Go right and climb to **Brund Fell**, the summit of Grange Fell.

Ascent from Rosthwaite 1

Via Puddingstone Bank →*2km/1¼ miles* ↑*350m/1150ft* ⏱*1hr 20min*

The popular bridle path over Puddingstone Bank to Watendlath provides the ideal springboard for an ascent from Rosthwaite.

8 Cross the **Stonethwaite Beck** bridge, north of the post office, and fork left, facing the entrance to Hazel Bank Hotel. Pass above Dinah Hoggus camping barn. The lane winds up to a gate. An open trail, which has received some restorative treatment, leads up the slope. Take opportunities to look back from

11 GRANGE FELL

time to time, as the view over upper Borrowdale improves with every stride and is quite superb. Two gates on, the track levels as it approaches the watershed. Bear left after the second gate, keeping the wall to your left. Reach the low ladder-stile over the wall, which you duly cross, and wind up to the summit outcrop.

Ascent from Watendlath 15

Via Puddingstone Bank →2km/1¼ miles ↑170m/560ft ⏲45min

The easiest route of all: stride out on the bridle path traversing Puddingstone Bank.

9 From the National Trust car park (with adjacent toilets and farmhouse tearoom) walk through the hamlet to cross the packhorse bridge at the outflow of **Watendlath Tarn**. Take the main path, left, via the hand-gate, signposted to Rosthwaite, observing the antics of ducks and fly-fishermen afloat on the tarn. The track climbs steadily, with lovely views back to the hamlet and tarn. Just short of the gate at the pass go right, accompanying Route **8** to the top. Keeping the wall to your left, you can either cross the first ladder-stile on the

Watendlath, as seen during the ascent of Brund Fell

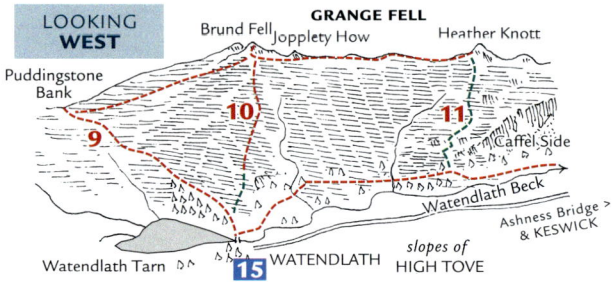

left and ascend the pathless slope direct to the summit or – probably better – keep with the wall to the low ladder-stile at the top.

Direct ➜ *1.5km/1 mile* ↑*170m/560ft* ⏲*35min*

This route avoids the walking traffic on the Puddingstone Bank bridle path.

10 An early branch right, just above the shore of **Watendlath Tarn**, leads up the bank, with a fine view down the Watendlath Beck valley towards Skiddaw. A narrow path leads through a hand-gate. Ascend, with a wall over to the right and sporadic evidence of a path. With some wet ground on the rise to the wall junction, go left along the ridge path, rounding the wall on the right, to the low ladder-stile, from where you can make your final approach to the summit.

Via Heather Knott ➜ *2.5km/1½ miles* ↑*190m/625ft* ⏲*1hr 20min*

Enjoy the fantastic views in solitude from Grange Fell's shiest summit, Heather Knott.

11 Go through the gate, take the first right after the packhorse bridge and follow the path down the valley. Immediately before the second hand-gate and before the short flight of steps, go left to clamber up the pathless rough fellside, en route peering over the craggy ramparts of **Caffel Side**. Climb with a wall, then a fence, to the right, onto the upper slopes, to reach the ridge-top stile at the fence junction to join the ridge path from Brund Fell. Cross the stile and work left, round and up the tough herbage, to the summit of **Heather Knott**.

eye being drawn south along the green strath of Borrowdale to the mighty Scafells, north beyond Derwentwater to Skiddaw, and near west to the craggy precipices and over to High Spy.

Safe descents

The roughness and confusing terrain of the upper fell may be a concern in misty conditions. The easiest line of escape is E. Cross the low ladder-stile and from thereon aim S (**8**), beside the descending wall, to the top of Puddingstone Bank. On meeting the track either go right (W) to Rosthwaite, 1.6km, or left (E, **9**) to Watendlath, 800 metres.

Ridge route

Great Crag →*2km/1¼ miles* ↓*90m/295ft* ↑*40m/130ft* ⏲*45min*
Head E, cross the low ladder-stile and from thereon aim S, beside the descending wall, to the top of Puddingstone Bank. A continuing path leads S, via the hand-gate, winding across intermittently marshy ground, with patches of bog myrtle, to a further hand-gate in a cross-ridge wall. The path bears slightly left to link up with the path rising from the lane on the W side of Watendlath Tarn. Now bear right, skirting the marsh, to a hand-gate. Thereon the path climbs towards Dock Tarn; take the first clear turn right before the tarn to ascend to the top.

12 GREAT CRAG 452M/1483FT

Climb it from	Rosthwaite **1**, Watendlath **15** or Stonethwaite **14**
Character	The upper slopes – a tangle of heather and rock – ensure all paths are tricky to find and follow
Fell-friendly route	3
Summit grid ref	NY 269 147
Link it with	Grange Fell or Ullscarf
Part of	Around the Jaws of Borrowdale

Observed from Stonethwaite, Great Crag appears to be a mass of trees, a gloriously pleated deciduous skirt. Hidden from view are its roughly textured upper slopes, luxuriant with heather, marsh and volcanic rock. The fell forms an intriguingly rough bridge between Grange Fell and the high central plateau of Ullscarf and is a backdrop to the much-loved lake-end scene at Watendlath. If your idea of a good time on the fells includes a spot of intense tanglefoot exploration, then this is your kind of top. It attracts few visitors and most actually ignore the summit, content with the shy charm of lily-endowed Dock Tarn on the lovely path between Stonethwaite and Watendlath.

↑ *Watendlath from the summit (photo: Maggie Allan)*

12 GREAT CRAG

Paths are few. Indeed, apart from the north–south traverse by Dock Tarn and sundry minor diversions to the summit, the fell is bereft of confidence-giving trails and the fellwalker must rely mostly on the instinctive twists and turns of sheep for any comfort. The most common line of approach is via the Puddingstone Bank bridleway (1–2) which links Rosthwaite and Watendlath, but the fell can also be climbed from Stonethwaite to the south (4–5) or on a more direct line from Watendlath (3).

Great Crag actually has higher companion parts: the cairn on Green Comb is proud of Great Crag's summit by the considerable margin of 28m. Green Comb offers superior views into the Watendlath valley and to Ullscarf, to which it might strictly be thought to belong, though by character it rests fairly and squarely in this chapter. Down to the southwest of the summit the lower-tier ridge of Knotts might attract the attention of explorers; however, this area is well defended by bracken and is inferior to the main summit as a viewpoint.

Ascent from Rosthwaite 1

Via Puddingstone Bank →*2.7km/1¾ miles* ↑*355m/1165ft* ⏱*1hr 30min*

The perennially popular path over Puddingstone Bank to Watendlath provides the ideal springboard for an ascent.

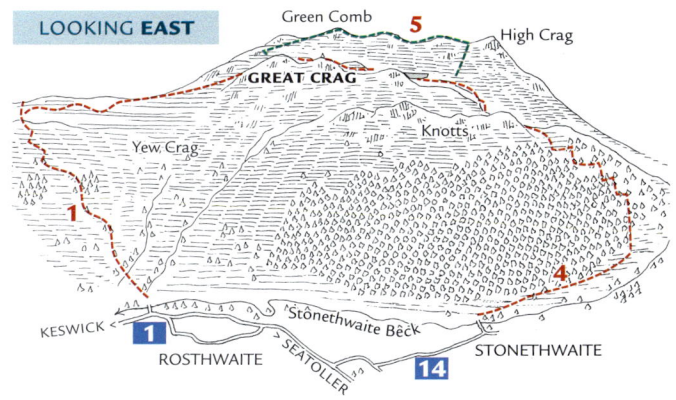

1 Cross the **Stonethwaite Beck** bridge, north of the post office, and fork left facing the entrance to Hazel Bank Hotel. Passing above Dinah Hoggus camping barn the lane winds up to a gate. An open trail leads up the slope; take opportunities to look back from time to time as the view over upper Borrowdale is quite superb. Two gates on, the track levels as it approaches the watershed. Bear right, off the bridle path, to the kissing-gate, then wind across intermittently marshy ground, with patches of bog myrtle, to a further

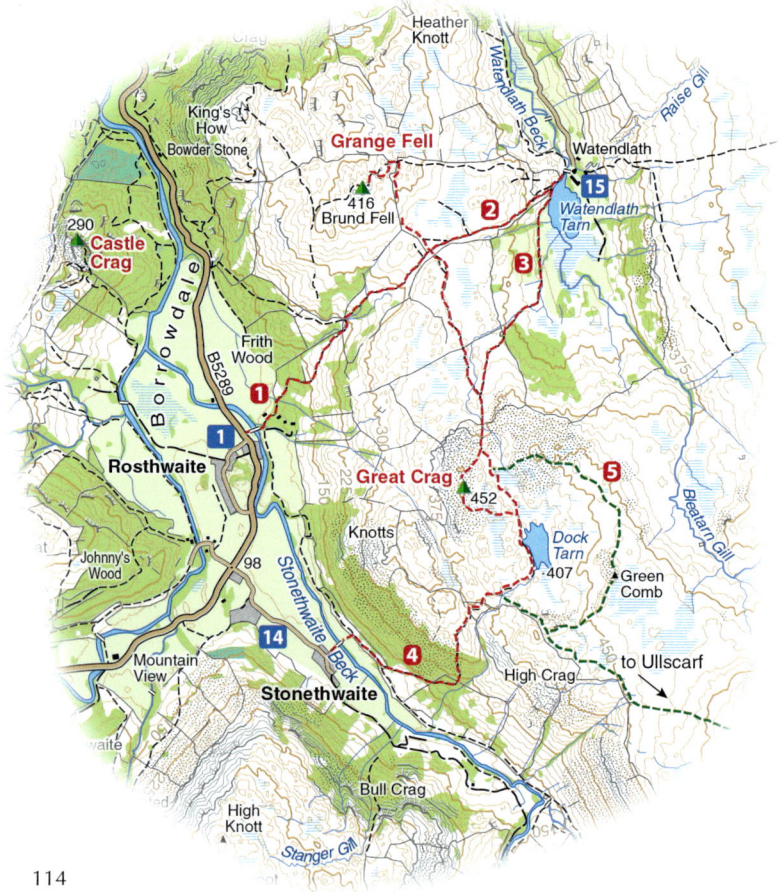

12 GREAT CRAG

kissing-gate in a cross-ridge wall. The path bears slightly left to link up with the path rising from the lane on the west side of Watendlath Tarn. Now bear right, skirting the marsh, to a hand-gate. From here the path climbs towards **Dock Tarn**. Take the first clear turn, right, before the tarn to ascend to the top.

Ascent from Watendlath 15

Via Puddingstone Bank →*2km/1¼ miles* ↑*195m/640ft* ⊕*1hr*

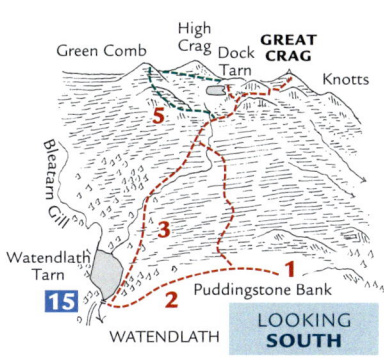

2 From the National Trust car park behind the farmhouse tearoom cross the packhorse bridge at the outflow of **Watendlath Tarn**. The main path goes up to the watershed then branches south via a kissing-gate. Continue along a clear path over boggy ground, with a considerable growth of bog myrtle, which is noted for its midge-deterrent properties. At another kissing-gate the trail drifts left to meet up with the path climbing direct from Watendlath Tarn (Route **3**).

One path leads on via yet more marsh, curving right to a wall-stile and climbing through a weakness in the Great Crag facade. The main thrust of the path wanders on towards the western shore of **Dock Tarn**. Watch for the cairned branch path to the right, climbing onto the first top; the second is the true summit.

3 Alternatively, from the fork in the track beyond the initial gate after the packhorse bridge (see Route **2**), follow the gated lane, rising above the tarn, and finally wind up a pasture, via gates, onto marshy ground and meet up with the former ridge-top path. Here join Route **2**.

Eagle and Sergeant's Crags from the ruined bothy on Lingy End

Ascent from Stonethwaite 14

Via Lingy End →2km/1¼ miles ↑355m/1165ft ⏱1hr 15min

Quite the most absorbing climb, steep-stepped through native woodland onto rank-heather moor, visiting an enchanting pool en route to the scenic summit

4 Park your car along the approach road, not in the hamlet. Entering the community, bear left at the kiosk, signed 'Greenup and Grasmere'. Cross Stonethwaite Bridge to reach a gate and join the main valley bridle path, coincident with Wainwright's Coast to Coast Walk. Go right, via the gate. After the sheepfold, which forms a delightful foreground to views of Eagle Crag, the lane dips. At the low wall opening, after some 50 metres, bear half-left and rise up the pasture on a turf trod, between swathes of bracken, to a wall-stile. The path goes left, rising to a wall-stile. From here the path climbs purposefully through the deciduous woodland on a stony staircase, switching away from Willygrass Gill.

Emerging from the canopy, take an approving view south to Eagle Crag and Sergeant's Crag, dramatically seen at their very best. Rising onto the appropriately named Lingy End, climb by the heather banks and ruined shepherds'

12 GREAT CRAG

shelter. Skirt round the re-entrant of Willygrass Gill, and the view is of the inaccessible High Crag above the eastern fork of the cascading gill. Cross over the wall-stile and continue to the shores of **Dock Tarn**, seeking the path leading left at the northern end of the tarn. On this path wind northwest to the summit.

This indulgent 2km circuit of the arc of tops east of Dock Tarn, culminating on Green Comb, is thoroughly absorbing.

5 Branch from the Lingy End route (Route **4**) where the ridge route to Ullscarf fords Willygrass Gill, following the ascending wall. Branch onto the pathless ridge and wind northeast to the cairned top of **Green Comb**. Continue naturally in a westward arc, with lovely patterned rock to inspect en route to fording a gill and uniting with the path from Puddingstone Bank (Route **1**).

The summit

Heather, sadly lacking on so many fells, makes repose in this vicinity quite delightful, especially when in full late-summer bloom. To the north, beyond a short depression, a large cairn rests on a rock-step. Further cairns mark a subsidiary top, blessed with a superior northward prospect towards Grange Fell and Skiddaw.

Great Crag, carpeted with heather (photo: Maggie Allan)

Safe descents

The consistent path running alongside Dock Tarn gives security for descents to Watendlath (**2–3**), 2km, Rosthwaite (N, **1**), 3.2km, or Stonethwaite (S, **4**), 2.4km, so head E from the summit to join it.

Ridge routes

Grange Fell →*2km/1¼ miles* ↓*40m/130ft* ↑*90m/295ft* ⏱*45min*
A path leads N, over an adjacent cairned top, then bears right, dropping NE to join the path from Dock Tarn. This now continues down to a wall-stile and, bearing half-right, avoids marshy ground resplendent with bog myrtle. At the path fork go half-left to a kissing-gate, and more marshy ground is crossed en route to a second kissing-gate. Cross the Puddingstone Bank track, ascending with the wall to your left to a low ladder-stile. Cross it and wind up to the summit, which is the second top after the apparent summit, marked by a cairn on a sharp pike.

Ullscarf →*4.3km/2¾ miles* ↓*15m/50ft* ↑*400m/1310ft* ⏱*1hr 30min*
To minimise rough and seriously boggy ground head SE to follow the main path beyond the outflow of Dock Tarn. Where a wall is seen rising left, bear off, ford the outflow gill, ascending with the wall to your right, and cross the saddle to the left of High Crag. As you descend enjoy the marvellous views of Eagle and Sergeant's Crags, as well as the long view up Langstrath to Bowfell. The wall dips right; contour to pick up the wall again along the edge above Greenup Gill. As the wall rises and falls, follow it until you round a knoll. Spin off E, climbing the fellside to Low Saddle and, picking up the ridge path, continue SSE to High Saddle and the ridge fence. Cross the flimsy stile near the acute corner to reach the summit.

13 GREAT END 907M/2976FT

Climb it from	Seathwaite **12** or Wasdale Green **34**
Character	A commanding viewpoint above a forbidding northern rim of crags; the best place from which to survey upper Borrowdale
Fell-friendly route	2
Summit grid ref	NY 227 084
Link it with	Scafell Pike

Whether viewed from Wasdale Head or Borrowdale, Great End is clearly the abrupt conclusion of the high plateau, linking naturally to the southwest to Broad Crag and Ill Crag. From Sprinkling Tarn, its shadow-darkened north face, etched with gullies and renowned for its winter ice climbs, is seen to perfection.

Worthy objective though it is, for fellwalkers as much as climbers, if you stand at the brink of this sumptuous north-facing cliff to enjoy the uninhibited views you will most likely be alone with your elation. And despite its outward ferocity there are wonderful ways to discover Great End, up dramatic ravines and over ancient packhorse routes or perhaps following in the footsteps of thirsty travellers heading over from Borrowdale to partake in a pint at the Wasdale Head Inn and stumble back in the dark?

↑ *Great End from Sprinkling Tarn*

The fell is often added to expeditions from Great Langdale, conveniently bolted onto the journeys to and from Scafell Pike. The primary lines up to Styhead Pass and Sprinkling Tarn, however, are a gradual out-and-back up Lingmell Beck from Wasdale (6) and the two packhorse routes (1–3) from Borrowdale. There you can choose from three contrasting lines (2, 4–5) to the summit.

Ascent from Seathwaite 12 *off map N*

The lynch-pin for ascents from Borrowdale is Stockley Bridge.

1 The valley track leads from the farm, via gates, to this elegant single-span packhorse bridge, constructed stoutly on bare rocks, where Grains Gill forces through a modest but quite beautiful ravine, especially exciting when the gill is in spate. The gate on the west side is the point where two dale routes (Routes **2** and **3**) diverge.

Stockley Bridge

13 Great End

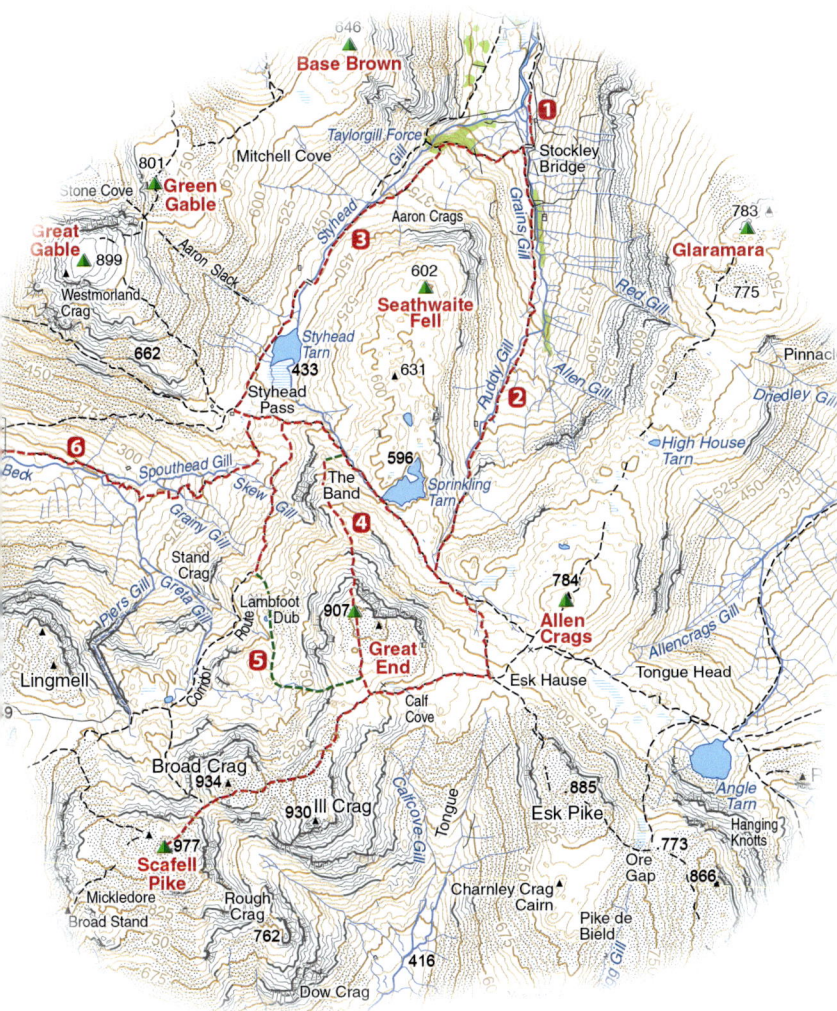

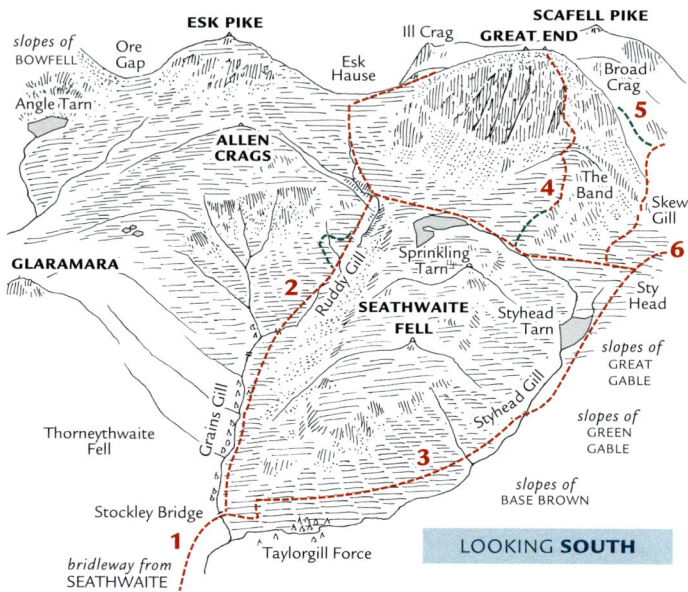

Via Grains Gill →*4.7km/3 miles* ↑*790m/2590ft* ⏲*3hr 45min*

Without question, this is the easiest route to the top.

2 This path has become the high-road to Esk Hause thanks to intensive pitching works. It crosses a footbridge as **Ruddy Gill** makes its final flight down a cleft to a secretive fall and a fuming waters-meet with **Allen Gill**, careering on as **Grains Gill**. At the second minor gill crossing you can drift up the rigg, half-left, onto the prominent shelf. This is the older packhorse route and makes an interesting soft staircase alternative to the hard pitching. If you do, then skirt the marshy ground on the shelf to the west side and link back to the modern trail. The upper section of Ruddy Gill runs through a deep ravine with some trees managing to grow unhindered by the Herdwicks!

Ford the gill to join the path ascending from **Sprinkling Tarn**, taking the right-hand fork to reach **Esk Hause** above the cross-wall shelter. Leading into the shallow combe of **Calf Cove**, a ceaseless flow of walkers ensures a clear path with a superfluity of cairns to boot. As the ground eases above this damp hollow, branch right, heading north up the broad semi-pasture ridge to the summit, thereby completely side-stepping the boulder-infested east slope.

Via Styhead Pass →*5.5km/3½ miles* ↑*800m/2625ft* ⏲*3hr 25min*

The setting of this ancient route is a stirring one and the popular rocky path is unmistakable.

3 The path winds up from the gate beyond **Stockley Bridge** (see Route **1**), via a rock-step, to a gate in the intake wall below Black Waugh, a broad, ice-smoothed grim-looking rock-face. The path continues, gradually easing in gradient though not necessarily in its roughness. Cross a footbridge and walk forward to glance by the western shore of **Styhead Tarn** – a popular high-level camp site. Arrive at the Mountain Rescue stretcher box at **Styhead Pass**, a natural rendezvous point. Go left, setting course for **Esk Hause**. The path, never in doubt, crosses the outflow of **Sprinkling Tarn**. Cross a low saddle to join Route **2** by Ruddy Gill.

Via the Band →*5.5km/3½ miles* ↑*800m/2625ft* ⏲*3hr 30min*

This ridge is nowhere near as intimidating a climb as might be thought at first sight.

4 Leave the route to **Esk Hause** (see Route **3**) when you reach outcrops on the slopes of Seathwaite Fell to your left and after a stretch of pitching. Climb to a small col as a grassy trod winds on up the ridge. The impressive Spouthead scarp close on the right gives magnificent views to Lingmell. A shallow gully marks the top of **Skew Gill**, a point of further divide. The direct mild scramble continues upward with a certain inevitable vagueness. Never fear, there is a simple line which draws up to a gully providing a fine view to Cust's Gully, identified by its huge chockstone. This gully, itself a demanding scramble, is not recommended, so it's best to give it a miss unless you have the necessary climbing skills. Instead tackle the final stretch of bouldery slope to reach the top. Make a point of skirting the cliff edge to see the top of Cust's and Central Gullies and the dramatic fell arena below.

Via Lambfoot Dub
→ *4.5km/2¾ miles*
↑ *805m/2640ft*
⏲ *3hr 40min*

This route starts with the busy Corridor Route but slips away, off-path, to find the tranquil Lambfoot Dub and a quiet western approach to the summit.

Looking down on the chockstone in Cust's Gully

5 Having started out with Route **3**, set off from the Styhead Pass stretcher box, heading up the Esk Hause path onto the first rise, to branch right to cross the vestige of a short wall, dip and contour to the mouth of the Skew Gill ravine. At Skew Gill, frequently a dry jumble of stones, mount the opposing slope and climb on, slipping through a short rock cutting. The pitched staircase is clear ahead. When you spot a round-headed knoll high above branch off the Corridor Route. Clamber up the predominantly grassy slope, slipping behind the knoll to find Lambfoot Dub. The pool is surprisingly clear and deep, a lovely spot to rest alone, blissfully gazing across to Great Gable, well above the chattering trekkers on the Corridor Route. Traverse into the nameless combe behind Round How, joining the headstream of Greta Gill, which curves up left to its source at the natural weakness in the scarp. This gives steep but simple access to the saddle above and thereby the summit, up to the left (north).

13 GREAT END

Ascent from Wasdale Green 34 *off map W*

Via Styhead Pass →*5km/3 miles* ↑*830m/2725ft* ⏲*3hr 30min*

Great End captivates the attention on the walk up Lingmell Beck from Burnthwaite, the high, rugged skyline a tempting call to arms – or to legs!

6 Leave the car park and follow the lane to Burnthwaite. Pass to the left of the farm buildings to a gate. Keep right. The obvious way heads on between varying walls, via a gate, to cross a footbridge spanning Gable Beck. Soon you face a choice of routes to Sty Head, both equally sound. The standard route sticks religiously to the rising path, which passes through a hand-gate before reaching scree. The smart route lies up the valley. (Alternatively take the scree on the way up and return along the valley for a little variety.) Either bear off as bracken begins to encroach or wait a further hundred metres to find a clear path slanting down to the hand-gate near the foot of a wall. Keep alongside **Lingmell Beck**, fording the stream just after the confluence with **Piers Gill**. A clear green trail winds up the rigg then fords a gill to the left. Slant across the next rigg to ford **Spouthead Gill** then zig-zag up to **Styhead Pass** to join Route **3**, **4** or **5**.

Great Gable from the north ridge close to Cust's Gully

The summit

Two tops of almost identical height vie for pre-eminence. The northwest cairn is further forward and so it better commands the northern prospect, although the Langdale Pikes and Lingmoor Fell are hidden from view from here.

Safe descents

Walk S to the depression, a little over 400 metres distant, to meet up with the path from Scafell Pike. Switch sharp left in the company of this popular trail (**2**), descending Calf Cove to Esk Hause. **Do not** walk S from this point. Find the cross-wall. It is only a short stride NE to Allen Crags hause – the 'false' Esk Hause – from here. Crossing the saddle E–W, a regular path leads to safety: E to Angle Tarn and Rossett Gill for Great Langdale and W for Ruddy Gill (**2**) and Borrowdale, or further to Styhead Pass for Wasdale Head (**6**).

Ridge route

Scafell Pike →*2.5km/1½ miles* ↓*100m/330ft* ↑*185m/605ft* ⏲*40min*
Descend S to the depression to join the path emerging from Calf Cove. Continue SW, soon encountering an awkward and unavoidable section of boulders. The ridge narrows, succeeded by a mild interval of gravelly trail slipping into the dip between Ill Crag and Broad Crag, and then, over the E shoulder of the latter, boulder-hopping resumes with a vengeance! Descend to Broadcrag Col and climb the facing narrow, greatly hammered ridge, with loose stones in abundance. Eventually matters ease and the walled summit stand comes into view. The best shelters from the wind are to be found on the E side, over to the left as you reach the plateau.

14 GREAT GABLE 899M/2949FT

Climb it from	Seathwaite **12**, Honister Pass **10**, Gatesgarth **9**, Black Sail Youth Hostel **8** or Wasdale Green **34**
Character	Tumultuously craggy, an iconic peak pivotal to Wasdale, Ennerdale and Borrowdale
Fell-friendly route	1 and 4
Summit grid ref	NY 211 104
Link it with	Green Gable

Great Gable is everything we desire of a mountain – a domed cathedral. From around the compass its good looks are quite distinct. Stand on Great End, overlooking Sty Head, and view the long Breast Route climbing to the near square-cut top. Stand on Lingmell and be thrilled by the illusion of vertical cliffs and scree on the Great Napes. But for many it is the composition from Wast Water, framed by Yewbarrow and Lingmell, that is most iconic and the emblem of the National Park.

Great Gable ranks as one of the most popular climbs in the district, alongside Helvellyn and Scafell Pike – the kind of hill that draws you back time after time. Central to its appeal is the Great Napes, a majestic mass of buttresses that draw up to a crest linking to the base of Westmorland Crags on the southern lip of the summit. Fellwalkers venture around it and scramblers visit such amazing features as Napes Needle, Sphinx Rock and Sphinx Ridge above it, out of Little Hell Gate.

↑ *Great Gable from Kirk Fell*

The South Traverse from Sty Head to Beck Head is a really fine high-level fell walk, especially when combined with the North Traverse under Gable Crag to make up the Gable Girdle (14). Whether from Buttermere (7), Borrowdale (1–5) or Wasdale (10–13), Great Gable is a serious day out, with lots of variants to choose from. Shorter approaches start from Honister Pass (6) or Black Sail Hut youth hostel (8–9).

Ascent from Seathwaite 12

Via Stockley Bridge and Aaron Slack or Sty Head
→6.8km/4¼ miles ↑780m/2560ft ⏲4hr

Stick to Routes 1 and 4 for a straightforward ascent, or start on Route 2 to take in a stretch of scrambling and finish on Route 3 to lose the crowds.

1 Walk straight on through the farm and follow the track, via gates, to cross **Stockley Bridge**. Keep with the main part-pitched path through two subsequent gates and, higher up, a footbridge, after a particularly stony beck-side passage.

2 The footbridge can also be reached by following the footpath running under the flanks of **Base Brown**. Turn right through the barn opposite Seathwaite farmhouse and cross the footbridge over the Derwent. Then turn left through a gate and follow the footpath upstream. The path drifts up from the stony river via a kissing-gate, with stony passages unavoidable. Cross a ladder-stile beside a sheep-creep and a pine, passing below an old fold and a wall and by large boulders, with Hind Crag prominent across the valley, shielding the western flanks of Glaramara. The path draws towards **Taylorgill Force** and mounts rocks to a hand-gate tight by a cliff, after which more earnest scrambling ensues – simple stuff when dry and reminiscent of a minor Jack's Rake. Fear not; the journey soon eases and the path scoops on with handsome views of the graceful

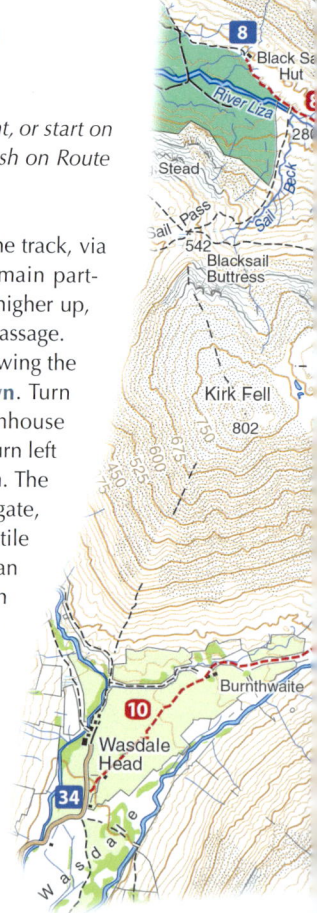

14 Great Gable

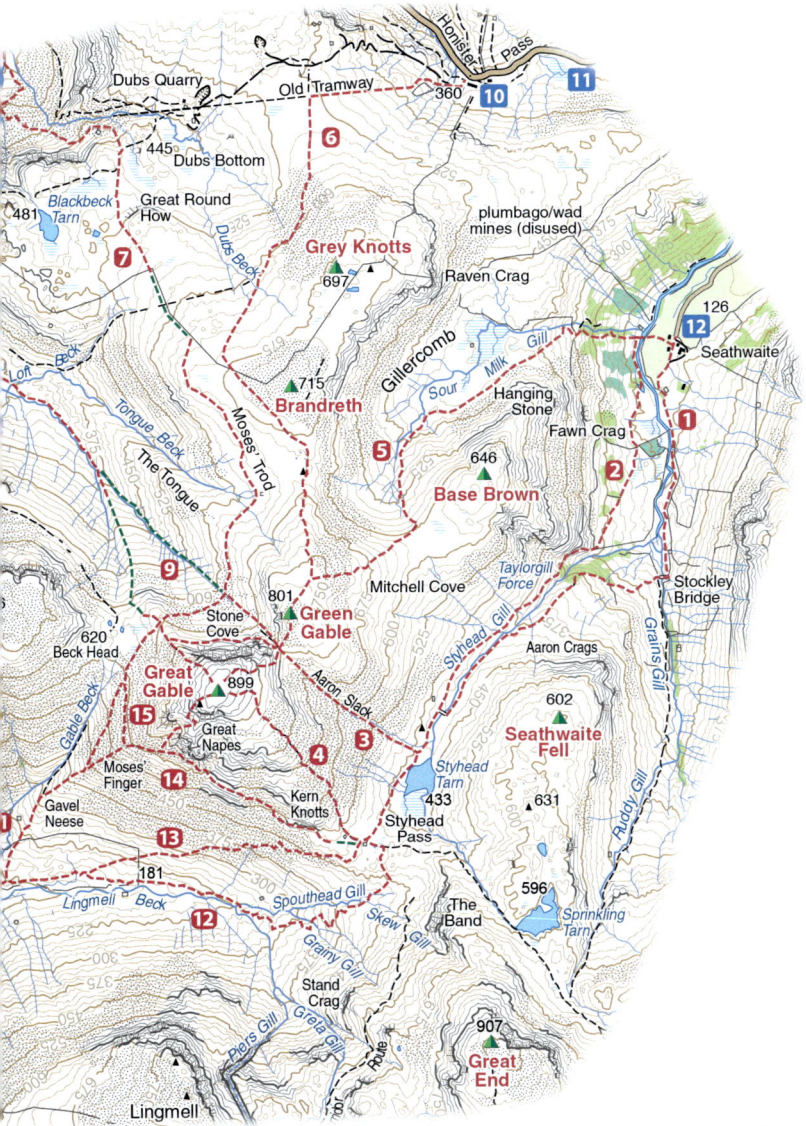

WALKING THE LAKE DISTRICT FELLS – BORROWDALE

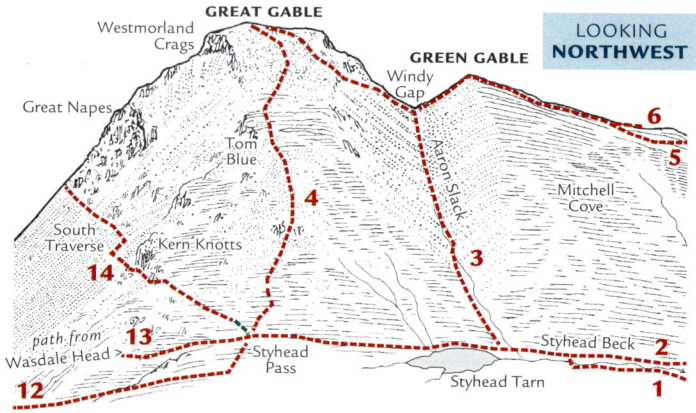

waterfall. (Steer well clear of the stony gully up to the right. It is not a means of ascent. Notice the huge boulders resting at the 'Y' fork constriction, above the broad lower screes, and the even narrower rift in the adjacent cliff.) Continue up **Styhead Gill** and past the footbridge.

3 Having started out with either Route **1** or Route **2**, approaching **Styhead Tarn** a ford marks the point of departure of the improved path up **Aaron Slack**, which rises and fords the gill to complete the ascent to **Windy Gap** on looser scree, there joining the ridge route from **Green Gable** en route to the summit.

4 Alternatively, pass on by **Styhead Tarn** to reach **Styhead Pass**, a veritable Piccadilly Circus of fell paths, the stretcher box a stark reminder of the latent perils of these mountains. From this point it is a 410m climb to the summit. Embark on the traditional tourist or Breast Route, which turns abruptly right (northwest), abundantly cairned. Higher, solid pitching has given stability to the path where it negotiates scree close under **Tom Blue**. There is almost no scope to lose the path, which leads directly to the summit.

Via Gillercomb →4.5km/2¾ miles ↑825m/2705ft ⏲3hr 45min

This popular route sets about earnest climbing from the start.

5 Turn right through the barn opposite Seathwaite farmhouse and cross the footbridge over the Derwent. At once the path gets to grips with a pitched ascent of **Sour Milk Gill**. Entering **Gillercomb**, the part-pitched path sweeps south up the western slopes of **Base Brown**, climbing to the ridge heading for **Green Gable**, latterly in harmony with the regular path from Honister. The quick loose descent to **Windy Gap** cairn is succeeded by a steady climb on a clear path, which has one short rocky section en route to the stony summit plateau.

Ascent from Honister Pass 10

Direct →*4.8km/3 miles* ↑*595m/1950ft* ⏲*3hr 30min*

The shorter winter months make this a particularly attractive option, with its lofty start and more gradual – if less exciting – approach via Green Gable.

6 From the car park begin with the quarry track, stepping up left on the realigned pitched path which soon reconnects with the **Old Tramway**. A few remnant sleepers are evident underfoot as you draw near to the ruined site of Drum House on the brow of the hill. Turn left and follow the chain of cairns, on a worn path, making easy progress across the flanks of **Grey Knotts**. Where the path forks keep left, and after crossing a fence-stile advance to the tarn-jewelled depression of Gillercomb Head. The path holds to a southerly course, climbing up onto **Green Gable**. Pause awhile and admire the impressive view of Gable Crag from

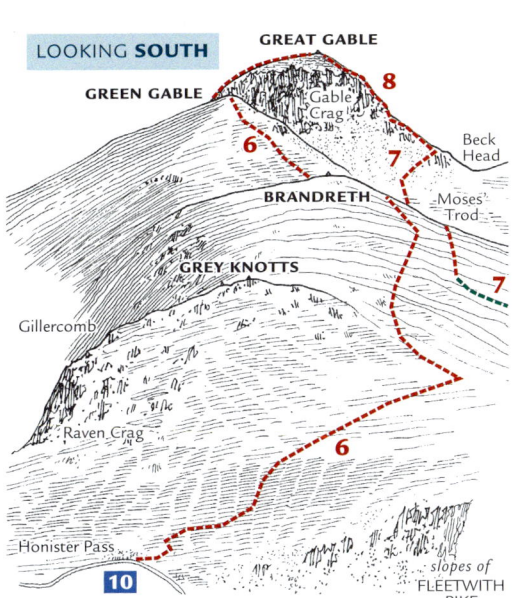

the wind-shelter, then head on south into the narrow defile of **Windy Gap** – invariably true to its name. From the cairn continue, now curving up on a southwest course and navigating a minor rocky scramble to reach the rock-strewn summit dome.

Ascent from Gatesgarth 9 *off map NW*

Via Warnscale and Moses' Trod →*6.4km/4 miles* ↑*855m/2805ft* ⏱*4hr 15min*

Climb up from the Buttermere valley on a steady gradient.

7 Follow the regular open track into the Warnscale valley, branch right to cross the broad footbridge and make your way up the old miners' path below the northern cliffs of **Haystacks** to Warnscale Head (bothy), working up to the brow left of Green Crag. Turn right with the popular path (as to Haystacks) but turn left at the next junction, ascending south, to the right of **Great Round How**, to meet and cross a fence by a stile. Bear up left with the fence. The next fence-stile marks the crossing of the course of the Coast to Coast Walk. Ignore this and continue up to the next fence-stile where an evident path breaks right; this is **Moses' Trod**. Follow this path above Brin Crag, round the head of **Tongue Beck** and along the upper slopes of **Green Gable**, on a contouring course. The track drifts into the aptly named **Stone Cove** and crosses below the dark shadow of Gable Crag, mounting to a shoulder, where it is joined by the North Traverse. Great Gable's northwest ridge ensues, requiring minor rock-hopping and scrambling to the top.

Ascent from Black Sail Youth Hostel 8

From the youth hostel at the head of Ennerdale you have two occasionally rough and pathless, but pretty direct, ways to choose from.

Via Beck Head or Stone Cove →*3.7km/2¼ miles* ↑*795m/2610ft* ⏱*3hr*

8 From Black Sail Hut stride southeast down the bank path towards the Liza footbridge. Short of the bridge a path contours left along the foot of the moraine. Ford **Loft Beck** close to its confluence with the newly born **River Liza**. Keep company with the north bank of the Liza on a modest path. At the first significant waters-meet, ford the beck and clamber up the steep bank

14 GREAT GABLE

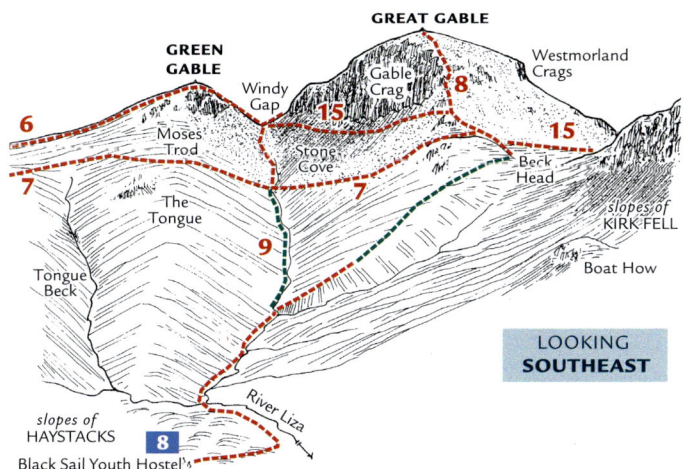

onto the grassy ridge, heading south-southeast. Typically, the path inevitably fades in the long grass. Aim to the right of the prominent outcropping towards the top to reach the broad saddle of **Beck Head**. Turn left and follow the clear – if loose – path onto the northwest ridge and to the summit.

9 Keep with the irregular path tussling up beside the confined Liza gill. This crosses the well-marked **Moses' Trod** and continues into **Stone Cove**. The higher path is subject to wear and is loose underfoot. Reaching the large cairn in **Windy Gap**, bear right (joining Route **5**) to complete the ascent.

Ascent from Wasdale Green 34

The lane leading up to the valley head (Route 10) is the starting point for a handful of contrasting approaches. Route 11, if you choose to take in the scree scramble that is Little Hell Gate, is the most direct approach to the fell.

Via Gavel Neese and Beck Head →*4.1km/2½ miles* ↑*825m/2705ft* ⏲*3hr 30min*

10 Follow the lane leading northeast from Wasdale Green by Lingmell House. Pass St Olaf's, a charming little place of worship sheltering amid yews and tombstones. The lane weaves through the irregular stone-walled enclosure

WALKING THE LAKE DISTRICT FELLS – BORROWDALE

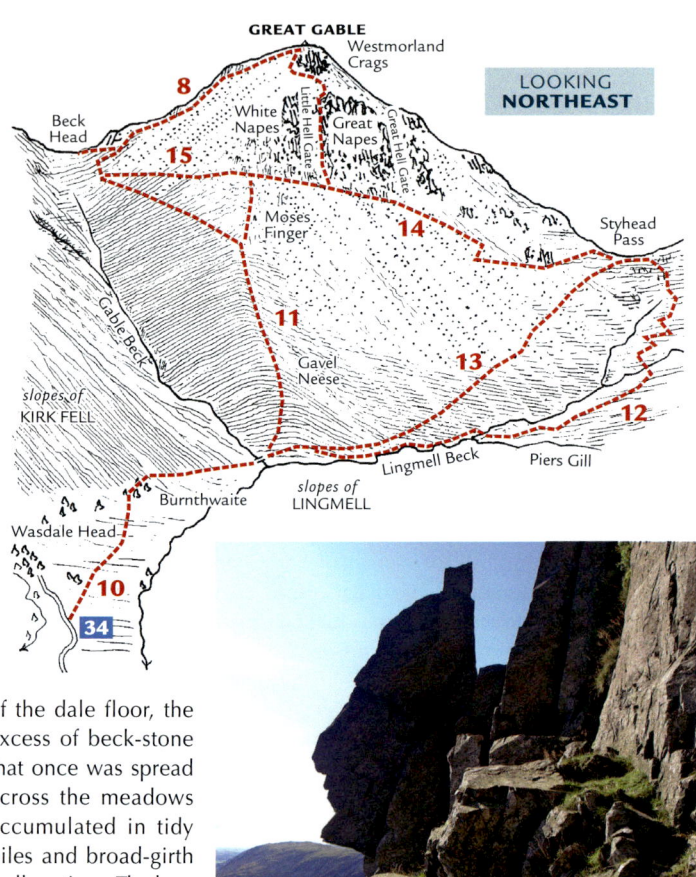

Striking profile of the Sphinx Rock

of the dale floor, the excess of beck-stone that once was spread across the meadows accumulated in tidy piles and broad-girth wall sections. The lane enters the environs of **Burnthwaite Farm**. Angle left, passing through a gate into an irregular walled drove-way which leads on, by a hand-gate, to reach the footbridge spanning **Gable Beck**, where you can join Route **11** or **12**.

Stony path off Gavel Neese, leading to Beck Head

11 You can confront the fell right away by climbing **Gavel Neese**, climbing either to Beck Head or onto the South Traverse. Step up left, climbing steadily via a hand-gate, with intermittent stone pitching. The large waterfall in **Gable Beck**, seen from Burnthwaite, is inconveniently obscured from the path. Ignore the first branch path, which moves into the upper confines of Gable Beck. Continue until the turf gives way to loose rock.

Here you have two options. Bear left and climb under the considerable scree spilling from the upper portion of **White Napes** to reach **Beck Head**. From the broad saddle, between Kirk Fell and Great Gable, the path then holds to the right-hand slope, rising to mount by the northwest ridge (with Route **7**). The second option is to continue up from Gavel Neese to pass the stump of rock known as **Moses' Finger**. The going can be mitigated by keeping to turf patches. The ascent lands you on the lateral section of the South Traverse path, with the option of trending left to Beck Head or contouring right to encounter Little Hell Gate (both on Route **15**). This tidal flow of scree can be ascended but there will be many a faltering step on the loose stone. The actual rock-squeeze 'gate' comes quite high up, from where you can trend left or right onto easier ground before angling left to round Westmorland Crags and reach the summit. The confident scrambler will see that it is possible to step from just below the throttle point onto the Sphinx Ridge to the right. **Do so only with due caution** – the upper section is quite

WALKING THE LAKE DISTRICT FELLS – BORROWDALE

Westmorland Crags from the top of the Sphinx Ridge

sensational, placing you right on the 'nape', a grassy ridge leading up to the base of **Westmorland Crags**.

Via Styhead Pass ➔ *6.4km/4 miles* ↑*830m/2725ft* ⏲*3hr 45min*

The more pleasant option of these two, and by far the less trafficked, is the Pony Route (12).

12 From the **Gable Beck** footbridge (see Route **10**) follow on with the level bridle path. As the main path becomes challenged by bracken and starts to ascend, break right when you choose to, following the dale-floor wall/fence adjacent to **Lingmell Beck**. Pass through a wall-gate and advance over progressively stonier ground to a ford, some 100 metres beyond the confluence of **Piers** and **Spouthead Gills**. The old bridle path is largely evident as a green trod, with some pitching, winding up the mid-ridge in harmony with Spouthead Gill. This fords **Grainy Gill** then **Skew Gill** as it climbs over grass to the skyline brow of **Styhead Pass**.

13 Most walkers stick resolutely to the bee-line path to **Styhead Pass**, largely because they are unaware of the old route, but there is a penalty. The path, working up the scree-clad southern slopes of Gable, is excessively worn and so there is much pitching to cope with on the rise to Sty Head. At the stretcher box you can join the Breast Route (Route **4**).

The Gable Girdle →*4.8km/3 miles* ⊕*2hr 10min*

Whether you arrive from Borrowdale (Routes 1 and 2) or Wasdale (Routes 12 and 13), the South Traverse is a real treasure to find and follow. The route is especially fine if linked with the North Traverse, bound for Windy Gap. The whole tour undulates between the 460m and 760m contour lines.

14 From the stretcher box the first objective is **Kern Knotts**. The path begins without much evidence on the ground. Aim due west and a path becomes evident on rising to the brow. This trends towards Kern Knotts, but watch for the awkward rock-step down. Where the path forks, keep left below the crag, rounding the massive boulders, then come up below the face on a clearer path. This path has one exaggerated zig-zag before contouring. (Watch for a cave with a fresh spring just above the path – to be appreciated on a hot day.) Anticipation mounts as the path nears Great Hell Gate, with **Great Napes** towering awesomely ahead. Fear not; the path works over the loose scree and keeps to a firm footing thereafter.

Climbers have made their own scrambling paths up from the traverse, notably a way to gain Napes Needle. Walkers with a definite head for heights can ascend Needle Gully and reach the tiny platform called the Dress Circle, up the final cleft. From this spot you can admire – and perhaps converse with – climbers tackling the famous pinnacle climb. Good scramblers can 'thread the needle' by squeezing through the gap behind Napes Needle. The author traversed west from the Dress Circle – a delicate move – and afterwards descended a steep cleft at the foot of Eagle's Nest Gully before clambering up to the Sphinx Rock. You need both a calm day and a calm head for such antics. You can move over the ridge immediately below the rock to enter Little

Climbers complete the ascent of Napes Needle, with Great End in the background

Hell Gate. The South Traverse, on the other hand, avoids all the tricky stuff but still provides handsome views up to these remarkable rock features. Little Hell Gate can be climbed to reach the summit (see Route **11**).

15 The South Traverse continues across Great Hell Gate, running under **White Napes** and stepping over boulders along the scree-strewn western flank of the fell to merge onto the grassy saddle of **Beck Head**. Keep up right, climbing to a shoulder, where Moses' Trod skips down into Stone Cove. Ignore this, keep up right and climb to the next definite step before the real onset of rocks on the northwest ridge. A small cairn indicates the point of departure of the North Traverse. This angles down to run directly beneath Gable Crag. The path completes its mission at last at the large cairn in the tight depression of **Windy Gap**. (The full girdle then descends **Aaron Slack** to regain **Styhead Pass**.)

The summit

The highest point is a small outcrop, given special grace by the Fell & Rock Climbing Club plaque dedicated in 1924. It bears a roll of honour to those members who lost their lives during the Great War. The spectacular view from the summit is completed by the views from two other tops on the edge of the plateau. From the brink cairn above Westmorland Crags to the south-west, Scafell and Lingmell are superbly displayed, but the crème de la crème is Wasdale. There is a jigsaw of fields, beyond the Screes and Wast Water, within which the golden light of late afternoon can shimmer, or it may be seen glinting on the distant Irish Sea and Isle of Man. A fine outlook also awaits anyone who wanders to the brink of Gable Crag on the northern edge of the summit plateau, overlooking the upper realms of Ennerdale.

Safe descents

From the summit there are three directions to choose from. To the NW is a path (**8**) leading down the rocky ridge to Beck Head, convenient for Ennerdale, and, by Gable Beck, Wasdale (**11**). To the NE a well-cairned trail leads down by a short rock-step into Windy Gap (**3**), from where you can descend Aaron Slack for Borrowdale or climb over Green Gable for Honister (**6**) or Gillercomb (**5**). Finally, to the SE the Breast Route sweeps in from the E to descend predominantly SE to Sty Head (**4**) for Borrowdale and Wasdale.

Ridge route

Green Gable →*0.8km/½ mile* ↓*150m/490ft* ↑*50m/165ft* ⊕*30min*
Cairns guide NE and ensure a secure course is held, via one short rock-step, on the descent into Windy Gap. Climb the worn trail directly NNE to the summit.

WALKING THE LAKE DISTRICT FELLS – BORROWDALE

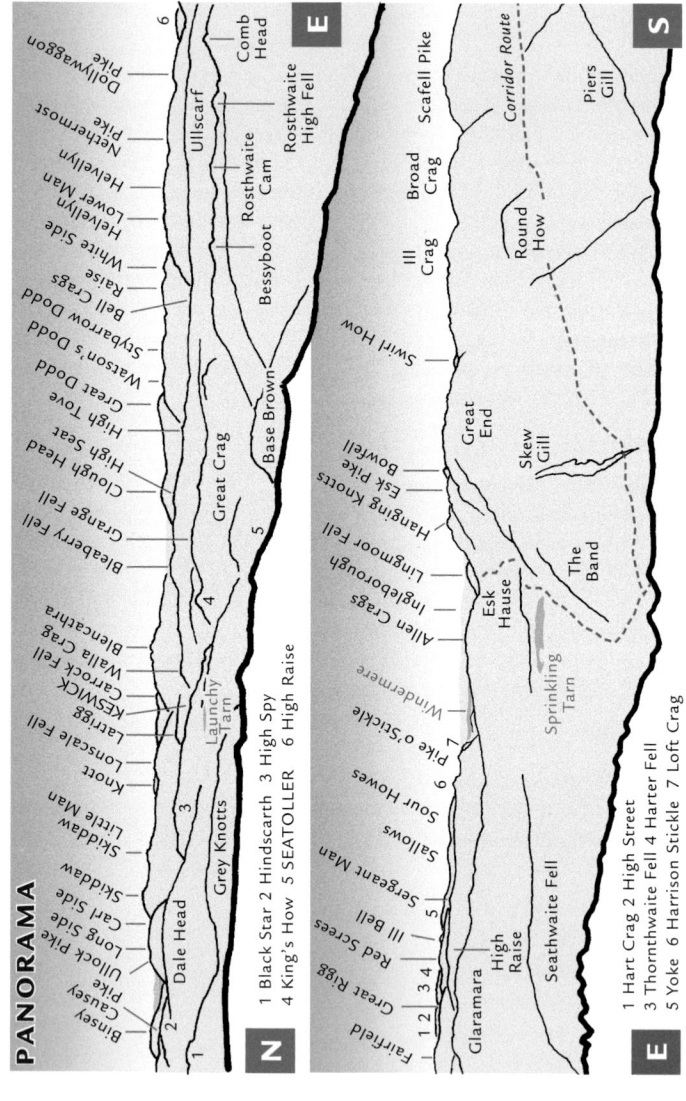

14 GREAT GABLE

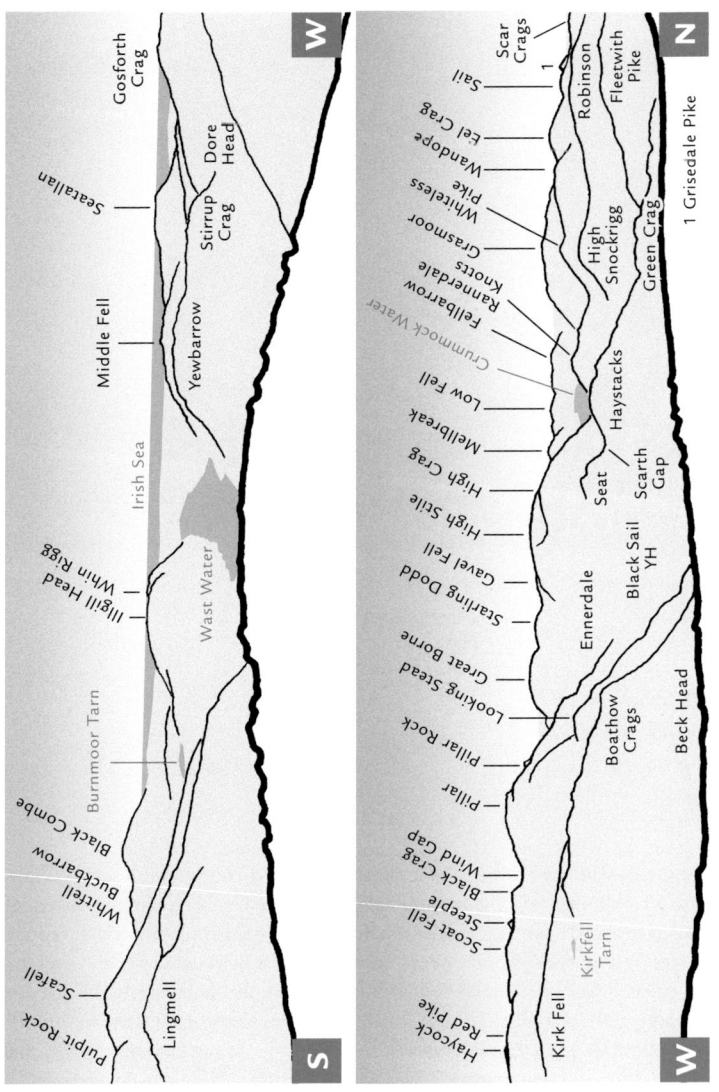

15 GREEN GABLE 801M/2628FT

Climb it from	Seathwaite **12**, Honister Pass **10** or Black Sail Youth Hostel **8**
Character	All northern ascents are unimpeded whereas southern approaches are uncomfortably loose; the summit is a terrific viewpoint
Fell-friendly route	4
Summit grid ref	NY 214 107
Link it with	Base Brown, Brandreth or Great Gable
Part of	The Gillercomb Skyline

Shepherds will have coined the fell name to draw a contrast with Great Gable, Green Gable's all-rock big brother, which, although a fine mountain, is a poor grazing ground. From east and west witness a trim gabled summit which, were it not for its mighty neighbour, would be considered a thoroughly worthy objective for a day's hike. Yet, like the South Col on Everest, for the majority this is but a stepping-stone – a place to pause, gain refreshment and take stock before the final climactic push. The fell has one notable crag, on the Ennerdale flank, and its fair share of scree, running down Stone Cove and spilling into Aaron Slack.

↑ *Green Gable, viewed from across Stony Cove*

15 Green Gable

Many walkers will opt to climb the fell from Seathwaite, either via Styhead Gill (2–3) or from Gillercomb (1). However, the pathless western slopes can be tackled from the Ennerdale valley (5–6), and Route 4 from Honister Pass offers an easier option, the high start cutting out a lot of the ascent.

Ascent from Seathwaite 12

Via Gillercomb →*3.7km/2¼ miles* ↑*685m/2245ft* ⏲*2hr 10min*

Since the majority of visitors to Green Gable will have their mind set on Great Gable, the approach from Seathwaite via Gillercomb will be commonly undertaken – often as the out-leg of a circuit that will invariably return by Styhead and Stockley Bridge.

1 Bear right through the mid-barn gate opposite the farmhouse at Seathwaite Farm. Follow the short lane to cross the new gated footbridge spanning the River Derwent. Go straight ahead, rising to cross the curious low-angled ladder-stile. Beyond, the pitched path winds up in harmony with **Sour Milk Gill**

Raven Crag from upper Gillercomb

and provides several pleasing aspects on this startling cataract – although only a few moments where you can get really close. A short, embowered scramble up a cleft leads ultimately to a left turn, crossing an ice-scoured rock shelf to reach a hand-gate in the intake wall. Continue up, passing a final major spout, to emerge in the hanging valley of **Gillercomb**, with great rock slabs over the wall to the right and, ahead, the massive face of Raven Crag (Gillercomb Buttress). The popular trail curves left, hugging the flanks of **Base Brown**, and ultimately clambers

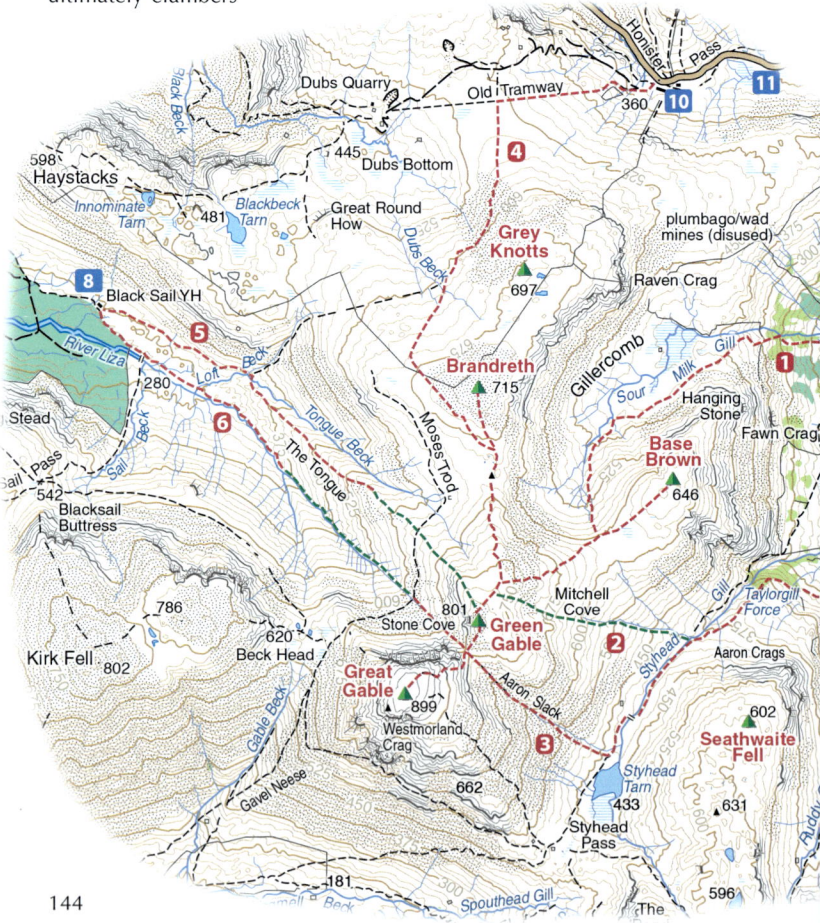

15 GREEN GABLE

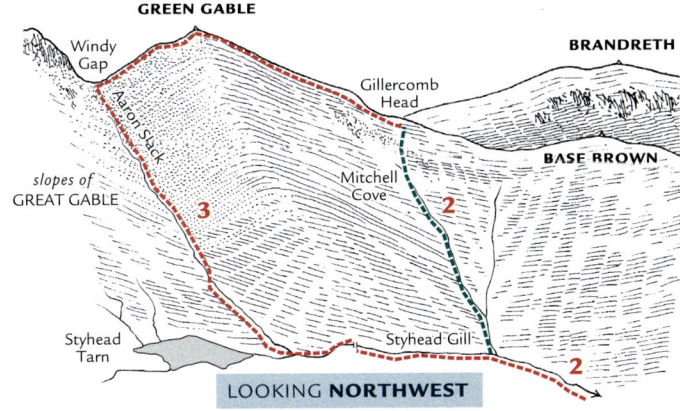

out of the combe onto the ridge where Base Brown and Green Gable connect. Bear right (southwest) and, aside from a brief rock-step, continue easily, curving to the west to unite with the path from Honister, with cairns so plentiful you can be assured of finding your way even in the thickest fog.

Via Mitchell Cove or Aaron Slack →4.8km/3 miles
↑685m/2245ft ⏲2hr 45min

This route offers a quiet side-door to the top and is mostly on grass, the only rock on the pitched path above Stockley Bridge.

2 Pass through the farmstead and follow the gated track to **Stockley Bridge**, continuing up the rock-steps beyond and coming above the pine copse sheltering **Taylorgill Force**. Come level with the large cascades in **Styhead Gill**, ford the gill immediately above them and follow **Mitchell Gill** into the shallow combe. You can keep to grass at the head of the combe by following the left-hand side of a rash of scree and thereby unite with the main ridge path directly above the meeting of the Honister and Gillercomb paths. Complete the ascent, left (southwest).

3 The more common option continues with the **Styhead Gill** path (see Route **2**), crosses the footbridge and, 150 metres short of **Styhead Tarn**, branches right with the next feeder gill, ascending **Aaron Slack**. The path has been improved and, a third of the way up, fords to the north bank, continuing, with some unstable scree, to **Windy Gap**, where you turn north up the ridge and continue to the summit.

Ascent from Honister Pass 10

Direct →4.1km/2½ miles ↑475m/1560ft ⏲2hr

For a gentler ascent take advantage of the high start offered by Honister Pass.

4 From the car park begin with the quarry track, stepping up left on the realigned pitched path, which soon reconnects with the **Old Tramway**. A few remnant sleepers are evident underfoot as you draw near to the ruined site of Drum House on the brow of the hill. Turn left and follow the chain of cairns, on a worn path, making easy progress across the flanks of **Grey Knotts**. Where the path forks keep left, and after crossing a fence-stile advance to the tarn-jewelled depression of **Gillercomb Head**. The path holds to a southerly course, climbing up onto Green Gable.

Ascent from Black Sail Youth Hostel 8

Direct →3.7km/2¼ miles ↑500m/1640ft ⏲2hr

This is the purists' route, entirely focused on Green Gable, starting from this wonderful little outpost in the hills.

5 Follow the path commonly adopted by walkers leaving the hostel engaged on the Coast to Coast Walk. This runs east-southeast along the upper edge of the moraine, along the flanks of **Haystacks**, to ford **Loft Beck**. Promptly switch right at the prominent cairn and ford **Tongue Beck**. A clear path now angles up left, duly gaining **the Tongue** ridge, a grassy expanse composed of morainal debris sashes. A fine waterfall is seen ahead in Tongue Beck but the path gives no encouragement to visit it. Should you wish to visit, be aware that the route is over steep ground, with little more than the faintest of sheep trods, but the

15 GREEN GABLE

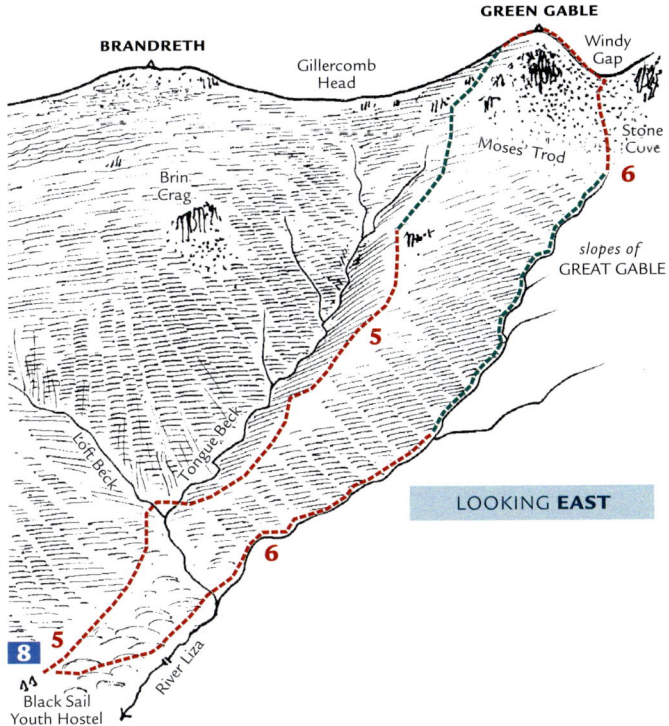

base of the fall is a particularly fine sight. The ridge path moves to the left of the skyline outcrop before dissolving in the prairie of grass above. Maintain course, crossing the deeply etched **Moses' Trod** path and aiming to the left of minor outcropping on the higher ridge to gain the summit.

Via Stone Cove and Windy Gap →*3.2km/2 miles* ↑*700m/2295ft* ⏲*2hr 15min*

You can follow the Liza gill right up to Stone Cove, although the path dwindles on the latter part of the ascent.

Ennerdale from the summit

6 From the Black Sail Hut march southeast down the bank path towards the Liza footbridge. Short of the bridge a path contours left along the foot of the moraine. Ford **Loft Beck** close to its confluence with the newly born River Liza. Follow the north bank of the Liza, on a modest path. Keep with the irregular path tussling up beside the confined Liza gill. This crosses the well-marked **Moses' Trod** and continues into **Stone Cove**, now ever more consistent to the name. The higher path is subject to wear and is loose underfoot. Reaching the large cairn in **Windy Gap**, bear left with the ridge path to gain the summit.

The summit

Standing by the wind-shelter, your attention is focused on Gable Crag. To the west the eye is drawn down the long trough of Ennerdale towards Kirk Fell and Pillar, and over Haystacks to the Buttermere vale, with the Northwestern Fells beyond. Eastwards see the Scafells and, left of Allen Crags, the Langdale Pikes. The skyline of the Helvellyn range runs to the north of Glaramara, leading to Blencathra and Skiddaw. Not a bad view in itself… now try Great Gable!

15 Green Gable

Safe descents

All five routes of ascent work well in reverse. For Seathwaite Route **1** is comfortable enough, although the final steps down Sour Milk Gill can be trying after a hard day. The better option is to descend Aaron Slack (**3**), the path now greatly improved.

Ridge routes

Base Brown →*1.6km/1 mile* ↓*190m/625ft* ↑*40m/130ft* ⏲*30min*
Head NE with the cairned path and watch to bear right at the critical path fork. This leads down, ENE, via one minor rock-step, after which the path veers back NE. In the shallow depression leave the more obvious path, which here departs left down into Gillercomb, and keep along the level ridge, with a tangible path. Stepping over peaty ground, rise easily to the summit rock plinth.

Brandreth →*1.6km/1 mile* ↓*145m/475ft* ↑*55m/180ft* ⏲*30min*
Depart NE, keeping left on the regular trail at the path fork, now heading N down the ridge to Gillercomb Head. Pass to the right of the tarns in this broad saddle, rising by small outcrops to the summit, which is the cairn by the isolated metal stakes.

Great Gable →*0.8km/½ mile* ↓*50m/165ft* ↑*150m/490ft* ⏲*40min*
Descend the worn trail S into the narrow dip of Windy Gap. Pass the cairn and continue on the regular path, bearing up W and clambering over an area of modest outcropping to gain the summit plateau.

16 GREY KNOTTS 697M/2287FT

Climb it from	Seathwaite **12**, Seatoller **13**, Little Gatesgarthdale **11**, Honister Pass **10** or Gatesgarth **9**
Character	A fine objective summit, though dangers lurk in the form of Raven Crag, the stupendous cliff that overlooks Gillercomb, and the tunnel entries of the plumbago mines
Fell-friendly route	5
Summit grid ref	NY 217 125
Link it with	Brandreth
Part of	The Gillercomb Skyline

Many a Lakeland height is known for its upper-fell detail, its characterful crags and distinctive summit. For all Grey Knotts' lack of obvious individuality, it does not falter when it comes to such detail and excels at lower levels too, for well below the massive Raven Crag, colloquially known to climbers as Gillercomb Buttress, can be found secrets of a famous and unique mining enterprise, and down at dale level is a group of ancient yew trees.

The plumbago mines were the source of a rare pure graphite, which was worked from the early 17th century for nearly 200 years to its deepest extent.

↑ *Eastern summit of Grey Knotts*

16 Grey Knotts

This soft lead was known locally as 'wad' and formed the basis of the local pencil-making industry, with which Keswick is synonymous. The mineral was so highly prized that miners were watched lest they stole any in their clothing.

The Borrowdale Yews, located close to the River Derwent downstream from Seathwaite, are known as the Fraternal Four. This compact group of yew trees has stood in this upper-dale situation for some 1500 years. In 2002 the Tree Council designated the senior specimen as one of 50 Great British Trees, in recognition of its place in the national heritage.

Down on the western side of the fell Dubs Bottom is a great hanging valley which harbours its own secrets worth seeking out. Rain drains into this hollow and lingers long among the accumulation of peat, with the draining beck running in excess of 2m deep in places. The pond-life here is a thing of tremendous fascination. This is the last place where ice would have lingered during the final phase of the last Ice Age.

Route 1 visits both the Borrowdale Yews and the plumbago mines, and the longer Route 6, from Gatesgarth, takes in Dubs Bottom. Other routes lead via the east ridge (2–3) and direct from Honister Pass (4–5).

Ascent from Seathwaite 12

Via the plumbago mines →*2.4km/1½ miles* ↑*575m/1885ft* ⏱ *1hr 40min*

A route full of interest, visiting the ancient Borrowdale Yews and the plumbago mines which once fed Keswick's pencil-making industry

1 There are two paths to the foot of the slope. You can approach direct from Seathwaite Farm, passing through the mid-barn arch and lane. After crossing the **Derwent** footbridge turn right. Cross two successive broken walls, with Newhouse Gill (dry in summer) between, to find a broader grass area. Alternatively, approach along the riverside footpath which leaves the road at Seathwaite Bridge. Two quick gates lead on to a low-canopied yew tree. Beyond the kissing-gate you can visit the fenced **Borrowdale Yews** up to the right or simply continue to the broad grass area, with the camping ground and trees lining the bank over the river on the left.

Especially when the bracken is up, the start of the ascending path is obscure. But stride up through the bracken and a path is quickly found. This angles slightly right in the light tree growth and then weaves left and ever

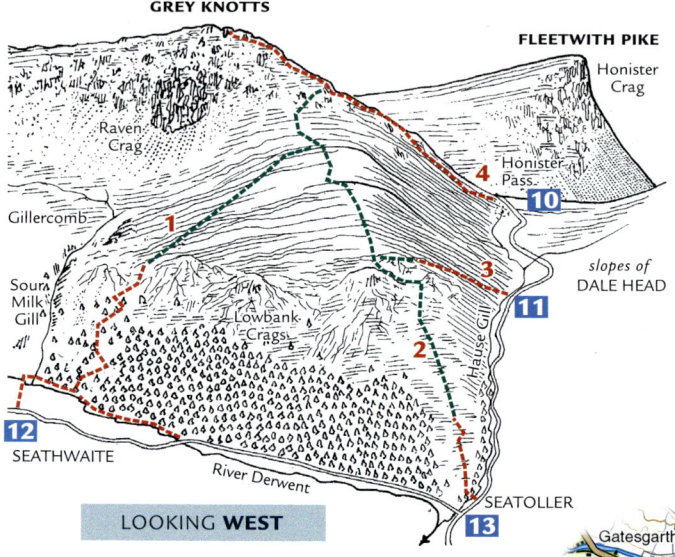

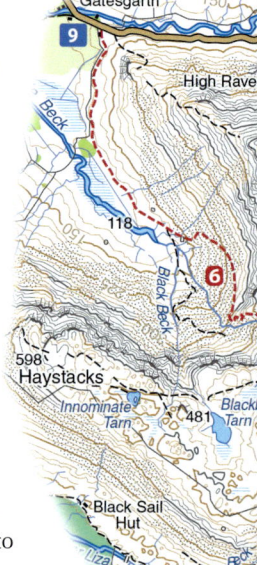

upward, avoiding the mine spoil. Keep your eyes peeled to spot a slate gravestone, which serves as a guide to the line of the path.

To the right find the lowest mine level, with spoil spilling steeply down the slope. This area and that above are not suitable for ascent or descent, so keep off for your own comfort. The path bears left, running level some 10 metres below the gravestone before rising in tight zig-zags, short of the gill, to a prominent shelf in front of a mine level. Peering in, notice a shaft of illuminating light from a slightly higher access. **Beware: this and other levels are treacherous.** (You can find out more about these workings in *Seathwaite Wad*, written by Ian Tyler, available from the Keswick Mining Museum).

Swing above the level to the right and reach further gallery accesses close beside the gill. Climb up to

16 GREY KNOTTS

Entry to a wad-mine level – dangerous shafts lurk not far within

the top level and, above this, find a ladder-stile, to the right of which the foundations of the guard-house dwelling are visible. Cross the wall bounding Seatoller Common and rise through the open excavations onto the grassy fell. Ascend the ridge, and as the outcrops increase trend right to link up with Route **4** beside the rising fence. This leads naturally via stiles to the summit.

Ascent from Seatoller 13

Direct →3.7km/2¼ miles ↑580m/1905ft ⏲2hr 15min

2 Walk up the street to cross the little bridge over **Hause Gill** on the left. Short of the cottage row, step off the track to the right and advance to the wall-gate (no waymarking). Keep left early on, beside

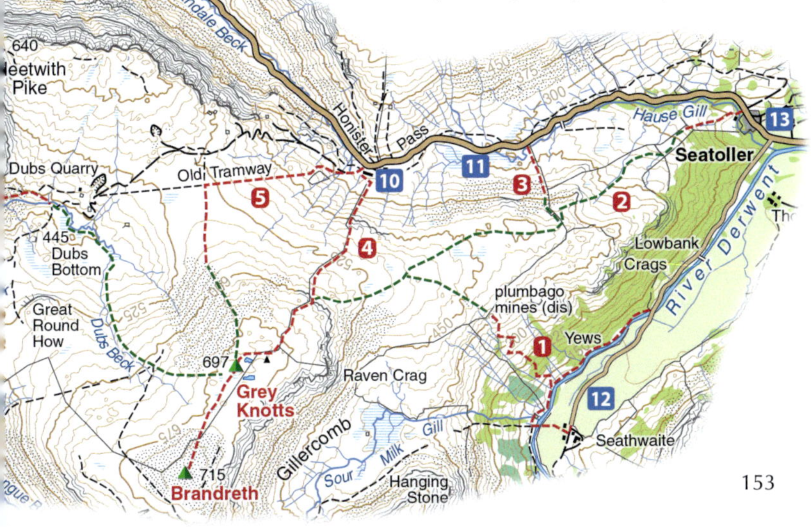

Base Brown from the Seatoller Common ridge

the wall, and follow the track up the rise to come through a gateway (now with the wall on the right). Coming by a sheep-creep and stile, bear up left through the bracken to pass beside the fence to a gateway. Now ascend the bank enclosure, finding the sheep-trod passages through the bracken and marshy clearings to gain height, then crossing low broken walls to ultimately arrive at a ladder-stile at the top left of the rough enclosure. Step over the ladder-stile and embark on the grassy ridge, linking up with Route **1**.

Ascent from Little Gatesgarthdale 11

Direct →2.8km/1¾ miles ↑400m/1310ft ⏲1hr 30min

An altogether simpler route, with the advantage of an elevated start point, leaves the Honister Pass road above Seatoller.

3 There is scope for casual car parking along the verge, shortly after the Honister Pass road emerges from the steep section and crosses the cattle grid. Ford Hause Gill and follow the rising wall bounding Seatoller Common. An

16 GREY KNOTTS

evident path shows the way. At a wall junction on the far side of the adjacent wall, notice an Ordnance Survey benchmark on the large boulder at its base. Come through a twin-compartment sheepfold to reach the ladder-stile used by Route **2**. Ascend the ridge with Routes **1–2** and revel in the fine views down to Honister Pass from the knolls.

Ascent from Honister Pass **10**

Direct →*2km/1¼ miles* ↑*350m/1150ft* ⊕*1hr 15min*

Two routes set off from the pass and may be considered the basis of a short, elevated circuit. Route 5 is a really pleasing little route.

4 From behind the sheds a path begins over a stile, with the rising fence right, and crosses some rocky ground on the climb to the brow. It crosses the fence at three points near and at the top.

5 Begin with the 'path most travelled' that leaves the car park off the mine track. A pitched path leads up to join the Old Tramway incline, which once served the mines. The track-bed leads through a shallow rock cutting to reach the retaining walls associated with the old **Drum House** winding gear on the brow of the ridge. Turn left and follow the heavily used path – the common route to Great Gable. As this starts to gain height up the slope, break left, southeast, by a large cairn and, easily evading outcropping, venture to the summit outcrop.

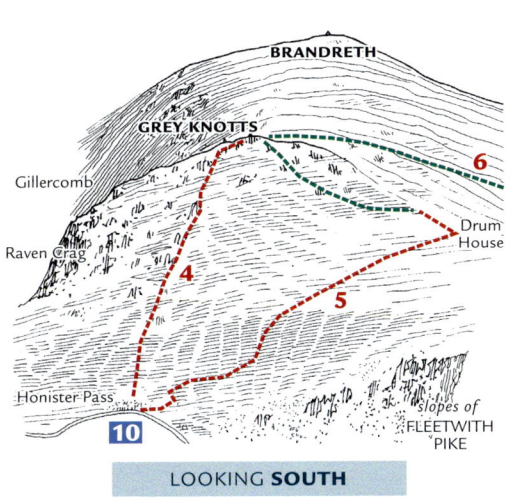

LOOKING **SOUTH**

Ascent from Gatesgarth 9

Direct →4.1km/2½ miles ↑580m/1905ft ⏲2hr 30min

This lovely route may also be considered ideal for the return leg on a circuit that begins with Fleetwith Pike.

6 Follow the track off the open road above the tree-sheltered farmstead. This leads round into the Warnscale valley. Ignore the path that forks to a footbridge. Keep to the main track, which switches left and right after a ruin to steadily gain height across the growing slope of **Fleetwith Pike**. This comes to a tightly engineered bend above the ravine of Warnscale Beck and winds up towards **Dubs Quarry**, but short of the quarry, ford the beck at the obvious convenient point and leave the path. Branch left, following the right-hand peaty bank into **Dubs Bottom**. There is no path and this area is rarely explored. The going is not inviting but the deep watercourse is quite fascinating. Advance to the solitary split-rock feature, an isle in the midst of the marsh, then continue with the right-hand feeding beck, which becomes a conventional stony gill. Ascend the heather bank to cross the popular lateral path in the vicinity of a junction of paths. Keep straight on up the pathless fellside to the plateau summit ridge and go left to complete the ascent.

The summit

There is some case for saying that the fell has two summits. Twins in many ways, two distinctly grey, rocky eminences are crowned by cairns some 55 metres apart, separated by the ridge-top fence and one marshy pool. The visitor can feel perplexed to know the difference, especially in misty conditions when, but for the fence, it would be difficult to know where you are – and with

Poised boulder close to the summit

so much rock about that could be an issue. The western top is, on balance, the better viewpoint. There are several other rock tors and intervening hollows with pools, which together make this a pleasing place to idle awhile.

Safe descents

The angle in the fence is a most useful landmark: this is where the ridge fence turns from a southerly course to due E. Bearing in mind that the one real concern for anyone leaving the summit – namely, Raven Crag – lies to the E, then this fence serves a vital directional role. With this in mind the safest recourse is W (**6**), picking a way through shallow outcropping down to the popular path to Great Gable from Honister. Turn right for the Drum House and Route **5**; a left turn leads to Warnscale and Buttermere, while the right turn leads down the incline direct to Honister Pass itself. Ignore the fence-side path down to Honister as this is uncomfortable and is becoming unsightly too. If you wish to find your way down to Borrowdale the best advice is to get onto the N side of the eastward-trending section of fence. Where this switches N follow on beyond the fence junction to slip through the fence and follow the fence down only to a point below the first set of rocks. Then veer right (**2**) across the rocky slope and down onto the more level moorland. Upon encountering the intake wall follow this left (**3**), down to ford Hause Gill and join the open road. Go right over the cattle grid and descend to Seatoller.

Ridge route

Brandreth →*0.8km/½ mile* ↓*15m/50ft* ↑*30m/100ft* ⏲*25min*
Our old friend the ridge fence gives all the guidance needed. There are paths on either side but that to the W has the better of the marshy ground. As the fence veers SW cross a light stile to reach the summit.

17 HIGH RIGG 355M/1165FT

Climb it from	Tewet Tarn verge **21**, St John's in the Vale Church **22** or Legburthwaite **25**
Character	An inviting little fell, explored with only modest effort. Nevertheless, the plethora of cliffs are hazardous, so watch your step!
Fell-friendly route	3
Summit grid ref	NY 308 220

High Rigg is an ideal 'first fell' for novice walkers. An end-to-end ridge walk delivers such variety you can come here when bigger brethren are lost in cloud and still have fun. Most visitors content themselves with a quick up and down from the church in the hause, the summit an ideal place to indulge in calm contemplation, away from the madding crowd. While contrasting in their scenic qualities, the eastern and western flanking valleys do at least have the commonality of draining into the Greta.

   Being a low ridge, ascent routes on High Rigg are well defined. There are two northern lines direct to the summit (3–4), an approach which can be further enhanced and extended by including Tewet Tarn and Low Rigg (1) as an aperitif,

↑ *Part of the Castlerigg stone circle, backed by High Rigg and Helvellyn*

17 HIGH RIGG

and one pure ridge walk (5) from the south (which has a westerly variation, 6, en route). Running along the fell base to east (8) and west (7) are footpaths which enable walkers to sample the two beautiful adjacent dales and so compose lovely fell-and-dale circular walks. The grandest circuit would introduce Castlerigg stone circle into the equation, across Naddle Beck, and approaching the stones in this way provides the greatest visual impact.

Ascent from Tewet Tarn verge 21

Direct →*2.5km/1½ miles*
↑*215m/705ft* ⏲*1hr 30min*

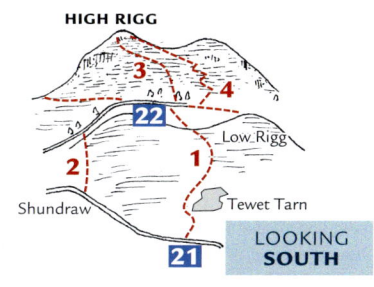

1 A footpath is signed from a gate, leading up a small field to a gateway. Continue, guided by a wooden waymark post by a curious rift feature, presumably laboriously cut for piping linked to the tarn. Aim left of **Tewet Tarn** and cross the wall-stile to the left of the fenced gateway. Quite naturally many visitors circle the tiny tarn, admire the backdrop of Blencathra and watch the coots weaving among the weeds. The path strides on via a fence-stile and over a dip in the **Low Rigg** ridge to a wall-stile, and on down to a stile opposite **St John's Church**, which rests among a shroud of trees.

The footpath linking Yew Tree Farm with Shundraw is useful as an alternative back-tracking route from the summit (hence it is described south to north).

2 From the church follow the approach road down, via the gate, by the tiny Yew Tree Cottage, and at the road bend bear off left through the double gates signed to Row End. The track leads between the house and barn to the gate with a 'footpath' plate. Head straight across the ensuing rushy field, skipping over the open ditch mid-course, to a stepped wall-gate. Keep the wall close right until you reach a short, gated lane beside the huge bank-barn at **Shundraw**, very like the barn back at Yew Tree Farm. Emerging onto the road, head north to return to your start point.

WALKING THE LAKE DISTRICT FELLS – BORROWDALE

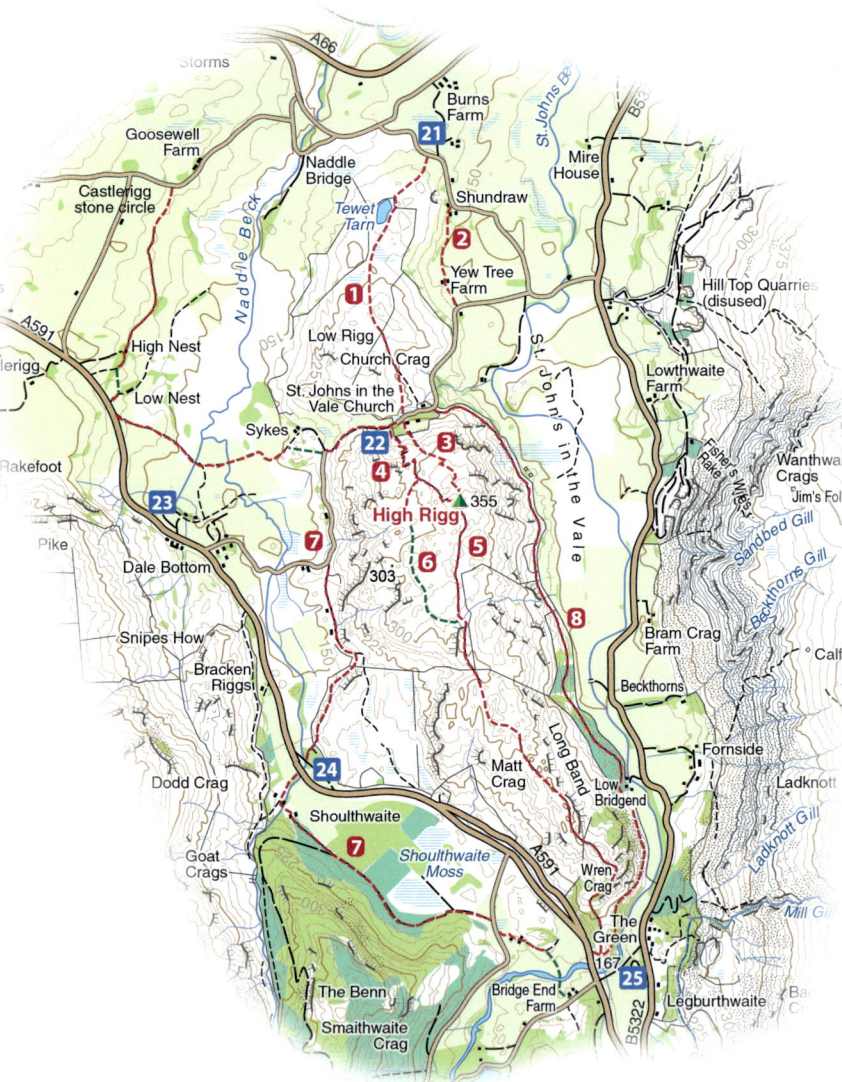

17 HIGH RIGG

St John's Church, a romantic setting for a wedding

Ascent from St John's in the Vale Church 22

The quickest way to the top

3 Embark on the path rounding the west end of the main centre building, which leads up to a kissing-gate and continues as a steady uphill trod. The bracken has been suppressed by the regular pounding. In its later stages the path swings round the left-hand side of the final summit knoll, thereby approaching the cairn from the south.

4 Alternatively, go further along the hause road to the kissing-gate, where the road deteriorates to a track 'unsuitable for motor vehicles'. Now bear left by the seat, rising above the enclosure copse and water tank, on a zig-zagging path which straightens onto a semblance of a ridge and reaches the top with alacrity and no little elation.

WALKING THE LAKE DISTRICT FELLS – BORROWDALE

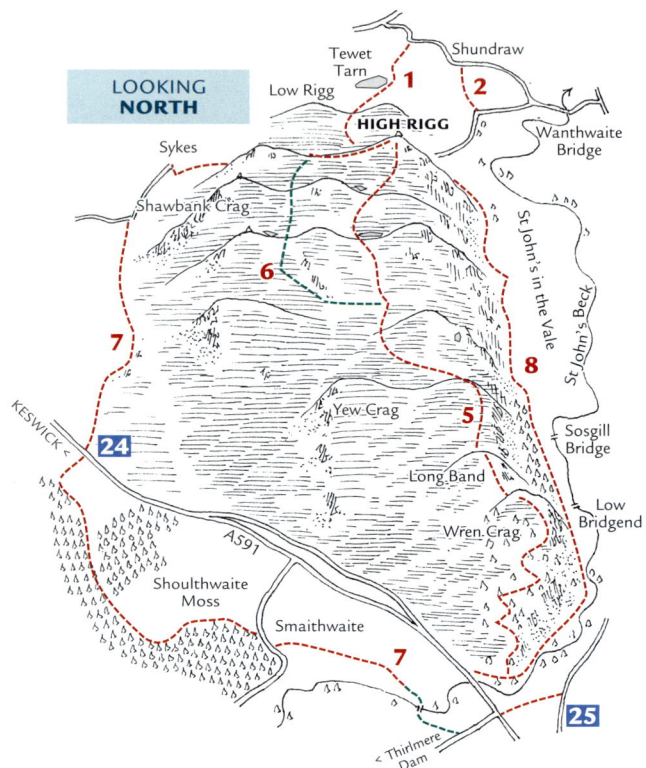

Ascent from Legburthwaite 25

Via the spine of the ridge →*3km/1¾ miles* ↑*230m/755ft* ⏱*1hr 40min*

On this route you see the very best of High Rigg, and the journey is given impetus by the magnificent surroundings, with eyes inevitably drawn to the most handsome fell of all, Blencathra.

5 The walk leaves the **A591** at a ladder-stile/hand-gate at NY 315 196, 100 metres north of the bus shelter; to reach this spot from the Legburthwaite

17 High Rigg

United Utilities car park follow the old-road cycle-way lane. A popular path sets off, ultimately bound for St John's Church, but within 50 metres the ridge path branches left. Early on, relish a delightful rising ridge garnished with Scots pines and giving superb views of Castle Rock of Triermain. Above the pines the first knoll provides a stunning panorama.

The path, showing signs of erosion, slips through a dip in the ridge, via a wall-gap, and clambers onto an attractive rocky step in the ridge. Passing a cairn perched on a splintered rock, stride along a lovely narrowing of the ridge above **Long Band**. At a wooden post the path is ushered left to a fence-stile. The regular path sweeps to the left of the next knoll, although you can stroll up, with the fence to your right, onto a cairned top above a pool, following its outflow to rejoin the main path, which leads down to a ladder-stile at a wall junction. Once over the stile there are two options, the first described here; the second is Route **6**. The ridge path heads up with the wall to the right. At the marshy hollow skirt left to cross the narrow outflow stones under Moss Crag, then either curve right, resuming beside the wall, or climb straight up the fell to the ridge-top, bearing right to rejoin the main path beyond the wall end. The summit beckons ahead.

6 Alternatively, from the ladder-stile on Route **5** branch left across the bracken slope on a sheep trod. Once level with the ash tree curve right, under the outcrop, and gain a shallow rigg, rising to the saddle. Briefly bear left

Blencathra from Long Band (photo: Maggie Allan)

to a viewpoint cairn with adjacent pool. Continue from the saddle with the slightly more apparent sheep path, and at the next saddle spur left again to the cairn at the top of **Shawbank Crag**. Both cairns enjoy lovely views across the Naddle valley to the shapely prow of Dodd Crag, foremost limb of Bleaberry Fell. The path, even more sure, advances across the broad hollow to link up with the popular path at the last lower saddle. This is the path rising from the St John's Church hause (Route **4**): turn right to proceed to the summit.

Two valley variations

Useful for creating a circular tour

7 The western trail (5km) leads off from the church centre via Piper House, Rough How Bridge, Shoulthwaite Moss and Smaithwaite to Bridgend Farm. The route turns down the road to the left from St John's hause (from the gate the road is unsuitable for vehicles). At the foot of the zig-zags follow the tarmac road left. Pass Piper House, a quintessential Lakeland cottage with a superb backdrop of Bleaberry Fell. Where the road turns right ignore this. Keep the wall to your right as you follow the byway past Shaw Bank, overlooked by **Shawbank Crag**, and Brownbeck.

Soon afterwards the road ends and forks into two bridle paths. The left-hand path rises invitingly to a ladder-stile but there is little merit in the succeeding trail across a bracken hollow, though a footpath veering right along the back of the rigg may come to your rescue if, by error, you chose the wrong option at the fork. It is better to take the right fork, via a stile; a rocky path dips to a smooth green track and a gate, where the footpath from over the brow on the left rejoins. The track leads through open woodland. Spot the old arched Rough How Bridge spanning Shoulthwaite Gill at the point where it becomes **Naddle Beck**.

Cross the road and follow the lane to **Shoulthwaite farm**, passing through by the camp site to enter Thirlmere Forest at a hand-gate. A path leads on, merging with a track from the right. This is now a well-graded track, leading past **Shoulthwaite Moss** onto a minor road. Go right and then first left with the signposted footpath, which leads, via gates, through the part-restored **Smaithwaite** farmyard. The path leads down by a fence to a footbridge over **St John's Beck** and rises to meet the road at **Bridge End Farm** (camp site opposite).

8 The eastern trail (4.5km) is part bridle path, part footpath, and, while sheltered and shady, it does have two notably appealing pluses: its fine view

Lonscale Fell and Tewet Tarn from the summit (photo: Maggie Allan)

of Wanthwaite and Bram Crags, invariably bathed in sunlight, and the **Low Bridgend** tea-garden! The green track starts down immediately east of the church, via a gate/stile. From there navigation is an unnecessary fussiness; the paths just flow naturally as you walk upstream.

The summit

A solitary cairn rests among the outcropping on a modest top, sufficient in area to give a party plenty of room to sit and consider the visual feast all round them! A large, shapely rock will no doubt take centre stage for photographic compositions.

Safe descents

The main caution is that serious crags bound the fell to E and W. The palpable paths leading smartly down NNE to St John's Church and youth centre (**3–4**) are without question the best options if in doubt or deteriorating weather. While the ridge path S (**5**) has little to cause trepidation, it is nicer, in foul conditions, to trace the fell-foot trails (**7–8**). A particular incentive on the eastern trail (**8**) is Low Bridgend tea-garden.

18 HIGH SEAT 608M/1995FT

Climb it from	Causeway Foot (Naddle valley) **23**, Rough How Bridge **24**, Ashness Bridge **17**, Surprise View **16** or Watendlath **15**
Character	Grand high-point on the ridge north of Ullscarf, with damp ground hard to avoid
Fell-friendly route	8
Summit grid ref	NY 287 180
Link it with	Bleaberry Fell or High Tove

The spine of the Central Fells dips from Ullscarf, switching northeast on Bell Crags, then runs its way due north, raising its head upon three summits – the middle one, High Seat, being the highest. From a distance the fell-top does indeed look like a bench so the 'seat' analogy is appropriate, a definite knoll perched above a general undulating marshiness. The eastern slopes drain into the Naddle valley via Shoulthwaite Gill, giving Thirlmere short shrift. The western slopes spread along the road all the way from Ashness Bridge to the hamlet of Watendlath, with Gowder and Reecastle Crags the main sporting outcrops. The lovely native woodland about Surprise View and Hoggs Earth softens Watendlath Beck's break for freedom through the Lodore gorge.

↑ *Summit OS column on High Seat (photo: Maggie Allan)*

18 HIGH SEAT

Of all the ascents, that from Reecastle Crag (8) is the most direct and least prone to wet ground. The more commonly followed ascent (5, 7) climbs from Ashness Bridge, the best of this journey being to the edge at Dodd, as the moor beyond is peaty indeed. The back route from Shoulthwaite (1–4) is peaceful and an ideal out-of-the-way experience. The more adventurous walker may be tempted to trace Middlesteads Gill, which provides a quiet novel line, with all the excitement confined to the gill and its minor arête; as the slopes thereafter are unexciting this has not been marked or described here.

Ascent from Causeway Foot 23 *off map N* or Rough How Bridge 24

Via Shoulthwaite Gill →*3.5km/2¼ miles* ↑*455m/1495ft* ⏲*2hr*

Eastern ascents inevitably stem from Shoulthwaite Gill, a valley whose praises are seldom sung and yet there is no doubting its beauty.

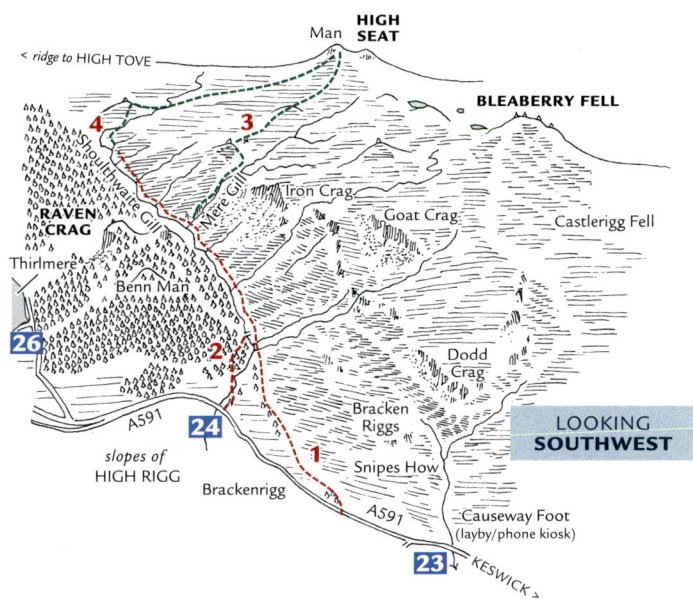

167

WALKING THE LAKE DISTRICT FELLS – BORROWDALE

168

18 HIGH SEAT

1 Follow the footpath from the ladder-stile off the main road south of Dale Bottom. This runs above **Brackenrigg** to a gate beside the footbridge and old weir.

2 This point can be reached more efficiently by starting from the Rough How Bridge layby and passing up the lane by **Shoulthwaite farm** and on through the farmyard (footpath waymarking) to a tall hand-gate entering Thirlmere Forest. Branch immediately half-right from the lower path, via a second tall hand-gate, cutting up to a forest track. Go right to where the track forks and bear right, exiting the forestry via the tall kissing-gate to cross the broad plank bridge. (It is not unreasonable to consider following the forest track up to the Raven Crag and Castle Crag viewpoints and either beating a way down from the duck-boarding to a ladder-stile directly beneath Castle Crag or continuing to exit the forestry off the track near the head of the gorge.)

The preferred route keeps with the footpath running up the west side of the gill itself. The cliffs above are striking; note particularly the fall spilling from a high crag, then the bold profile of Iron Crag. Pass an old sheepfold close to where the route of Castle Crag is met and soon afterwards encounter **Mere Gill**. At this point you can choose between Routes **3** and **4**.

Litt Memorial stones

3 From the end of Route **2** ford and follow the impressive little ravine of **Mere Gill**, climbing quite steeply west, with the minimum of inconvenience. As the gill opens bear left to a cairned knoll, below which are located two slate slabs, like fairy gateposts. This is the Litt Memorial, a person of no known significance. There is nothing but a sheep trod pursuing the shallow ridge and, as far as possible, avoiding damp ground on the rise southwest to the outcrop called **Man**. The true summit lies just to the west.

4 Alternatively, from the end of Route **2** continue with the gill-side path, which falters as it moves away from the forest. This is just as well, as the upper reaches of **Shoulthwaite Gill** promise no more than peat and mire, so make a random right-hand move, heading due east for the skyline fence and the summit.

Ascent from Ashness Bridge 17

Via Ashness Gill ↑*3.2km/2 miles* →*440m/1445ft* ⏱*1hr 45min*

Two routes, sharing a common start, depart from the Watendlath road: one the common way; the other far less so. Both benefit from good early stages but the second gains commendation for having the driest line.

5 From Ashness Bridge (car park) a footpath climbs directly beside the wall, via an early stile. As the wall gives way to a fence you can continue ahead, climbing to a kissing-gate in the intake wall and then climbing on by a solitary rowan to come level with the brink of an impressive waterfall. Alternatively, bear half-left to accompany **Barrow Beck** up to a hand-gate. The path rises through the bracken along the edge, overlooking the formidable dale-head, to unite with the main path. The

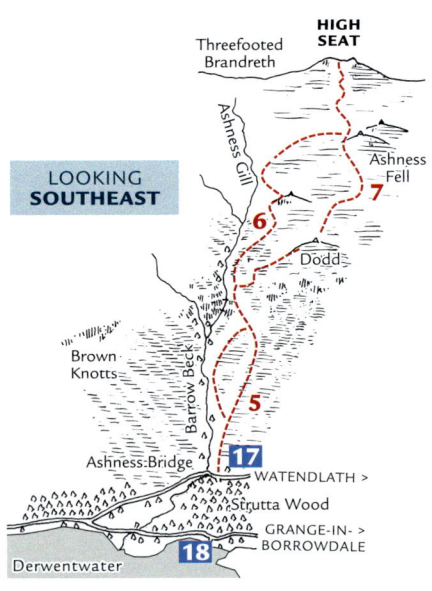

Derwentwater from the head of Barrow Beck

more intrepid may fancy keeping even closer to the beck's bouldery course, though near the top the going gets tricky. The waterfall makes a worthy spot to pause and admire the broader scene. From this point choose from Routes **6** and **7**.

6 From the waterfall (see Route **5**) the old path, less obvious and therefore less commonly trod, keeps strict company with the beck a little further before drawing out onto the heather moor to pass to the left of a knoll crowned with a cairn. Continue, again quite near the gill, until an old wall is met. Keep close to the wall's foundations, which is useful where it traverses bog, to reach the point where the popular path (Route **7**) crosses, near the ridge-top. Proceed along the path to the summit.

7 Alternatively, the ridge-top can be gained from the end of Route **5** by climbing the newly pitched path leaving the environs of the waterfall, which eases as it approaches the prominent cairn on the brink of the fell. (As is evidenced by a path, some walkers, unaware of the craggy edge below, appear to have tried to descend directly – they must have rued their presumption!) The path is forced to meander by encounters with marsh as it follows on up the ridge to the wall crossing. The fell summit is clearly in view but more marsh has to be rounded before the final rise to the old stone-built trig point.

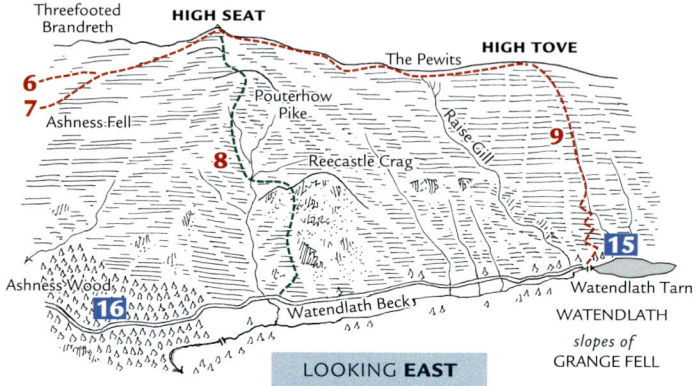

Ascent from Surprise View 16

Via Reecastle Crag →3.5km/2¼ miles ↑350m/1150ft ⏱1hr 30min

Quite the most direct route to the summit is to be found taking a surreptitious line out of the Watendlath valley from the foot of the imposing Reecastle Crag ridge.

8 Park either at Watendlath or Surprise View car park. The popular road climbing into the hanging valley from Derwentwater, via Ashness Bridge, twists and turns through gorgeous woodland to emerge at a cattle grid. The road is unenclosed on this side. After passing Thwaite House the road crosses Thwaitehouse Beck.

The climbers' approach is the key to this ascent and entails following a path that rises with a gill to the marsh beneath **Reecastle Crag**. The route keeps left. Aim for the skyline dip between two outcrops. There is no path, but keep to the rough line of thorns, en route passing a large, fractured boulder.

At the top ignore the hand-gate in the enclosure wall. Bear left along the edge, enjoying handsome views back over Reecastle Crag to Grange Fell. Pass an old sheepfold and ford Thwaitehouse Gill to reach a ladder-stile in the intake wall. Go half-right and ascend beside the gill and broken wall. Near the skyline, as the wall curves left, slant right to crest the prominent outcrop.

This is **Pouterhow Pike**, an excellent viewpoint. The summit is in view to the east-northeast and the intervening ridge has but one small marsh and the occasional sheep path.

Ascent from Watendlath 15

Via High Tove →4km/2½ miles ↑365m/1200ft ⏲1hr 45min

The high route is not necessarily the dry route!

9 High Seat is a natural destination from Watendlath. The infamous bog of The Pewits (lapwings) is newly tamed with a stone-flagged path; the wet and wilderness given a new lease of life, since walkers can skip along the ridge segregated from the jewelled sphagnum moss.

The summit

The fell-top was formerly open grazing but unfortunately is now crossed by a fence, albeit periodically graced with stiles. The fence may be considered a blessing in mist to act as a guide, but in the main it would be deemed an

High Seat from Heather Knott

eyesore, for all its practical stock-proofing intent. It partitions off the summit from the eastern knoll, called Man. The boss of rock that forms the summit hosts a stone-built Ordnance Survey pillar; the science of surveying may have rendered it redundant, yet this well-made pillar lends a touch of order to the scene. And what a scene it is too, an unusually good all-round panorama, sufficient to cause you to idle many minutes, mentally ticking off the tops… while your mates plough on up through the bogs!

Safe descents

All lines of ascent work in reverse, the quickest route to a useful road being Route **8**, heading due W via Pouterhow Pike and slipping below Reecastle Crag.

Ridge routes

Bleaberry Fell →*2km/1¼ miles ↓30m/100ft ↑50m/165ft ⏲30min*
In years gone by the normal practice was to follow the general line of the fence, but it has to be admitted that this is now less satisfactory, except in mist, as it encounters the worst of the marsh. A better option is to avoid crossing the fence and instead dip off the NW edge of the summit on a path which, admittedly, splodges through some pretty appalling peat to reach a stile at the head of Ashness Gill and below Threefooted Brandreth. Thereafter the path winds N, with varying degrees of peatiness, keeping left of a large pool to duly rise onto the dry summit ridge.

High Tove →*1.6km/1 mile ↓100m/330ft ↑10m/35ft ⏲25min*
Head S and switch sides of the ridge fence to cross the stile/hand-gate at the fence junction. As the slope eases a stone-flagged path is joined, coming through a hand-gate onto The Pewits marsh. The stone flags weave a merry way through the once-horrid bog to a corresponding hand-gate. The path engineering continues, minimising soft ground to reconnect with the ridge fence to reach the top of High Tove. In mist know that the summit cairn is set some 100m to the east of the ridge gate.

19 HIGH SPY 653M/2142FT

Climb it from	Chapel Bridge (Little Town) **7**, Seatoller **13**, Rosthwaite **1** or Grange-in-Borrowdale **3**
Character	Extremely well defended to east and west; however, the spine of the ridge affords wonderful walking and spellbinding mountain views
Fell-friendly route	1
Summit grid ref	NY 234 162
Link it with	Maiden Moor
Part of	The High Spy ridge

Travellers coming into Borrowdale by Lodore will get a solid view of High Spy, with Blea Crag a pronounced peak, although the summit is unseen. As a whole, the fell forms the craggy, somewhat confused backdrop to the west side of the famous Jaws of Borrowdale. (Although Castle Crag is, in fact, a dependency of High Spy, it is treated as a separate fell in this guide.) This eastern declivity, centred on Goat Crag, suggests scope for adventurous ascent, and such routes are described here. Only two conventional routes exist – one created by shepherds (White Rake, 7) and the other by quarrymen (Rigghead, 4) – while the steep scarp sections of Routes 5 and 6 are straight out of the locker of fell adventure, being secure but pathless.

↑ *The upper Newlands valley aspect of High Spy from Hindscarth*

WALKING THE LAKE DISTRICT FELLS – BORROWDALE

Crags are not restricted to High Spy's eastern face for, with equal impact, the western escarpment is buttressed by Eel Crags, a popular venue for climbers. Generally, there is little hint of an easy ascent along the steep ground forming a wall to the upper Newlands valley, although one route has been researched and is described here (2).

Ascent from Chapel Bridge, Little Town 7

Via Dalehead Tarn →6.4km/4 miles ↑610m/2000ft ⏲2hr 15min

For all the verdant riches of Borrowdale, the absence of cars makes the upper Newlands valley prime fellwalkers' territory.

1 From the parking spot at Chapel Bridge walk back up the road towards **Little Town**, stepping over the stile on the right to come onto the open green track, which otherwise starts at the farming community from a gate. This old miners' way leads on along the dale floor. After 1.6km the track passes the Carlisle Mountaineering Club hut and enters the wild upper quarter, passing beneath the stubby spur of **Castlenook**. The track forks on the approach

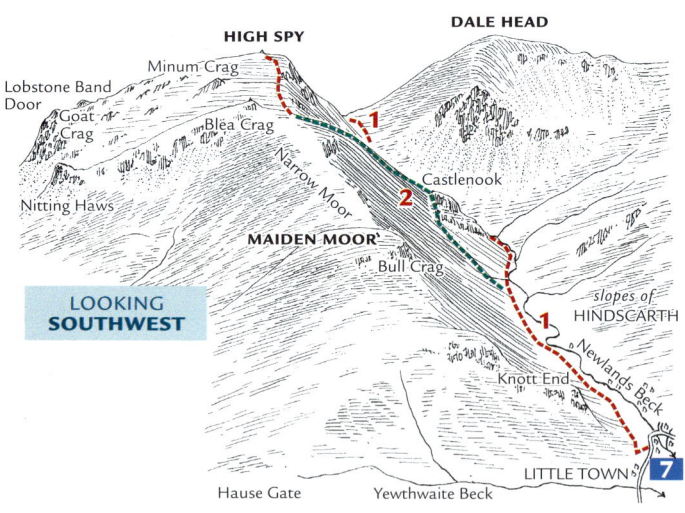

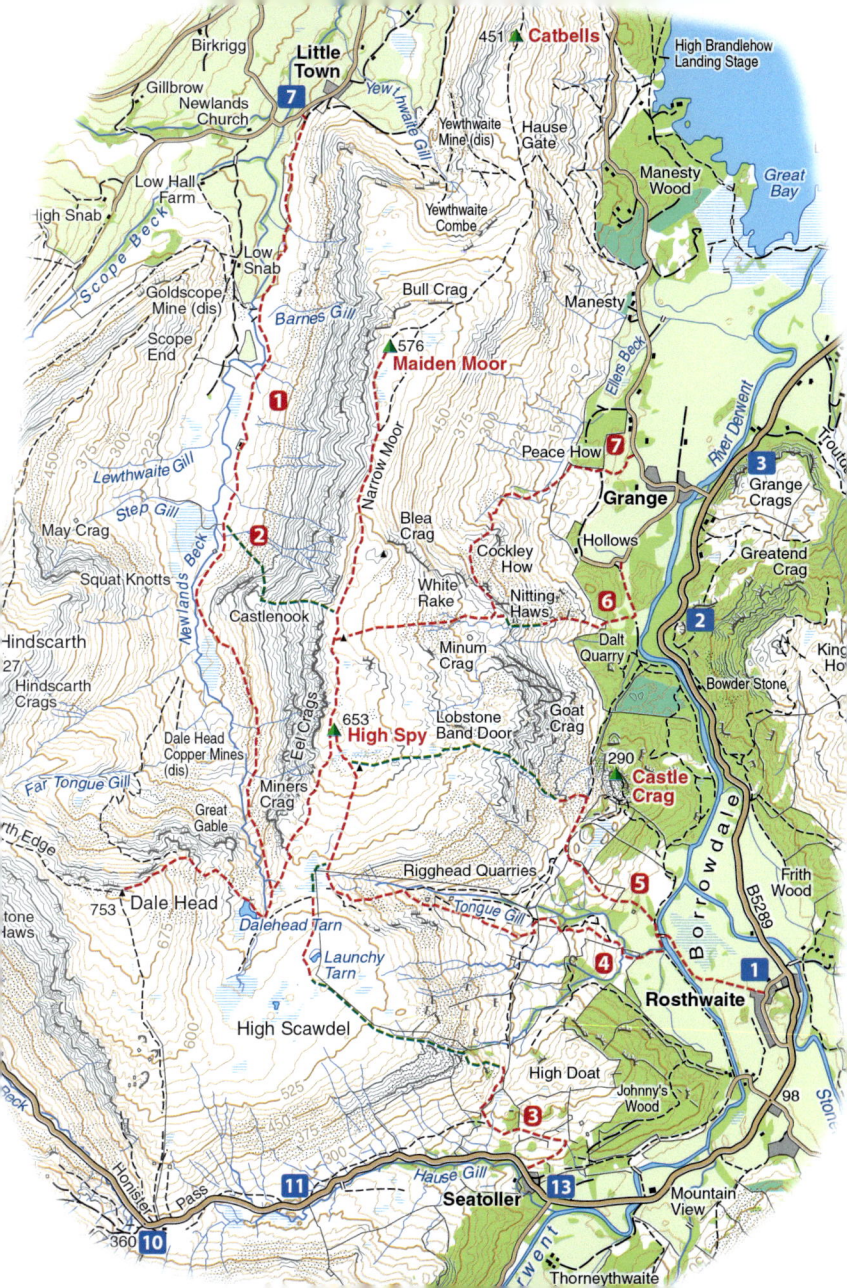

High Spy and Dalehead Tarn from the southeastern slopes of Dale Head

to a ford. Here bear uphill, climbing steadily over rough ground (you can keep beside the beck and inspect the impressive sequence of cascades, but the higher path is the preferred way). The route leads up beneath **Eel Crags** to come above the upper ravine, which is the outflow of **Dalehead Tarn**. As the fell opens cut back left up the well-worn ridge path, with its stirring cliff views, and climb, unhurried, to the summit.

Via Castlenook →4.8km/3 miles ↑610m/2000ft ⏱2hr 20min

If you are not deterred by rank heather and fancy an unorthodox climb, the Castlenook ridge presents a unique challenge.

2 Start out with Route **1** but leave the valley track shortly after passing the climbers' club hut and, before the wall ends, angle up the wide gill debris, bracken-free, working your way up the slope to the obvious, broad tilted rake at the top of the craggy **Castlenook** spur. At the base of the rake find a mine adit, a stooped entrance which invites a cautious entry. Continue up the rake. This is pathless terrain but there are no obstacles en route to the high shoulder, a fine viewpoint, with traces of a bield (shelter) showing that shepherds have been this way too.

19 HIGH SPY

Take a break to collect your energies, as from here on the climb – straight up – is pure heather for some 300 metres. The occasional lateral sheep trod provides brief respite but generally you are making headway on a spring mattress! You'll be hard pressed to do it without a few breathers, and the outward views never fail to reward the essential pauses. Arrival on the level ridge seems surreal: ridge-strollers cruise by as if on a seafront promenade, while you seek the stone seat to restore your sense of equilibrium! The handsome summit cairn lies 400 metres due south (right).

Ascent from Seatoller 13

Via Scaleclose Gill →*3.6km/2¼ miles* ↑*615m/2020ft* ⏱*1hr 45min*

3 At the head of the hamlet bear right at the first gate, opposite the bridge and track approach to a row of cottages on the left. Follow the rough, cobbled former toll road by two further gates or rise up the modern road a further 50 metres to the first bend and step up through the hand-gate to climb more directly. As the two routes come together veer up the grass-bank

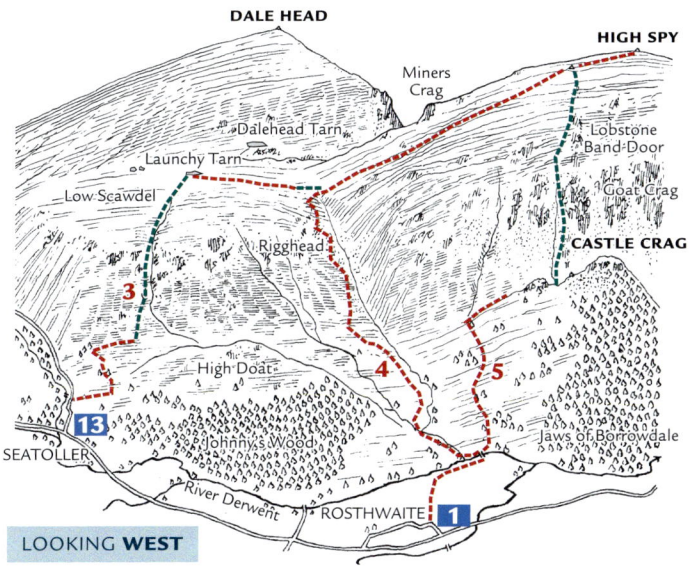

path to a hand-gate and follow on north beside the wall. Watch where three walls come together, set back to the right, and march on a further 60 metres to find a small boulder to the left of the path. At this point leave the path and climb the steep pathless bank, thus avoiding bracken and outcropping. As the slope eases find traces of a path, leading to a hand-gate in a stout wall. From this point there is little evidence of a path but the route simply follows the upper course of Scaleclose Gill and subsequent fence. The heather growth on the far side contrasts markedly with the grassy wet waste underfoot. Curve round the sharp fence-corner, bearing right to quickly pass **Launchy Tarn**. Head downhill (north), effectively beside the fence, passing the stile from Rigghead Quarries, to skirt round the right-hand turn in the fence. Here join company with the path rising from a stile in this fence and climb the open grassy fell. Come over a cairned brow to reach the summit through a hollow.

Ascent from Rosthwaite 1

Two choices: the regular and the rare

Both routes begin by following the lane from Yew Tree Farm to cross New Bridge.

Via Rigghead Quarry →*4km/2½ miles* ↑*580m/1905ft* ⏱*1hr 45min*

4 The regular route switches left to encounter the two-part footbridge beside the stony **Derwent** and slips over the stile in the middle to follow the flood-bank beside Scaleclose Beck. The path crosses a plank-bridge, then a stile, and winds up the pasture to a field-gate. It then veers up left, crossing the lateral track, to ascend the grassy rigg. Brushing through the bracken, climb to a wall-stile to reach the old quarry building, now a climbing-club hut. Pass on beyond it to naturally join the pitched path ascending **Tongue Gill**. The stepped path climbs through the lower spoil and adits of **Rigghead Quarries**, above which bear purposefully right to cross the fence-stile at the fence-corner. The fell path leads on up the open slope, passing over a cairned intermediate top, to reach the ultimate cairn.

19 High Spy

Via Lobstone Band Door →*3.2km/2 miles* ↑*620m/2035ft* ⏱*2hr*

The instinctive fell-explorer will relish this crafty route.

5 From New Bridge turn right, taking the first left-hand gate to enter a pasture. Head up the bank to reach a wall-gate, bear right and step onto the lateral bridle track linking Seatoller with Grange. Pass the fence-fold on the hause and start down the cobbled track – but only so far, as the aim is to gain the old slate cave up to the left. Get to the point approximately level with the right-hand regular path onto Castle Crag. A faint quarrymen's way winds up the left-hand ridge to the spoil and ruins in front of the walled slate cave. Having peered tentatively into the walled entrance, embark on the fell-climb proper on the right-hand side, ford the gill and maintain a right-hand bias, following the broken slabby edge to reach the rank heather, where the slope eases. The heather continues but sheep trods give comfort underfoot. A cairn top will attract attention but the greater interest is **Lobstone Band Door**, up to the right – a narrow gap in the rocky ridge. The fascination comes in the form of the coarse volcanic rock exposures: diverse concentrations of lava which have formed medallion-shaped nodules in a rock cement. Ascend, with a choice of boiler-plate outcrops and grassy passages, to reach the subsidiary summit, with its two cairns, then bear northwest to reach the tall summit edifice.

Pillow lava at Lobstone Band Door

WALKING THE LAKE DISTRICT FELLS – BORROWDALE

Ascent from Grange-in-Borrowdale 3

Via Nitting Haws direct →*4km/2½ miles* ↑*625m/2050ft* ⏱*2hr 20min*

6 Follow the **Hollows Farm** access road leading south from the middle of the community. Where the metalled road swings right veer left with the track, which provides access to two camping fields. Turn right through the first recessed parking area and follow the path, passing close by the site toilet block, to reach a hand-gate in the bounding wall. The steep fellside beckons. Follow the obvious path leading uphill. This ascends the bracken slope towards the rock headland, not towards the tumbling gill. Upon reaching a shelf of ice-smoothed rock the path is lost as boulders deny scope for a tangible way. Keep up left, close by the juniper shrubbery, on the large-boulder scree; avoid the small scree, which has been made loose by hasty scree-running descending walkers. Keep up by the rock wall and short shallow gully, on loose footing, to arrive by the side of **Nitting Haws**, where a simple stroll right brings the rock headland underfoot. The peak is the regular perch of many a resident raven

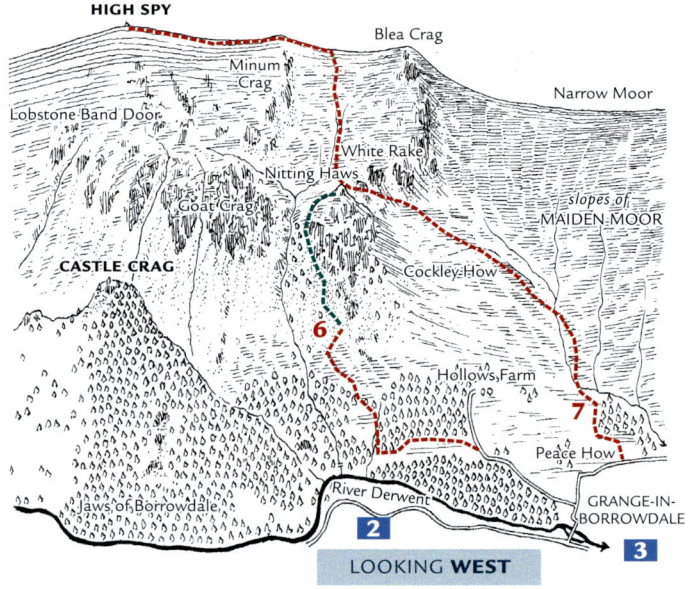

Looking northwest from the summit

and a wonderful spot from which the flightless fellwanderer can survey the setting of Grange and the wooded magic of the Jaws of Borrowdale. Wander back from the headland to join the regular path emerging from the undercliff of **White Rake** (Route **7**) and follow this to the summit.

Via Cockley How →*3.2km/2 miles* ↑*595m/1950ft* ⏱*1hr 40min*

This canny route, which breaks through the rocky armour of the fell, owes its origins to shepherds gathering their flocks from remote higher pastures.

7 Follow the road north from the village to find a footpath signed left, just short of Borrowdale Gates Hotel. From the hand-gate a path leads through the scrub and tree-dotted **Peace How** pasture to a gate, where a path continues by the walled woodland to pass to the left of a reservoir building. Go through the kissing-gate in the fence and embark on the ascending path. This follows up a ridge to ford the gill where it converges with another, then aims on up the steep grass slope to crest **Cockley How**. The top features a split block, an obvious foreground subject for the camera.

The path rises and slants half-left, passing beneath the crags of **White Rake** to come easily onto the higher pasture, close behind the **Nitting Haws** headland. It then curves right and ascends, with a gill, up the amphitheatre, a great unknown pasture which provides an easy line to the skyline and the regular ridge path. A left turn leads to the summit.

The summit

A stouter – if tumbling – version of the Dale Head summit cairn stands impressively back from the scarp edge. At your feet are flakes of splintered rock. The situation is every bit as grand and exciting as Dale Head, with that fell itself and Hindscarth greatly displayed. Indeed, with the high ground sustained for a considerable distance to the north, there are many fine situations to encourage a prolonged admiration of this fell theatre. To get the best view of Derwentwater continue north for a little under 1km, to the crest of Blea Crag.

Safe descents

The ridge path can be relied on N for Hause Gate, the depression beyond Maiden Moor, where paths lead left to Little Town and right to Manesty for Grange. A further chink in the armour of the fell lies 400 metres along this path, where, at a cairn amid a wide grassy space, lies the start of a path which leads down to the E (**7**). This comes into the secretive amphitheatre behind Nitting Haws, a little peaked spur, and bears left, short of the peak, following a shepherds' drove under White Rake Crag and down by the split boulder on Cockley How, direct to Grange.

Ridge route

Maiden Moor →2.4km/1½ miles ↓85m/280ft ↑10m/35ft ⊕40min
The almost level ridge heading N encourages a confident stride, with the scarp-edge views across the gulf of the upper Newlands valley to the fine fells at the heart of the Northwestern group putting an extra skip in your step. En route make a point of visiting the cairn on the peak of Blea Crag for its exceptional view over the great basin of Derwentwater. This cairn is set to the right of the main thoroughfare, just where it begins a more consistent descent. Come down to an obvious fork, where you take the left-hand path to keep along the western edge to reach the contiguous summit.

20 HIGH TOVE 515M/1690FT

Climb it from	Armboth **27** or Watendlath **15**
Character	An intersection of moorland ways, surrounded by marsh; a place to pause and admire the larks
Fell-friendly route	3
Summit grid ref	NY 289 165
Link it with	Armboth Fell, Bell Crags or High Seat

The age-old cross-ridge footpath (1–3) that linked Armboth Hall, beside Leathes Water (now lost under the lapping waters of Thirlmere), and the hamlet of Watendlath went against convention: instead of seeking a low point in the ridge it slipped precisely over the summit of High Tove, the reasoning being that it is high and dry. The tough tussocks of heather and rush must always have been taxing to the stride. There are moments when webbed feet would be a distinct advantage!

Water from the fell initially flows without due haste, then smartly spills into both Thirlmere and the exquisitely shy but far from secret Watendlath Tarn, a quintessential Lakeland tarn.

↑ *High Tove, unlit, seen from the bridle path to Blea Tarn*

Journeys from the summit to either Bell Crags or High Seat look nothing on the map but there is dismay awaiting the ill prepared. Good gaiters are a basic necessity, particularly when crossing the worst of 'the sponge', encountered at the hollow called the Pewits, which is more than a match for any Pennine peat bog! A period of drought or intense frost is a distinct advantage for any degree of comfort.

Ascent from Armboth 27

Direct →*1.5km/1 mile* ↑*350m/1150ft* ⏱*1hr 10min*

1 Leave the car park and turn right to the hand-gate, with footpath sign 'Watendlath', at the first bend in the road. There are two lines of ascent from this point. The made-way passes over the little bridge spanning **Middlesteads Gill** and continues to a hand-gate, then rises through the hurdle sheepfold on a green trail. As the forestry wall comes near pass a distinctive group of large boulders, after which the wall is replaced by a fence, partitioning the path from **Fisher Gill**. As the slope steepens below Cockrigg Crags the path makes exaggerated zig-zags and passes under a sycamore tree, with some juniper evident, and rises to a wall-gap at the top of the forestry.

Now follow the well-defined path leading west. Avoid fording the tributary gill as bracken is entered and keep uphill to ford a little higher. The path becomes far less certain and contrives to deliver damp ground underfoot as it nears the top, even in dry weather, though it offers nothing to match the bogginess of the Pewits. The summit cairn is your skyline target.

Via Middlesteads Gill
→*2km/1¼ miles*
↑*355m/1165ft*
⏱*1hr 20min*

This alternative involves more interest – and effort – than Route 1.

2 Route **1** can be joined from the hand-gate off the road by ascending by the

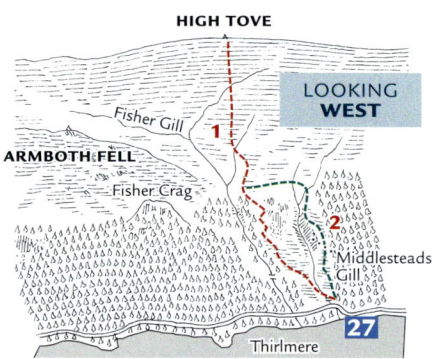

20 HIGH TOVE

right-hand forest fence, which is steep and has no path. As the slope scoops, angle half-left onto the arête overlooking the impressively deep **Middlesteads Gill** ravine, with natural tree growth enhancing the view to Fisher Crag and across Thirlmere to Helvellyn. Keep to the rim of the gill and eventually angle right to slip round the right-hand end of the fell-bounding wall where it all but abuts the forest fence. Go left, keeping this wall to your left, to reach the wall-gap and join Route **1**.

Ascent from Watendlath 15

Direct → *1.5km/1 mile*
↑*265m/870ft* ⏲*1hr 15min*

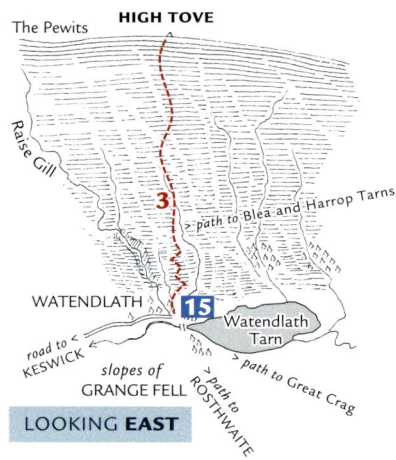

3 Start from the National Trust car park, crossing the ladder-stile, or go right from the point of entry, and by either means reach a gate. The waymarked footpath fords **Raise Gill** and soon commences the zig-zag ascent of the steep bank, grooved by centuries-old sled trails used to convey peat from High Tove for domestic heating. The path is in a well-repaired state and rises onto the pasture beyond the wall corner. Where the old bridle path meets the brow the **Harrop Tarn path** departs right. Continue up the easier ground due east. The occasional cairn reflects the idle boredom of pedestrians rather than navigational need, though in mist the lack of landmarks lends them a certain credibility. There are worn sections higher up – watch for sly holes – on an otherwise tedious journey to the hand-gate in the ridge fence and the summit.

The summit

A solitary cairn rests on the eastern edge of the summit as a skyline marker and a sure guide for wayfarers traversing the ridge from east to west. The hand-gate in the fence, some 50 metres further west, rests on slightly higher ground. The view is remarkably good for all the modesty of the setting. Westward, the array of tops will keep you amused for several minutes, though the stronger horizon is east, from Blencathra through Helvellyn to Heron Pike. Catstycam makes a cheeky appearance over the saddle south of White Side, in much the same way as Raven Crag and Castle Rock of Triermain raise their heads further north above the thoroughly hidden Thirlmere. In fact, the

Looking west from the summit cairn (photo: Maggie Allan)

only named water in view is the Solway Firth, which sneaks into shot over the left shoulder of High Seat.

Safe descents

Compass bearings E (**1**) for the Armboth road and – better – W (**3**) for habitation at Watendlath are the only sane options. All else is ankle-twisting bewildering misery in mist.

Ridge routes

Armboth Fell → *1.3km/¾ mile* ↓*75m/245ft* ↑*45m/150ft* ⏱*30min*
Dismiss all thoughts of a beeline. The heather is cruelly rank and the hollow at the source of Fisher and Launchy Gills is on a par with that at the Pewits – which is saying something! Follow the eastward course of the traversing footpath, bearing SE after the first hint of a gill to meet, ford and follow upstream Fisher Gill, then bearing half-left to the prominent summit outcrop.

Middle Crags, on the ridge path to Bell Crags

Bell Crags →*3.2km/2 miles* ↓*10m/35ft* ↑*50m/165ft* ⏲*1hr 10min*
The ridge fence S provides the guide, but there are too many marshy moments to call this a joyous escapade.

High Seat →*1.6km/1 mile* ↓*10m/35ft* ↑*100m/330ft* ⏲*40min*
Again the ridge fence largely does the navigation for you. Considerable engineering has been done to the path, which dips briefly then swings right over flag stones cutting a fence corner and re-joining it to pass through a hand-gate. At this point embark on the once-treacherous bog charmingly called The Pewits. The traverse is now enchanting, especially fun for walkers who love to study sphagnum dryshod. From the second hand-gate the stone flags continue a little way up the steepening slope, then shortly go left through the fence by a stile/hand-gate to reach the rocky crown of High Seat.

21 MAIDEN MOOR 576M/1890FT

Climb it from	Chapel Bridge (Little Town) **7**, Grange-in-Borrowdale **3** or High Brandelhow Jetty **4**
Character	A lovely ridge to wander upon, with swathes of heather, extremely steep on the west side and only slightly less so on the east
Fell-friendly route	1
Summit grid ref	NY 237 182
Link it with	Catbells or High Spy
Part of	The High Spy ridge

Standing back from the plaudits of Catbells, the next step up the growing ridge, Maiden Moor, may lack a great lake view and is often bypassed by ridge walkers on the Newlands Horseshoe, yet fellwanderers will love its summit as the most intimate and telling viewpoint for the Newlands fell scene.

In contrast to the western declivity, which is steeper and mightily buttressed, the eastern slopes sweep down to Grange-in-Borrowdale. The ridge tightens, running south from the summit to its union with High Spy on Blea Crag. The fell shares with Catbells custody of Yewthwaite Comb, scene of considerable lead-mining activity – as the bare debris attests.

↑ *The Newlands Beck aspect of Maiden Moor from Hindscarth*

WALKING THE LAKE DISTRICT FELLS – BORROWDALE

Of the routes to the top all attention is directed at two northern lines: the connecting ridge with Catbells (1) and, for a spot of spicy adventure, the stepped Knott End ridge (2) above Little Town. The popular lines from the east embark from Manesty (3) and High Brandelhow Jetty (4) to join the ridge at Hause Gate.

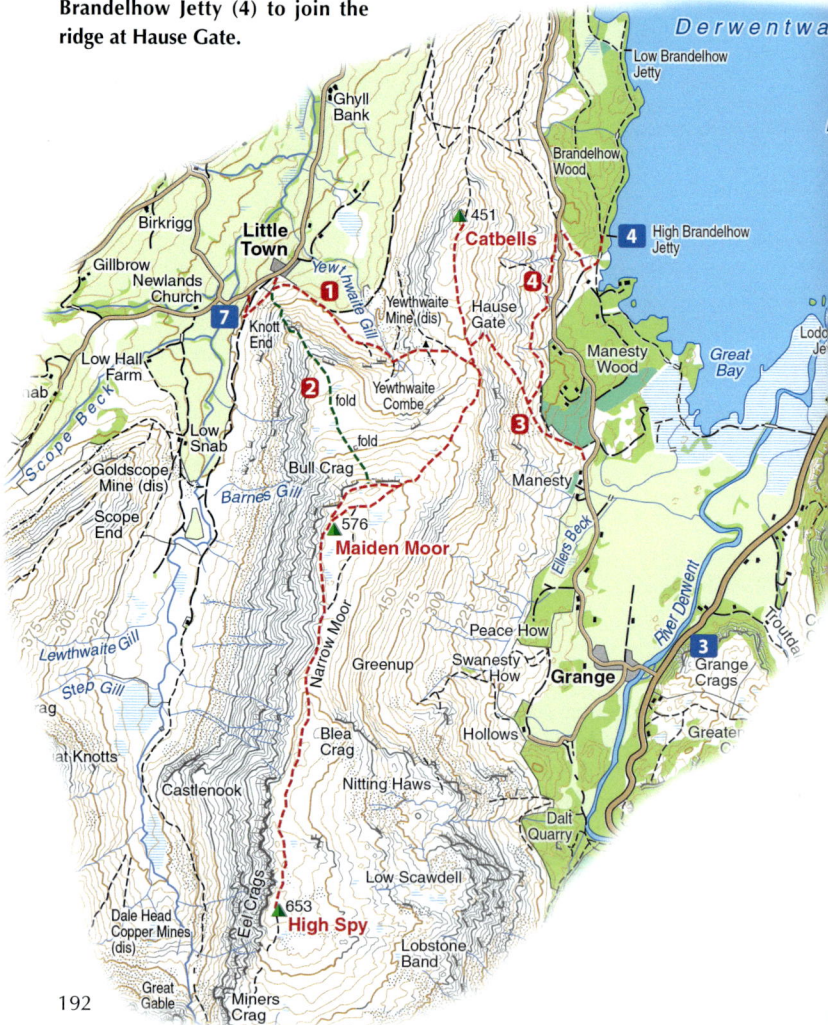

21 MAIDEN MOOR

Ascent from Chapel Bridge, Little Town 7

There are two inviting routes: one commonly followed in shepherding and mining days and reassuringly simple; the other gifted to enthral the seasoned fell-explorer.

Via Yewthwaite Comb →3.2km/2 miles ↑380m/1245ft ⏱1hr 30min

1 You can leave the road at the gate in the hamlet or, if parked up at Chapel Bridge, ascend the road and skip over the fence-stile where the wall ends and step up to the track; go right and then switch left with the higher green track to meet up with the way from the Little Town gate at the first hairpin.

Head east on the green track, coming by the intake wall. Watch for the bridleway breaking right, parting company with the wall and rising steadily south. This bears left, fording Yewthwaite Gill beneath a waterfall, and the level section of path is pitched. Hop over the second ford to embark on a broad rough path, rising to a sheepfold at the upper workings of the old Yewthwaite Mine. The path now comes onto grass and angles easily half-right to the saddle in the ridge, where you turn right and follow the trail of the multitude. Early on there are fine views down to Derwentwater. Typical of many another, the popular path sweeps onto the ridge oblivious of the actual summit, so as the ground eases look to take either one of two clear paths breaking half-right, which will take you to the summit at the brink of the impressive scarp.

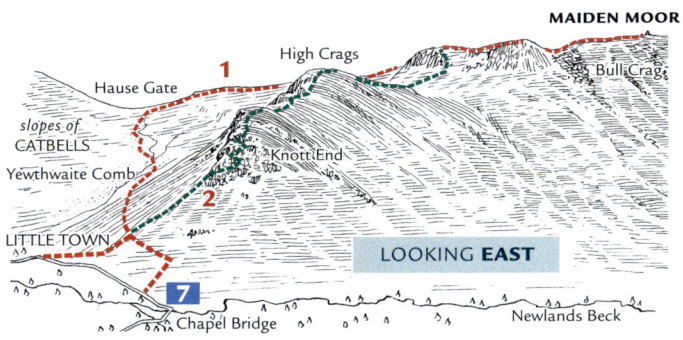

Catbells from the northern edge overlooking Yewthwaite Comb

Via Knott End →*2.4km/1½ miles* ↑*380m/1245ft* ⏲*1hr 10min*
2 From the hairpin (see Route **1**) leave the regular path and aim for the solitary tree in a low crag directly above, with bracken an issue in summer. Pass to the right of the tree then angle up to the crag above, aiming to the immediate left of the holly tree on Knott End. You can scramble onto the ridge here or drift a further 50 metres left to angle onto the ridge on slightly easier ground. Either way, tussle with the heather and simple rock ridge with happy abandon – there are no difficulties if you stick to the ridge. There is no evidence of a path: in fact, the only imprints are those made by resident Herdwick sheep. There are two distinct steps to the rising ridge and the second clambers over the ambitiously named **High Crags**. The view of Catbells is superb from this top. Descend to pass a small tarn and above this locate a small sheepfold. Continue, on a rising line, to a second larger fold on the slope ahead, from where you can either clamber straight up or slant left, by either means coming into union with the regular skyline path. Bear right to follow the edge onto the impressive viewpoint of **Bull Crag**. The next easy rise brings the summit underfoot.

21 MAIDEN MOOR

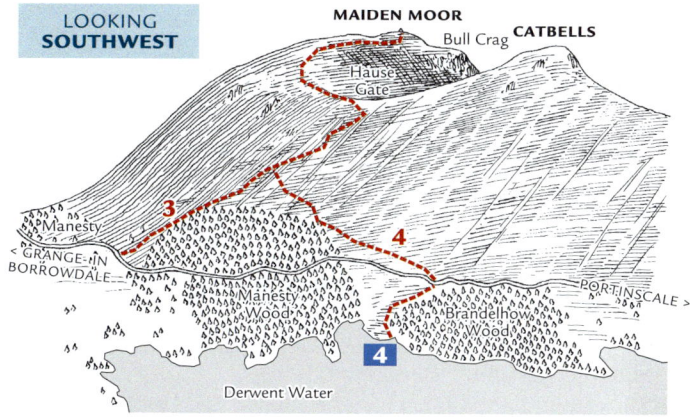

Ascent from Grange-in-Borrowdale 3

Via Manesty →*2.4km/1½ miles* ↑*495m/1625ft* ⏲*1hr 50min*
3 Follow the road north from Grange; this is a popular stroll in spite of the passage of cars and Honister Rambler buses! After **Manesty house** find a signposted path stepping off the road on the left. This rises via a gate and climbs steadily to the **Hause Gate** saddle, with lovely views back to give you plenty of cause to take it easy from time to time. Follow the ridge path south; a heavy flow of walkers has ensured a torn trail. Higher up, watch to keep right along the brow in order to reach the summit, along the scarp edge over **Bull Crag**, rather than be lured by hasty Newlands Horseshoe walkers who race past this first major step, more intent on High Spy.

Ascent from High Brandelhow Jetty 4

While there are numerous suitable verge spaces along the road above Brandelhow Wood, there is no denying the immense pleasure of approaching the adventure from the Keswick Launch.

Via Hause Gate →*3.2km/2 miles* ↑*500m/1640ft* ⏲*1hr 50min*
4 Step off the jetty and bear left on a woodland track to a hand-gate, from where a path leads forward before bearing uphill, alongside the old

Narrow Moor

Brandelhow lead mine, to step onto the open road. Cross and join the graded path leading left from the old quarry. This leads past a seat and plaque to the writer Sir Hugh Walpole, who lived in the house below, Brackenburn. The path comes to a wall above woodland and forks. Take the rising line to join the Manesty path (Route **3**), climbing, via the saddle of **Hause Gate**, to the summit.

The summit

This is not a summit for walkers who love peaks, as the sense of being at the highest point on the fell is less convincing than on many other occasions. Yet, with a small cairn resting innocently on a flat mat of grass a few paces from the brink, there are sufficient makings of a summit to satisfy. From the near edge revel in a bird's-eye view into the exciting upper Newlands Beck valley. Peer down upon the spoil of Goldscope Mine and across the greater gulf to an array of ridges from Dale Head round to Causey Pike, with the stately presence of Hindscarth warranting special attention.

21 Maiden Moor

Safe descents

Aim NE to join the main pedestrian thoroughfare to Hause Gate, and here either turn right for Manesty (**3**) or left for Little Town (**1**). Both paths are reliable.

Ridge routes

Catbells →*2.4km/1½ miles* ↓*215m/705ft* ↑*90m/295ft* ⏱*45min*
Head NE, the route quickly merging with the shortcut ridge path from Narrow Moor, which draws down to the grassy depression of Hause Gate and continues easily N, via a minor rock slab, onto the bare rock summit. To be alone here is unusual.

High Spy →*2.4km/1½ miles* ↓*10m/35ft* ↑*85m/280ft* ⏱*30min*
A clear path leads S, with the constant pleasure of the profound escarpment always close by on the right. There is but one slight rise en route to the summit, passing to the right of the crest of Blea Crag, a top that should be visited for its commanding view over Derwentwater.

Maiden Moor from the ridge path to High Spy

22 RAVEN CRAG 463M/1519FT

Climb it from	Thirlmere Dam 26, Armboth 27 or Rough How Bridge 24
Character	Defined by a great cliff and a mantle of conifers
Fell-friendly route	4
Summit grid ref	NY 303 188

The great buttressed bluff of Raven Crag, for all its smothering of trees, commands avid attention, especially from travellers crossing the Thirlmere dam. The summit is not a viewpoint for it is consumed by trees, but the brink of the cliff most certainly is.

Tucked under its eastern slope is a rocky hillock, Castle Crag, complete with Iron Age ramparts. Due north a bare-topped crest called Benn Man, although not often visited, is a fine viewpoint for the forbidding crags across Shoulthwaite Gill and for Raven Crag itself. The coniferous slope between Middlesteads Gill and Shoulthwaite Farm comes within the domain of Raven Crag and offers a mixture of ascents and gradients. These woods are famous for their indigenous population of red squirrels, but recent sightings of grey squirrels, which carry a virulent virus that kills the reds, have brought about a community watch campaign to stem these unwelcome intruders.

↑ *Helvellyn and Thirlmere from the Raven Crag scarp (photo: Maggie Allan)*

22 RAVEN CRAG

The direct route (1) climbs steeply through the forestry from the Thirlmere dam. However, there are plenty of options for a longer line and a back-door approach, either from Armboth via Middlesteads Gill (2) or Fisher Gill (3), or from Rough How Bridge (5). It is also possible to create a grand tour of the minor tops hereabouts (4), taking in Castle Crag, Raven Crag, Benn Man and Great How.

Ascent from Thirlmere Dam 26

Direct →*0.8km/½ mile* ↑*305m/1000ft* ⏲*1hr*

This is the hot route to the top: the steepest, shortest and most popular.

1 The path leads off from the small car park at the road junction west of the dam. Go right, then after some 100 metres go left at the hand-gate into the mature plantation. The path rises to a forest track. Either cross it, via the tall kissing-gate, or go left, sweeping round the fenced enclosure and thus getting a close-up view of Raven Crag from below – this route is often followed in descent on a there-and-back outing. The direct route winds up through the young plantation in the deer-excluding enclosure

Raven Crag from Thirlmere Dam

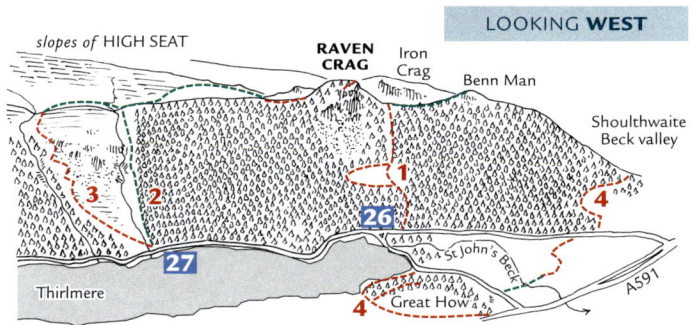

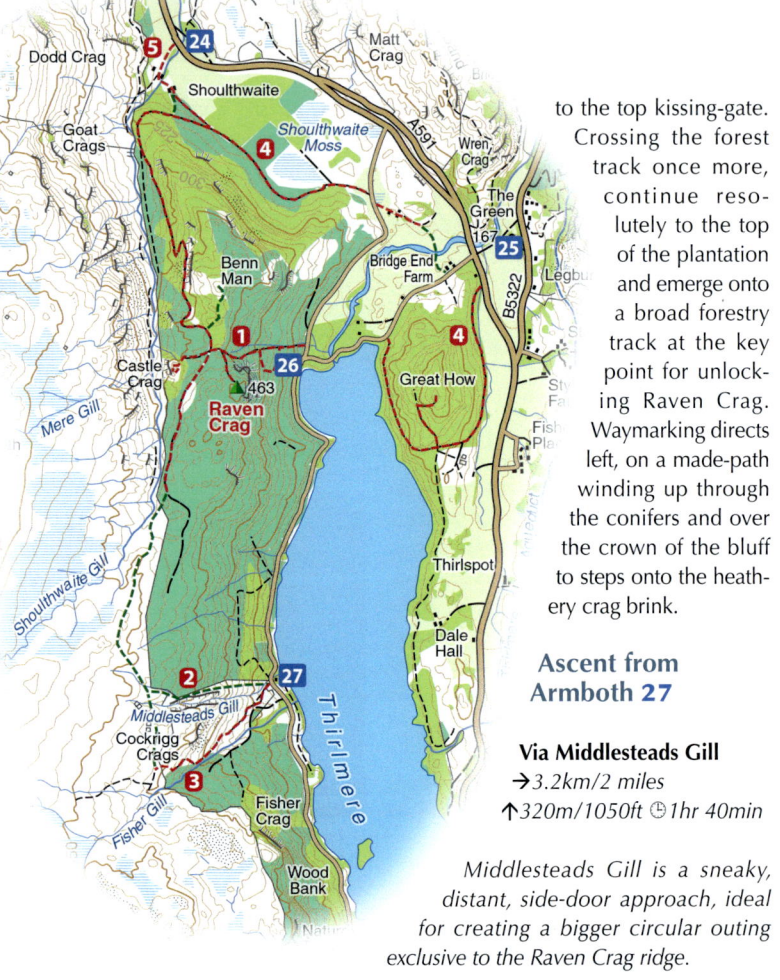

to the top kissing-gate. Crossing the forest track once more, continue resolutely to the top of the plantation and emerge onto a broad forestry track at the key point for unlocking Raven Crag. Waymarking directs left, on a made-path winding up through the conifers and over the crown of the bluff to steps onto the heathery crag brink.

Ascent from Armboth 27

Via Middlesteads Gill
→ 3.2km/2 miles
↑ 320m/1050ft ⏱ 1hr 40min

Middlesteads Gill is a sneaky, distant, side-door approach, ideal for creating a bigger circular outing exclusive to the Raven Crag ridge.

2 Leave the Armboth lakeside car park and follow the road right (north), going through the kissing-gate at the first bend, at the beginning of the Watendlath path. Ignore the inviting path over the 'sma' brig', and while you can ascend the footpath rising above **Fisher Gill** and follow the wall, right, at the top (**3**), the more inviting line climbs directly from the road beside the right-hand forest fence. It is steep going, and you hug the fence to help avoid the bracken. As the slope scoops, angle half-left onto the arête overlooking the impressive **Middlesteads Gill** ravine, enhanced by natural tree growth.

Keep to the rim of the gill and eventually angle right to slip round the right-hand end of the fell-bounding wall where it almost abuts the forest fence. Bear up right by the gill and fence, and at the next corner angle up the slope to top the length of ascending wall and thus gain the low ridge. Advance beyond a cairn, on a descending line, to the gate entering the forestry. Follow the main track left, with further fine views down the Shoulthwaite Gill valley towards the Glenderaterra Gap. Arriving at the broad turning area, you can go left to follow the made-path to **Castle Crag** or right to take the similarly prepared trail to Raven Crag. If you continue down the track, also consider branching half-right, just before the track begins to descend, to join a narrow path leading through the pines to the top of **Benn Man** (see summit section).

4 All three viewpoints – **Castle Crag**, **Raven Crag** and **Benn Man** – can be included in a grand tour of 11.7km which would continue north with the forest track and sweep round in the valley by **Shoulthwaite Moss** and Smaithwaite, then orbit **Great How** (you could include the summit, though the view is blanked out by trees!) to reach the dam, all on firm paths (see map).

Ascent from Rough How Bridge 24

Direct ➔ *2km/1¼ miles* ↑*335m/1100ft* ⏱ *1hr 25min*

The climb does not have to be a slog; there is another way. The track rising from Shoulthwaite to the north is as sweet a route to the top as could be devised.

5 From the layby cross the busy **A591** into the lane leading to and through **Shoulthwaite farm** (footpath waymarks), entering Thirlmere Forest at a tall gate as from between the barns. Either follow the level bridle path ahead to the open track and then turn acutely right, via the

Birches near Shoulthwaite farm

deer-fence gate/tall hand-gate, rising with the forest track, or branch off immediately, via the tall hand-gate in the deer fence, following the impromptu path, shortcutting up to the forest track, which you follow to the right.

The main forest track is signposted 'Raven Crag, Fort and Viewpoint' and leads, via a sweeping zig-zag, under Sipping Crag and via a later bend to the turning area on the saddle, from where the made-trail can be followed to the summit.

The summit

The United Utilities signboards are correct; the brink of Raven Crag is a viewpoint. The whole of Thirlmere reservoir can be seen, backed by the high rolling skyline of the Helvellyn range, with tantalising glimpses south over Dunmail Raise and north to Skiddaw and Blencathra. To complete the viewspotting you need to move around to evade the trees, an activity hampered by deep heather and the knowledge that the cliff is all too close at hand. This is not the summit of the bluff; there is a cairn to be found among the ragged trees behind the viewpoint. A further cairn marks the viewpoint itself. Close by are the remains of a wall from the days when sheep needed to be discouraged from risking their necks grazing too close to the edge. This is the ideal picnic place.

There are two other special viewpoints in the vicinity, well meriting a visit. Castle Crag, replicating Legburthwaite's more famous Iron Age site, is waymarked from the track at the saddle. A made-path, with duck-boarding, leads to a low rampart embracing a rocky knoll, with a narrow path via the rampart circling clockwise over the bluff (rock-step). Retrace the approach to continue. Benn Man (or the Benn), the second high point on the ridge to the north, is reached from the track just before it shapes to descend. Bear right, on a narrow path through the pines and larches, and climb the heather-and-bilberry hillock for a superb summit prospect back to Raven Crag and westward to the crags lining Shoulthwaite Gill, most notably, Iron Crag.

Safe descents

All routes of ascent can be comfortably reversed.

23 ROSTHWAITE FELL 551M/1808FT

Climb it from	Stonethwaite 14 or Seatoller 13
Character	A crag-bounded and somewhat confusing ridge, calling for good navigation skills and constant attention to topography
Fell-friendly route	4
Summit grid ref	NY 258 125
Link it with	Glaramara

Undeservedly, Rosthwaite Fell gets little attention from walkers. There are no popular paths on this intricate tangle of rough fell, and there is only a sketchy ridge path to give a clue as to the passage of the occasional intrepid soul. The fell is sheer delight in clear weather but – beware – something of a nightmare in swirling hill fog!

Since the ridge rises in steps it is no wonder that there are several piked tops. Bessyboot, the traditional summit, is only the second of four. High Knott forms the northern crest, quickly followed by Bessyboot, then beyond the hollow of Tarn at Leaves the slope mounts to a distinctive undulating east–west crest, with Rosthwaite Cam the eye-catching western top, some 70m higher than the acknowledged summit. A further depression is crossed before the fell yet again

↑ *Bessyboot, the acknowledged summit of Rosthwaite Fell (photo: Maggie Allan)*

reaches for the sky upon a mighty mass of craggy ground – this top some 6m higher still! It seems strange that this, the highest point on the fell, has not been credited with a name, so here it is given the dignity it deserves by ascribing it the name of Rosthwaite High Fell.

The plaintive call of peregrine frequently pierces the air around Rosthwaite Fell's craggy, tree-shaded northern slopes, which form a charming backdrop to the attractive hamlet of Stonethwaite. And it is this side of the fell that hides the one prime staircase to the top, by Stanger Gill (1), beginning from the entrance to the National Trust's Stonethwaite camp site. Elsewhere, scramblers may revel in the airy arête of Cam Crag and the sun-warmed curiosity of Dovenest Crag. Fellwalkers might also find interest in Dovenest (5), as well as two other side-slope approaches: via Dry Gill (4) out of Combe Gill and from Black Moss Pot (3) in Langstrath. The obvious re-entrant of Woof Gill proves even less appealing on close acquaintance, being defended by bracken on approach and remorselessly steep at its headwall.

Ascent from Stonethwaite 14

Via Stanger Gill →2.4km/1½ miles ↑460m/1510ft ⏱1hr 35min

1 This, the principal ascent, begins at a green gate opposite the entrance to the National Trust camp site, situated 400 metres east of Langstrath Hotel along the rough tracked lane. Climbing into light woodland, the partially

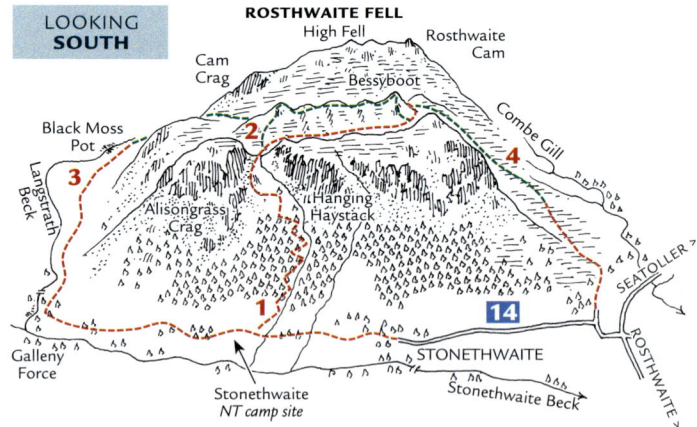

23 ROSTHWAITE FELL

pitched path rises close to **Stanger Gill**, slippery tree roots demanding caution when wet. Mount via a wall-stile as the path hugs **Bull Crag** by a minor arête-top col, the view back over the Stonethwaite vale providing all the excuse needed for frequent pauses to catch your breath – exacted by the height of the stone steps!

A final zig-zag brings the walker into a small amphitheatre. Keep right via a wall-end and pass on to ford the gill before a fall. Switch right then quickly

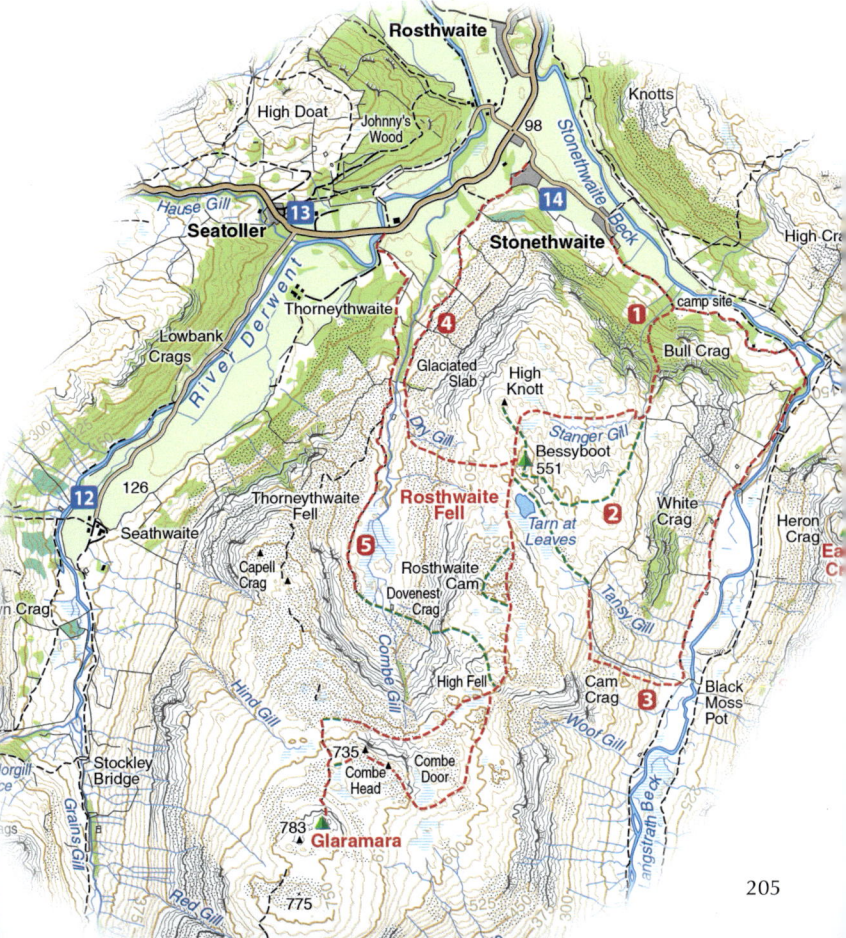

Rosthwaite Fell from Black Moss Pot

23 ROSTHWAITE FELL

left to ascend the damp slope, with the rock ribs of Racomb Bands up to the left. The path swings left at peat groughs, skirting boggy ground. You can visit the cairned top of **High Knott** just to the west, keep south on the shelf below Bessyboot or even scramble straight onto the rigg direct to the summit.

2 From the wall-end on Route **1** bear up left, squeezing through the tight step gap between the wall and an outcrop, and climb onto the pathless ridge – the route is not an exact science. The eastern top of Racomb Bands has a beautiful pool and a lovely view to Eagle and Sergeant's Crags. The ridge west undulates pleasantly to culminate on Bessyboot.

Via Tansy Gill →*4.7km/3 miles* ↑*460m/1510ft* ⏱*2hr*

An unusual 'catch-it-unawares' route via Black Moss Pot

3 Follow the footpath that continues from the **camp site** approach lane. Entering Langstrath, keep with the west-side track to the gate/ladder-stile at **Black Moss Pot**. Beyond bear immediately right, climbing by the fence fold. Ascend the gill, with a wall to your right; after this tackles a rock slab, find evidence of a path contouring right in harmony with the top of the wall to go through a gate in the fence. Keep beside the wall until the next gill then follow this, **Tansy Gill**, into the hollow wherein lies the enigmatically named **Tarn at Leaves**. Bessyboot, climbed from the ridge path, is encountered at the western end of the tarn.

Beyond Dry Gill →*2.4km/1½ miles* ↑*510m/1675ft* ⏱*1hr 40min*

Dry Gill offers a natural line, free from crags.

4 Follow the cul-de-sac by St Andrew's Church and pass through Chapel Farm, via gates. Bear off the track, left, to the gate in the left-hand corner of the field, entering the fringe of a shelter-belt of larch. Turn promptly left via the kissing-gate. The concessionary path goes right, passing through a gateway, washed by a gill. It then angles up half-left, with waymark posts, and contours as a green track above **Combe Gill**, via old wall gaps, to a gate by a partial fold. The path disappears, but no matter; angle up half-left up the rigg beyond the first watercourse, **Dry Gill** (a misnomer!). A path materialises during the ascent, emerging to lead into a nick in the ridge below a knoll surmounted by an erratic. The conical peak of Bessyboot, the fell's acknowledged summit, rises immediately left.

Ascent from Seatoller 13

Via Dovenest Crag →*4km/2½ miles* ↑*530m/1740ft* ⏱*2hr 15min*

The explorer's route

5 Begin from the National Trust car park in Seatoller. Follow the verge past the appropriately named Glaramara holiday centre. At **Strands Bridge**, beside the terrace of gabled cottages known as Mountain View, go right with the **Thorneythwaite farm** access lane. Watch for the gate on your left after 70 metres. Pass through and follow the rough track, rising up the lightly wooded ridge to a further gate in the intake wall. A fine waterfall in **Combe Gill** holds attention short of the path fork, which is marked by a cairn. A clear trod leads past the curious remains of an oval fold, set on a slope. The path leads into the moraine-fringed hollow at the heart of the combe and is most commonly used by climbers heading for Raven Crag, on which the severity of the routes is intensified by the lack of sun; Dovenest Crag, on the opposing

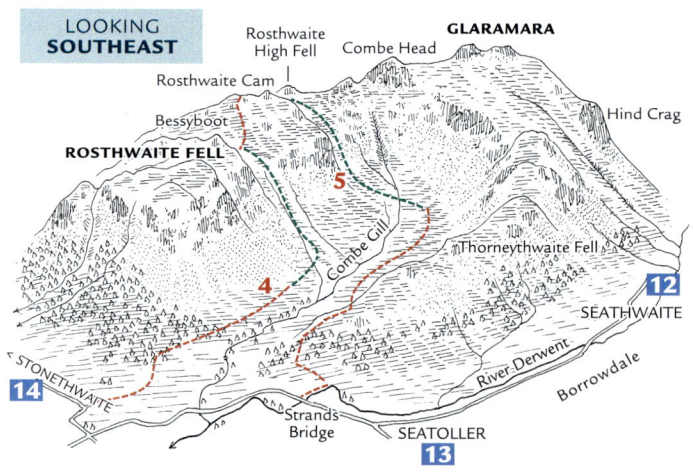

fellside beneath Rosthwaite Cam, is, by comparison, quite balmy. The caves that make the lower portion of the crag a place for brave speleologists might give you a reason to return another time. Depart from the path, aiming for the sheepfold.

From the sheepfold a steep slope presages the approach to the foot of **Dovenest Crag**. The vague hint of a path materialises as height is gained, slanting to the right of the cliff. The cliff has been a popular rendezvous for climbers and competent scramblers since the advent of recreational climbing. Walkers might make a cursory visit, clambering onto the shelf by the obvious cleft, but go no further. Ascend the steep ground beside the outcrops. Don't get caught in the short but wet gully; keep right. Above, as the cliff eases, clamber left to complete the ascent via the final brow outcrop. The marshy shelf at the top offers the option of visiting the two hen-comb crests of **Rosthwaite Cam**, left, and **Rosthwaite High Fell**, right. Rosthwaite Cam is a real characterful, chunky square boss of rock; access it only from the west side. A snaking path leads across the plateau to Bessyboot, the commonly recognised summit.

The summit

A cairn, set on a small outcrop, registers this as a place to rest and count the loot of a fine view. It is easy to forgive Rosthwaite Cam, and the backing Combe Head, for imposing a sense of inferiority on this knott. The avid fellwanderer will cast off such notions as they peruse the wonderful view. Pike o'Stickle will intrigue to the east, but it is the scene to the west that will induce the greatest admiration: Honister Crag, backed by High Stile, with Dale Head and the Northwestern Fells all held dramatically in a tight camera shot.

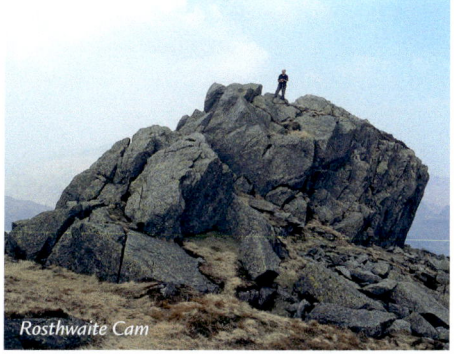
Rosthwaite Cam

Safe descent

In deteriorating conditions, the best way off is to reverse Route **4**, slipping down between Rottenstone and Dry Gills. Descend S from the summit to the initial nick, before the erratic-topped knoll. Descend due W; there is some rough ground but progress is uncomplicated. Short of Combe Gill bear right to the gate in a down-wall (and partial sheepfold). Joining a green track, contour N, en route to the valley pastures at Chapel Farm and St Andrew's Church.

Ridge route

Glaramara →3.2km/2 miles ↓85m/280ft ↑60m/195ft ⏲1hr 10min
A less-than-orthodox ridge turns navigation into a challenge in misty conditions. There are paths but they are never strong enough to give confidence that you are on the ridge path. Descend S, skirting the knoll W of Tarn at

Rosthwaite Fell from Combe Head

23 ROSTHWAITE FELL

Tarn at Leaves (photo: Maggie Allan)

Leaves. Slant half-left up the ensuing slope to cross the E shoulder of the Rosthwaite Cam ridge. There is a path that aims half-right towards a notch in the ridge, close to the Cam, if you wish to pay a visit to this eye-catching high point. The main path weaves on, rounding the bank beneath Rosthwaite High Fell; you'll know you've passed it as the path slips over a short length of broken wall immediately after.

Now you have two choices. The first option crosses Great Hollow diagonally half-right, mounting the ensuing bank. Contour along the shelf beneath Combe Door and directly above the top of the Combe Gill ravine to join the path climbing Thorneythwaite Fell, angling left to the summit bastion. Alternatively, from the broken wall keep left, skirting the marshy ground to avoid the apparently impenetrable ridge-top outcrop, and proceed up a ramp onto Combe Head from the E, then swing S to the summit.

24 SCAFELL PIKE 977M/3206FT

Climb it from	Old Dungeon Ghyll (Great Langdale) **30**, Seathwaite **12**, Wasdale Green **34**, Wasdale Head **33**, Brotherilkeld **31** or Wha House **32**
Character	Remote and rugged, daunting and deserving of great respect
Fell-friendly route	4
Summit grid ref	NY 215 072
Link it with	Great End

Scafell Pike must be the monarch of all Lakeland mountains, following hard on the heels of Helvellyn as the most popular climb of the major fells. It is, in every dimension, a real mountain. Crag and scree abound on all fronts, meaning that care is needed both in ascent and descent, and the summit contrives to keep itself remote from the gaze of valley observers.

It is not the most beautiful, does not have the very best ascent, does not offer the finest panorama and is not home to the most challenging crags, but Scafell Pike is the highest, roughest, toughest and assuredly the most revered ground. In a district simply bristling with shapely peaks there is inevitably a strong impulse to stand atop the highest of the lot.

↑ *Sunlight and shadow across the eastern cliffs of Scafell Pike from the ridge of Scafell above Foxes Tarn*

Your judgement on when to go, and by which route, needs to be tempered with much thought. The fell can be climbed from four directions: Wasdale Head (5–7), Seathwaite in Borrowdale (2–4), Great Langdale via Esk Hause (1) and lonely Eskdale (8–10). There are two hot-favourite ascents: two paths come together in the vicinity of Lingmell Col, from Lingmell Gill (6) and the Corridor Route (2). The other popular approach is from Great Langdale, via Rossett Gill and Esk Hause (1). Being closer to the M6, this route comes under disproportionate pressure, but it is nonetheless a grand route.

Ascent from the Old Dungeon Ghyll, Great Langdale 30
off map E

Via Rossett Gill and Esk Hause →*11km/6¾ miles* ↑*955m/3135ft* ⏲*5hr*

Scafell Pike is a distant, almost surreal, notion from the Old Dungeon Ghyll, with the added fear that it may be lost in the clouds. The adage 'better to travel hopefully' applies, as too 'retreat is the better part of valour', an option if, having reached Esk Hause, it is indeed befogged.

1 Starting from the Old Dungeon Ghyll, you can soon pick up your stride in Mickleden, but don't overdo it – energy levels will be tested today. Crossing the footbridge at the foot of Stake Gill, engage on the pony path which fords Rossett Gill, then, via an exaggerated double zig-zag, steps ascend to the saddle at the head of the gill. The path goes down to the outflow of **Angle Tarn**, a place to pause and study the reflections of Hanging Knotts in the hanging waters. The continuing path rises northwest up **Tongue Head**.

Closing in on the saddle, drift half-left to the cross-wall shelter. This is an important landmark and its existence is no coincidence: the terrain here has a nasty habit of confusing even confident ramblers, and it is a meeting of the winds too! Be aware that there are two saddles: the east–west link to **Sprinkling Tarn** and **Sty Head** and the higher col of **Esk Hause**, situated 250 metres southwest of the wind-shelter. Esk Hause, the broad depression between **Esk Pike** and Great End, is littered with cairns. Clearly many people come this way, bound for Calf Cove. Go west on the all-too-palpable trail. The path winds up the damp hollow, wherein lies a small shelter and the last running water.

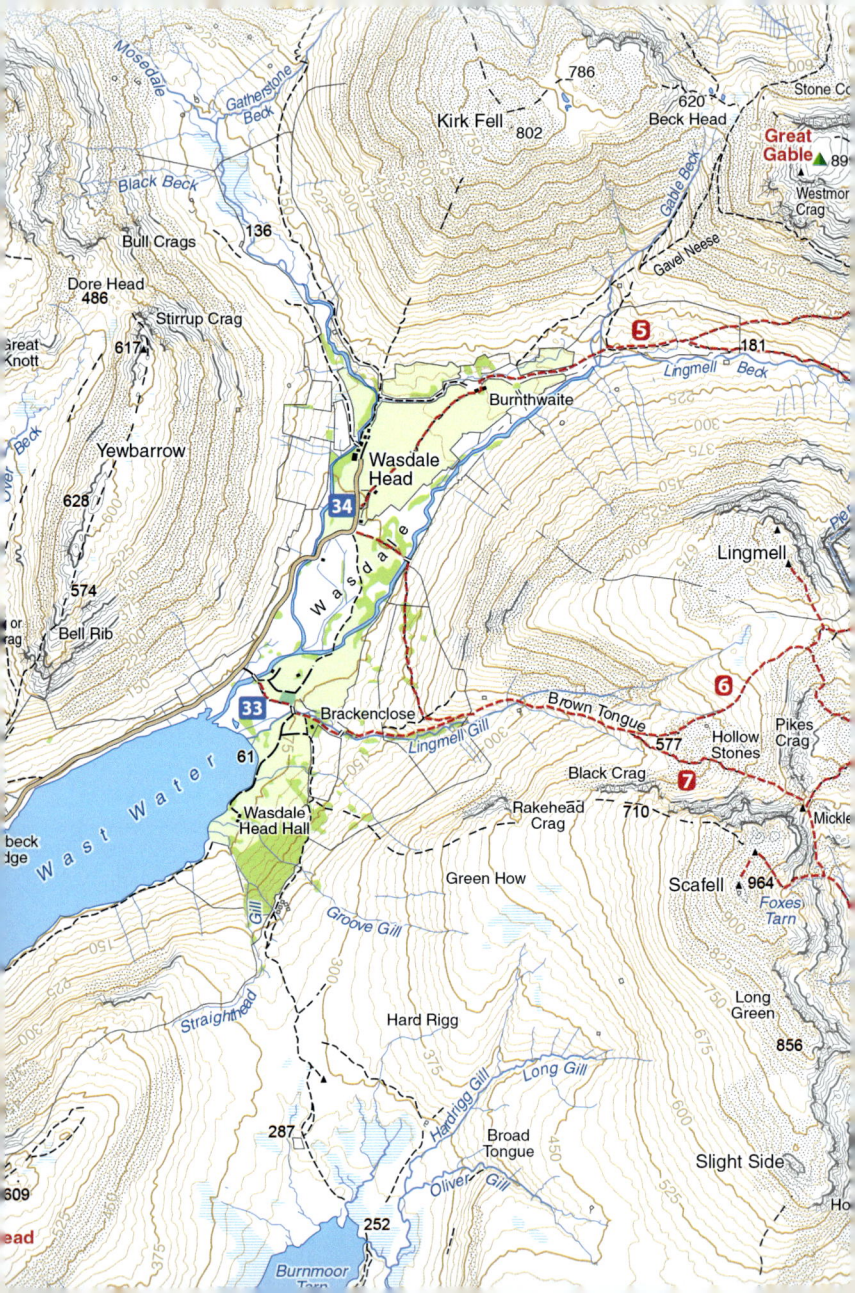

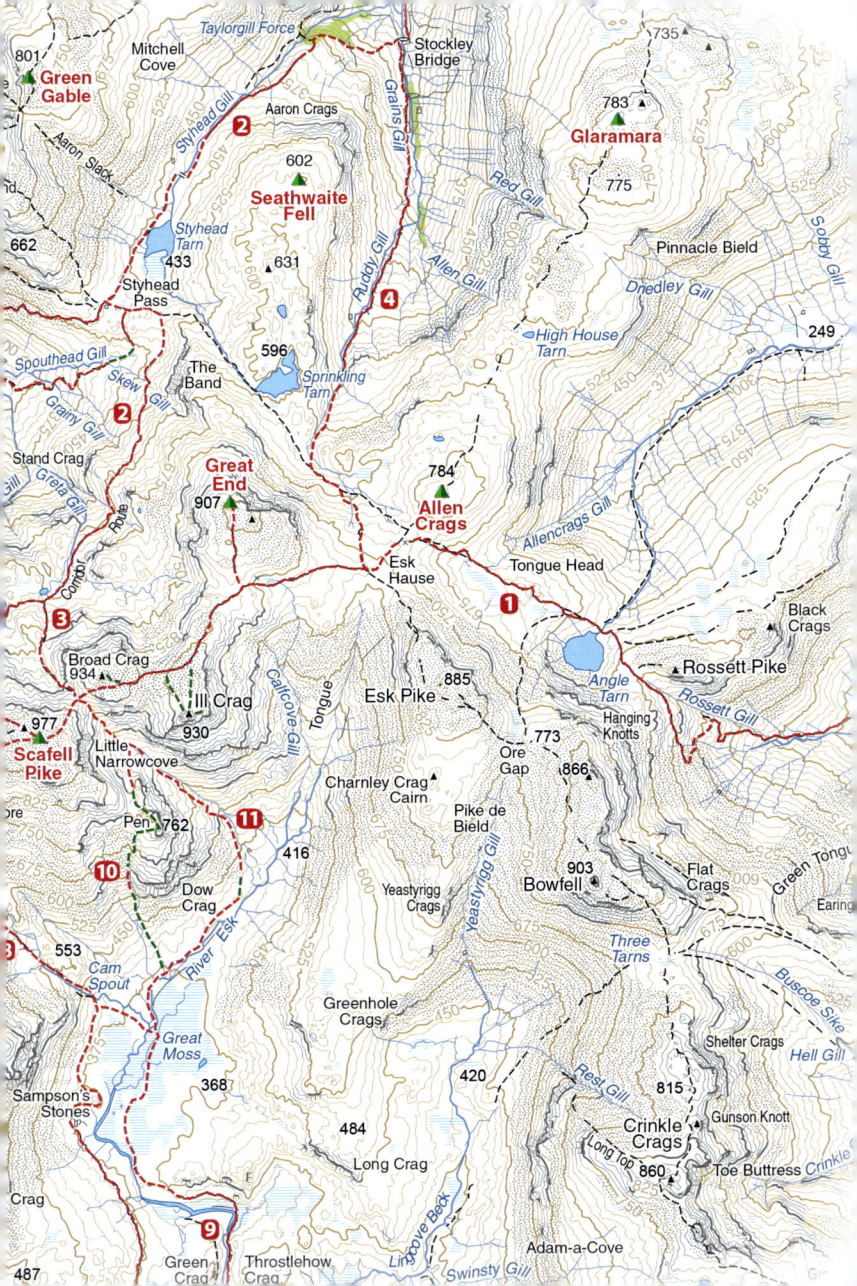

Climb onto the plateau saddle. So far so good, but the terrain is about to deteriorate. The ridge draws up southwest to an innominate rocky crest. Weave through the boulders, the path inevitably vague. The boulders relent as the summit of Scafell Pike comes tantalisingly into eye shot, more distant than you may have hoped! Here the path sweeps majestically over the gravelly shoulder of the **Ill Crag** plateau, dipping into Illcrag Col, before encountering yet more boulders on the traverse of the east shoulder of **Broad Crag** into Broadcrag Col. Views from the col, left down Little Narrowcove to Pen and right to Lingmell, are quite stirring. Wearying legs need to make one final effort on the sorely eroded scramble up the narrow arête leading to the summit boulder-field. All but the keenest walkers will dally on the summit, perhaps wandering to the various plateau brinks for differing perspectives, knowing that long rough crossing has to be repeated.

Sadly, the tiresome trek across the plateau causes most walkers to ignore Ill Crag and Broad Crag, both considered part and parcel of the Scafell Pike ensemble. In fact, they fully deserve the attention of well-informed fellwanderers and the high-country connoisseur. Broad Crag is a serious adjunct, serious in its utter rockiness; you can count the grass by the blade! The cairnless top lies only a matter of metres to the west of the ridge path, with easiest access from the north. Ill Crag is actually quite a separate entity, as you will clearly appreciate if you view it from Pen across Little Narrowcove, removed yet at one with the mountainous setting.

Ascent from Seathwaite 12 *off map N*

For all its tantalising distance from the target summit, a circular expedition can easily be created courtesy of the paths that fork at Stockley Bridge. The valley to the left (4) leads to Esk Hause, while that to the right (2) makes unerringly for Styhead Pass, thereby joining the Corridor Route.

Via Styhead Pass and the Corridor Route →*6.7km/4¼ miles* ↑*855m/2805ft* ⏱*4hr 15min*

2 From Seathwaite Farm follow the regular bridleway via **Stockley Bridge**. This bears up right, via gates, climbing above the trees of **Taylorgill Force**, with excellent pitching underpinning a heavily used trail. Though the way is stony on the approach to the **Styhead Gill** footbridge, a more comfortable trail ensues, passing **Styhead Tarn** to reach the pass, identified by the stretcher box.

24 SCAFELL PIKE

There is nothing passage-like about the **Corridor Route**: it is a deceptively long and quite tough traverse, frequently congested with human traffic. Ongoing pitching works on the steep open sections have made it more comfortable. You can start directly from the Sty Head stretcher box, angling half-left, shortcutting across the headstream of **Spouthead Gill**, but it's better to take the original route, which branches right after the initial rise on the eastbound path, as to **Sprinkling Tarn**. Cross the vestige of a short wall, dipping and contouring to the mouth of the **Skew Gill** ravine. Climb the facing slope and pass through a short cutting on a hard staircase, rising to a ridge crossing. Beware: the far-side step down is awkward. The path weaves on by two headstream fords of **Greta Gill** before a parting in the way.

Bear right to continue on the Corridor Route and ford **Piers Gill** just where it spills almost innocently into its notoriously deep and treacherous ravine. Eschew the dubious trace of a path that branches up the rough northern slopes west of Dropping Crag. The main path avoids the Lingmell Col. Work up among the outcrops to link with the path from **Hollow Stones** on the broad, stony, but otherwise unthreatening, northwest ridge to the summit.

3 Or, at the junction just after **Greta Gill** (see Route **2**), take a clear set of steps to the left which marks the start of a less-than-savoury direct route to

Scafell Pike and the upper portion of Piers Gill

Pool beside the Corridor Route looking to Great Gable

Broadcrag Col. The latter stages of the climb up the wild combe to the narrow rough saddle will test your tempo and temper. The route to the summit (**1**) lies up the blunt eroded arête to your right.

Via Esk Hause →*6.5km/4 miles* ↑*905m/2970ft* ⏲*4hr 40min*
4 The Esk Hause route follows the left-hand path from Stockley Bridge up **Grains Gill**, which becomes **Ruddy Gill** after a footbridge. Pitching is evident right up to the point where the upper ravine is forded. Link to the path rising from **Sprinkling Tarn** and **Sty Head**. Take the first path branching right, leading up to Esk Hause, to join Route **1**.

Ascent from Wasdale Head 33–34

Via Styhead Pass and the Corridor Route →*5.7km/3½ miles* ↑*915m/3000ft* ⏲*4hr 30min*

The direct route up from the head of Wasdale, with a choice of a steady ascent or a pleasant valley approach to Styhead Pass

24 SCAFELL PIKE

5 Leave the village-green car park, following the lane by St Olaf's to **Burnthwaite**. Pass to the left among the farm buildings to a gate. Keep right; the obvious way heads on between varying walls, via a gate, to cross a footbridge spanning **Gable Beck**. Soon you face a choice of two equally sound routes to Sty Head. The standard route sticks religiously to the rising path, which passes through a hand-gate before taking on the scree section. The passage of several hundred years has ensured a well-defined shelf has been padded down and, but for one brief stumbly section and a good deal of ballbearing gravel, the path delivers the walker with minimal fuss.

The more pleasant option lies up the valley. Either bear off as bracken begins to encroach or continue a further hundred metres to find a clear path slanting down to the hand-gate near the foot of the descending wall. Keep alongside **Lingmell Beck**, fording the stream just after the confluence with **Piers Gill**. A clear green trail winds up the rigg then fords a gill to the left. Cut across the next rigg to ford **Spouthead Gill** and then zig-zag up to **Styhead Pass** to join Route **2**.

Via Lingmell Gill →4.5km/2¾ miles ↑915m/3000ft ⏲3hr

Pikes Crag from below

Route 6 offers the shortest and most trouble-free ascent, while Route 7, up to Mickledore, will involve discomfort, if short-lived, but no navigational difficulty. The latter path may never have been all that sweet but certainly the relentless scouring of fell boots has taken its toll.

6 There are two prime approaches to the Lingmell Gill valley. Direct from the National Trust camp site follow the path, left, off the **Wasdale Head Hall** track by **Brackenclose**, rising beside the beck to a footbridge and subsequent hand-gates. From the village green follow the road back to the first bend, where a

WALKING THE LAKE DISTRICT FELLS – BORROWDALE

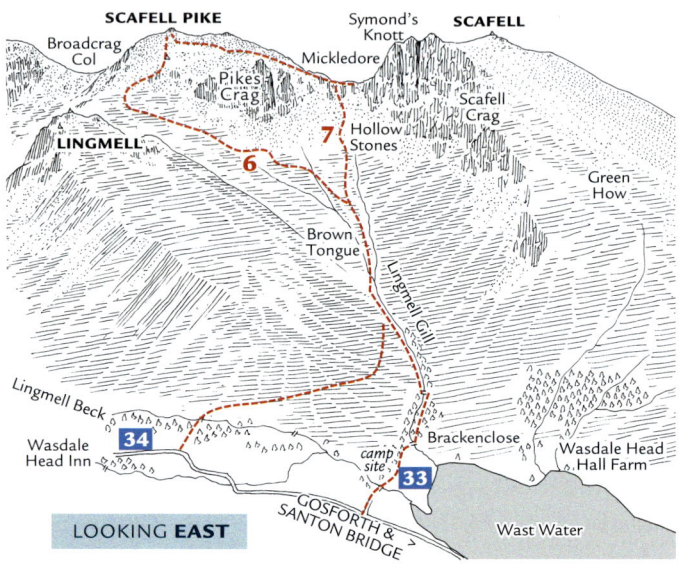

stile and footpath sign direct across the dale floor to a footbridge spanning the stony-bedded **Lingmell Beck**. The path bears right, gradually ascending across the fellside to draw over the ridge-end contouring into **Lingmell Gill**.

Where the path splits as the **Brown Tongue** ridge begins to flatten out, take the left fork. This leads to the well-worn trail below **Pikes Crag** and onto the northwest ridge, winding up to a large cairn on the lip of the summit plateau.

7 The right branch at the top of **Brown Tongue** leads up to a quite breathtaking intimacy with Scafell Crag on the way to **Mickledore**. Once on the narrow neck of ridge connecting the two great Scafells turn left, passing the Mountain Rescue stretcher box. The path to the summit remains clear. For a brief diversion, once on the plateau bear half-left and, with modest effort and a hint of bravery, clamber onto the top of Pulpit Rock. A cairn marks the spot. From here you can enjoy a jealously guarded and airy new angle on Scafell Crag.

24 SCAFELL PIKE

Ascent from Brotherilkeld 31 *off map S* or Wha House 32 *off map S*

There are two approaches to Cam Spout and then three choices thereafter: direct and scrambly up via Mickledore (8 and 9) or looping round via Broadcrag Col (10 and 11).

Via Mickledore →*8.5km/5¼ miles* ↑*1050m/3445ft* ⏲*5hr*

8 The speedier route to Cam Spout is via the Cowcove zig-zags. Embark either along the farm track from Wha House direct to Taw House or take the farm-track from Brotherilkeld from the old red telephone box, guided left of Brotherilkeld farmyard to a hand-gate, and, a matter of a few metres further on, go left, crossing the wooden footbridge spanning the wonderfully tree-shaded **River Esk**. Traverse the pasture, with a wall on your right, to a ladder-stile entering the farmyard at Taw House.

Leave the farmyard by the gate at its northern end and follow the lane to a gate, continuing thereafter on an open track, via two gateways, to a gate/ladder-stile below a ladder-stile at a sheepfold. A clear track continues to Scale Bridge, crossing the embowered cascades of Scale Gill. Ignore the direct path up from the bridge and take the footpath signed further up the track. Watch for the acute left turn up through the bracken. (The path is clear enough.) Higher, the zig-zags afford a view into the Cowcove Beck ravine, laced with birch and rowan, before entering the first of two marshy hollows. Keep to the dry western edge, crossing a plank over Damas Dubs. The path, well

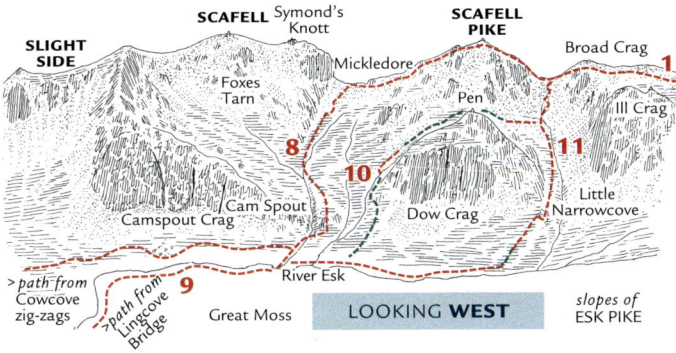

Cam Spout – the path scrambles up the slabs to the right (photo: Jonathan Williams)

evidenced underfoot, leads into the Esk catchment and meets up indistinctly with the west-side path. It then leads through a multi-penned sheepfold, curving round a low spur littered with huge erratics known as **Sampson's Stones**, set beneath the massive cliff of Camspout Crag. Keeping to the fringe of **Great Moss** marsh, the path now bears up half-left to reach the foot of **Cam Spout**.

Clamber up the bare rocks to the right of Cam Spout, ascending the increasingly rough combe above you, beneath Scafell's East Buttress. There is a path all the way, though it is inevitably loose nearing the saddle. From **Mickledore** head up the southwest ridge with Route **7** to reach the summit.

9 Alternatively, the main valley approach holds tight to the Esk beside a fence. A clear path leads via a gate in a wall, continuing to a ladder-stile beside a gate and a small fold, where a path that began above the cattle grid at the foot of the Hardknott road converges. The valley soon narrows, with three great cliffs catching the eye: Yew Crag up to the right on Hard Knott, and Brock Crag and Heron Crag to the left. The undulating path becomes smoother as it reaches the sheep-wash fold at the elegant single-span Lingcove Bridge. From here Eskdale Needle (aka the Steeple) to the south takes on the appearance of a thumbs-up. Cross the bridge and follow the path up Throstle Garth. As the mass of **Throstlehow Crag** is left behind we see the river taking wide meandering sweeps through a landscape reminiscent of a remote Highland glen, the path keeping close under Scar Lathing. As the vast amphitheatre surrounding **Great Moss** takes centre stage, spot a turf-topped wall close right. This is the remnant of a medieval deer compound built by the monks of Furness Abbey. Wet marsh is unavoidable but once the Esk shallows are forded the sponge is less of a problem, trending northwest to the foot of **Cam Spout**, the most handsome of pencil-thin waterfalls. Here join Route **8**.

Via Little Narrowcove →*8.7km/5½ miles* ↑*920m/3020ft* ⏱*5hr 30min*

Arguably the most impressive of Scafell Pike's chest of crags is Esk Buttress (Dow Crag), the Central Pillar face commanding upper Eskdale. It is quirkily surmounted by a pimple of banded rock bearing a distinctly Celtic name, Pen. The route to this fabulous little top is arduous and largely pathless but the summit well rewards the effort.

10 Bearing off right from Route **9**, a path contours along the edge of **Great Moss**, and, after fording two gills, it is time to bend to the ascent. The rigg tapers to a gill to the left of **Dow Crag**. A worn path materialises, the climbers' descent route off the back of the crag. Don't be drawn into the gully but keep to the steep rigg. As the slope gradually eases drift right to scramble to the top of **Pen**. There is a cairn and cause for much inner revelry at reaching this less-than-orthodox viewpoint. Ill Crag's stunning southern buttress simply steeples, even from this elevated spot. Briefly follow the spine of the ridge then work round to the left to find the breach in the ridge. A sheep path leads easily through into **Little Narrowcove**, where you can join Route **11** to proceed to the summit.

11 The direct route into Little Narrowcove does not hug the outflowing beck. To find the point of entry continue beside the infant **Esk**. After a large cairn angle up the rigg, left. A path emerges on approaching a gully. Clamber up, exiting right then left on a path drawing up beside Little Narrowcove Beck. The rarely seen beauties of this secret corrie deserve to be savoured. The final stages of the ascent zig-zag up the scree at the head of the combe to reach **Broadcrag Col**. It's a feather in your cap to have made this point by these means. Walkers' paths converge here from Esk Hause and up the combe from the Corridor Route but precious few ascend from Little Narrowcove! Turn left, southwest, for the summit.

The summit

A domed plateau, well blessed with boulders and a few precious grassy patches, culminates in a sturdy, circular drystone-walled platform, which displaced the Ordnance Survey from the actual crown of the fell. All summits with loose rock seem to attract windbreak-makers and Scafell Pike is no exception. There are several of the normal tumble-down type and one, situated towards the eastern brink, which lacks only a roof. It is worth making the effort to wander

Scafell Pike summit

around the plateau edge and enjoy some stunning new perspectives, the pick of the bunch that from above Dropping Crag.

Safe descents

For all its many year-round visitors, in nasty weather there can be no lonelier place than the summit of Scafell Pike. And once you've made it there, getting back is an altogether different proposition. Psychologically, the energy that drove you ever upward disappears in the instant you turn back, you might be tired and objectives are downbeat. Great Langdale, for instance, lies to the E, smack into the teeth of winter winds. Wasdale Head, in contrast, catches the prevailing ocean-borne breeze – by definition warmer, if potentially no less fierce.

For Wasdale Head (4km) start from the extra-large cairn on the plateau edge 250 metres W of the summit. Descend the cairned path down the NW ridge (**6**). Short of Lingmell Col the path veers left down into Hollow Stones, drawn naturally onto Brown Tongue and then into close company with Lingmell Gill.

For Seathwaite (6.5km) instead of veering left go right, off the NW ridge, following the Corridor Route NE to Styhead Pass (**2**). From the stretcher box the old bridleway leads unerringly down to Stockley Bridge.

The return routes to Great Langdale (**1**) and Eskdale (**8**) are altogether rougher and longer. In bad weather either don't embark on these routes in the first place or, if conditions unexpectedly close in, turn down to Wasdale Head or Borrowdale.

Ridge routes

Great End →*2.5km/1½ miles* ↓*185m/605ft* ↑*100m/330ft* ⏱*40min*
Descend N, via the narrow, sorely eroded arête, into the tight neck of Broadcrag Col. Traverse the ensuing bouldery shoulder into Illcrag Col and sweep up the gravel slope to a short boulder section, over a crest, and then down onto the broad saddle. Divert half-left, off the popular path to Esk Hause which leads down Calf Cove, and keep to the easy ground on the ridge, heading N to a choice of two summit cairns.

25 SEATHWAITE FELL 631M/2070FT

Climb it from	Seathwaite **12**
Character	An intricate little ridge, with jewel pools and rocky tops, easily accessed from the south but very steeply bounded on all other fronts
Fell-friendly route	5
Summit grid ref	NY 229 102

The highest point of Seathwaite Fell is situated north of Sprinkling Tarn, in famously the wettest sector of Lakeland. However, the traditional summit, as seen from Seathwaite Bridge, lies further north and is some 30m lower, an abrupt little pike crowning the slope above Aaron Crags and an exceptional viewpoint for upper Borrowdale. The ridge-top is quite irregular, pleasantly so if your visit coincides with fair weather, the pools and knobbly tops making this a joyous quest.

Resolutely defended east and west by crags and rough slopes, there is little encouragement for a walker to divert from either of the two popular paths that track up the flanking valleys of Styhead Gill (1–5) and Grains and Ruddy Gills (6). Where the fell merges with Great End the going becomes more lenient; at Sprinkling Tarn, which lies beside the Sty Head to Esk Hause trail, a path (5) weaves easily onto the undulating plateau.

↑ *Seathwaite Fell's summit outcrop*

25 SEATHWAITE FELL

Ascent from Seathwaite 12

Direct, via Aaron Crags →*3.3km/2 miles* ↑*475m/1560ft* ⏱*1hr 50min*

The primary valley route

1 Go through the farmyard, via gates, heading for **Stockley Bridge**, a typical packhorse bridge, well maintained and focal to two popular routes. Pass through the succeeding hand-gate and consider your options: either left via Grains and Ruddy Gills towards Esk Hause (Route **6**) or right via the ancient pony route towards Styhead Pass and Wasdale (Route **2**).

2 Take the right-hand path from the gate beyond **Stockley Bridge** (see Route **1**). After the next hand-gate you will see **Aaron Crags**. Go right with the main winding trail above **Taylorgill Force** (unseen from this angle). A minor ford gives the clue as to the direct route to the traditional summit. Follow

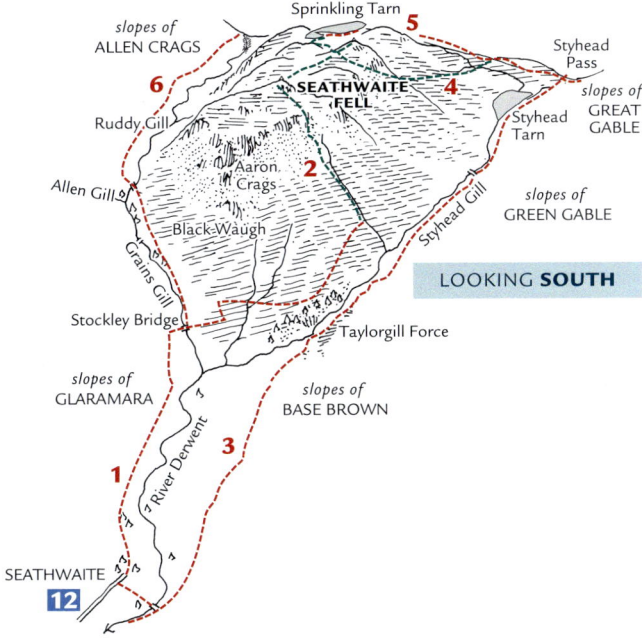

WALKING THE LAKE DISTRICT FELLS – BORROWDALE

the gill up the slope; there is no path on the ground. The gill dwindles as a natural break in the skyline's craggy facade gives cause for confidence that easy ground is at hand. The north-top summit knoll lies directly ahead, defended by modest outcrops.

The (higher) south-top cairn backed by Great Gable

Via Styhead Pass →*4.7km/3 miles* ↑*505m/1655ft* ⏱*2hr 30min*

Styhead Pass offers a useful means of creating a circular route and allows you to visit the higher south summit, should you so wish.

3 A walled lane leads right from the middle of the buildings (under the roof canopy) at Seathwaite Farm. On crossing the **Derwent** footbridge turn left via the hand-gate; the path traverses under trees and above marshy rough terrain to a ladder-stile crossing a wall at the top of a small plantation. Slant across the fellside to climb more steeply to a hand-gate as the gorge constricts facing the **Taylorgill Force** amphitheatre. A short scramble ensues, awkward in descent. The path continues on the true left bank until, at a footbridge, the pony route from Stockley Bridge joins. Keeping to the west bank, pass above **Styhead Tarn** to reach the stretcher box at Sty Head.

Styhead Pass is a point of elation and decision, a high saddle, subjugated by the immensity of Great Gable and the massive bastion of the Band leading up onto the Scafells. Here choose between Routes **4** and **5**.

4 Turn east from **Styhead Pass** (see Route **3**), mounting a bank, and, as you draw near a ravine to the left, slip across and slant up the pathless grass slope, passing under outcrops then rounding to reach the south top from the north.

5 Alternatively, for an even easier life, having followed Route **3** to **Styhead Pass**, keep to the main path to ford the outflow of **Sprinkling Tarn**, the first issue of the River Derwent. Follow the northern shore path, venturing onto the ridge. The path diminishes; keep right of the nameless tarn to avoid outcrops, skirting round to approach the south top from the east.

Via Grains Gill and Sprinkling Tarn →*5km/3 miles* ↑*515m/1690ft* ⏲*2hr 15min*
6 A left turn at the hand-gate beyond **Stockley Bridge** (see Route **1**) leads onto the path up **Grains Gill**. This leads via a hand-gate, and subsequently a footbridge, up the east bank of **Ruddy Gill** to meet the path from Sty Head to Esk Hause. Fording the gill as it bends southeast, follow this path, right, to reach the outflow of **Sprinkling Tarn** and accompany Route **5** to the summit.

The summit

Can a fell have more than one summit? The firm rule that a summit is the highest point falters where there are rising ridges of the character of Rosthwaite and Seathwaite Fells. It is hard to choose one high spot over another. There are perceptual as well as strict structural considerations at play. When viewed from Seathwaite Bridge, Seathwaite Fell culminates assuredly on the northern pike above Aaron Crags. Stand upon that pike and you know precisely why tradition has ordained this to be the summit: the view down Borrowdale is peerless. A new generation of fellwalkers may yet arrive seeking to overthrow the traditional perception and feeling no compunction in adopting the highest ground as a summit. The south top may be a brilliant viewpoint but it lacks that intimate visual relationship with upper Borrowdale. (You will note that the ridge path from the north top to Sprinkling Tarn has no truck with the ridge proper, nor the south top, preferring to wend near the eastern edge, a lovely link to higher things.)

Safe descents

Steep rough ground runs away from the summit, most notably to the N and E. In favourable conditions you can descend pathless Route **2**, W from the summit, then N from the scarp edge by the emerging gill. The better choice is to follow the ridge S (**5**), linking up with the Esk Hause–Sty Head path at the outflow of Sprinkling Tarn. This also gives options for your valley return, depending on prevailing winds, a stiff westerly encouraging walkers to track down the sheltered Ruddy and Grains Gill path (**6**) in preference to the more popular and more exposed Styhead Pass trail bound for Stockley Bridge and Seathwaite.

26 SERGEANT'S CRAG 574M/1883FT

Climb it from	Stonethwaite **14**
Character	A rock-shielded crest which is awkward to reach
Fell-friendly route	3
Summit grid ref	NY 274 114
Link it with	Eagle Crag

The comparatively uneventful northern fall of the fell massif from High Raise, the crest of the range, tapers to an eye-catching halt on Sergeant's Crag. Flanked by considerable crags overlooking Langstrath, the crag has one great pleat gully and several bold slabby pockets. It has a neighbour, Eagle Crag, to which and from which it can be compared and admired. Sergeant's Crag might today be the domain of climbers, but in recent centuries it has been mined and quarried – though the untrained eye would find it difficult to detect the residual spoil.

Conventionally, walkers approach the fell-top by following the ridge wall (1), having first tackled Eagle Crag. An alternative line, bereft of bracken and crags, can be found climbing from the footbridge at the foot of Stake Beck (4), its one and only merit the majestic view back across Langstrath to Rosthwaite Cam and Glaramara. Langstrath is a place to amble as well as stride, relished best on the circuit of the dale-floor paths (1–2) from Stonethwaite. A convenient back-door approach (3) can be made from the Greenup Gill valley.

↑ *The Langstrath aspect of Sergeant's Crag*

WALKING THE LAKE DISTRICT FELLS – BORROWDALE

Ascent from Stonethwaite 14

Via Eagle Crag →*3.6km/2¼ miles* ↑*480m/1575ft* ⏱*2hr 15min*

Amazingly, the state of the path suggests only a comparatively few undertake this initially steep, later intricate, but utterly exhilarating route.

1 From the centre of the hamlet follow the lane signposted 'Greenup Edge', which leads over the Stonethwaite Beck bridge. After the gate go right with the gated bridle track. Cross the footbridge immediately above the confluence of Greenup Gill and Langstrath Beck. Bear left and cross the fence-stile, taking care to keep to the low side of the flush marsh, which is abundant in delicate bog flora. The path brushes through bracken of potentially monster proportions; stay parallel with the Greenup Gill fence. Pass through a hand-gate in the down-wall, and, while a path continues low beside the wall and gill, continue on the shepherds' path, angling gently up the slope to a wall-gap.

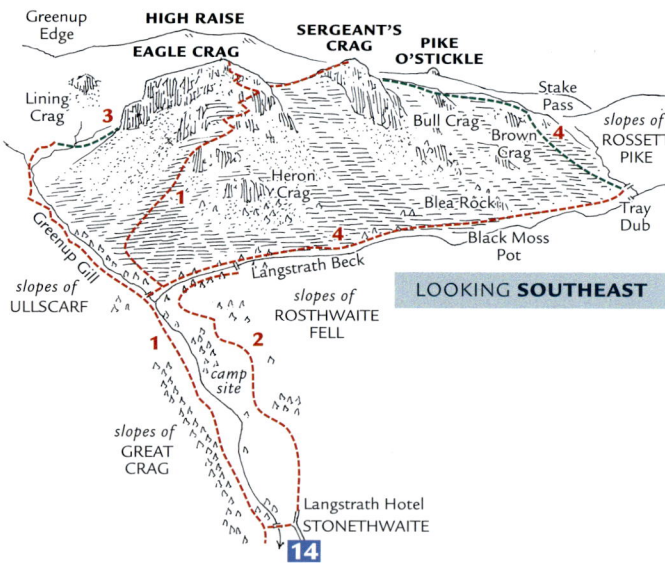

26 SERGEANT'S CRAG

At this point the climb proper begins. Keep the partly broken wall to your right, and the path, confirmed by modest cairns of transitory existence, winds up to a fragile stile at the top of the rising wall hugging the undercliff.

If your temper has been tested by the sweaty work up to this point, prepare for a fell-ecstasy lift-off. A narrow breach in the craggy defences permits a short stair climb.

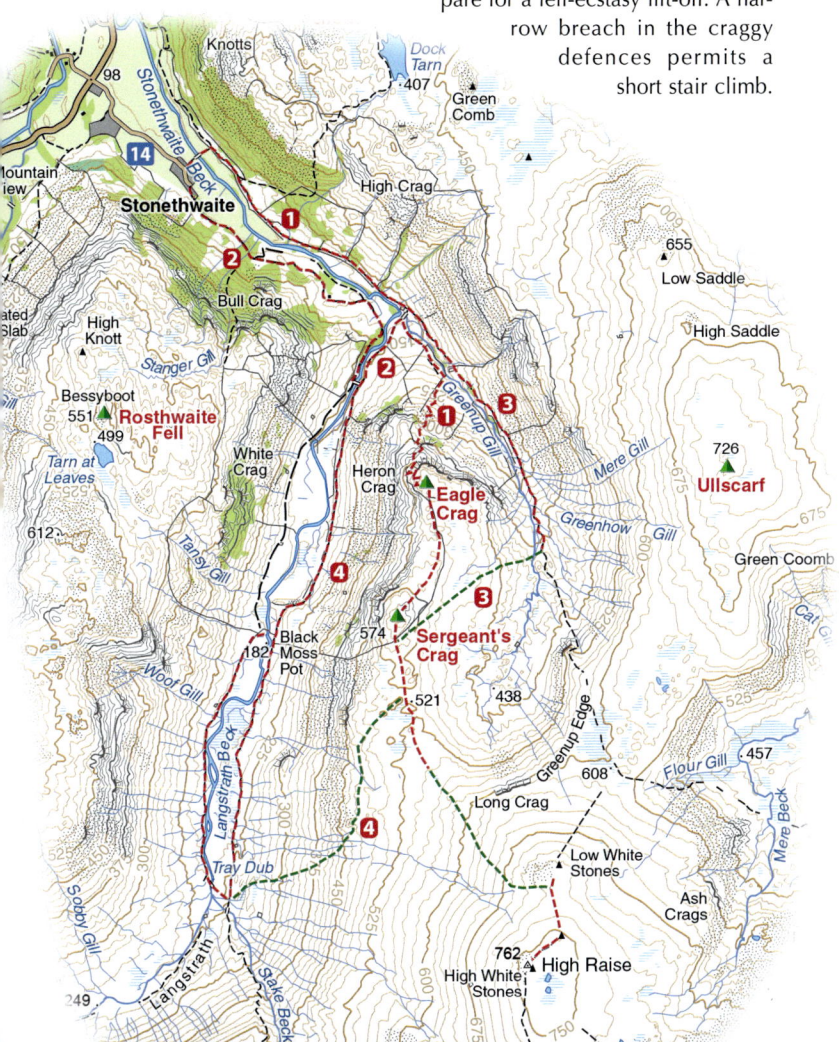

Solitary birch by Langstrath Beck

The way beyond suggests two options but in reality there is but one. The path leading up left ends abruptly but gives a handsome view of Pounsey Crag. Backtrack to continue; this is important, as there is no safe fellwalking ground further left. The prime route goes immediately right, along the ledge marked with ice-like fragments of quartz, and terminates with a fine full-height view of Sergeant's Crag. Now switch up, making several similar sharp turns to avoid rock bands, with much heather underfoot. Both the immediate and outward scenery is consistently exciting. Duly – and with no little sorrow for an end to the fun – the tilted summit slab of **Eagle Crag** is rounded. Follow the subsequent ridge onto Sergeant's Crag.

2 Follow the lane through the hamlet (noting the Langstrath Hotel for end-of-walk refreshment). The gated track passes above the popular camping meadow, latterly passing Alisongrass Hoghouse (camping barn). As you near the beck listen to the roar of Galleny Force down in the tree cover, left. The track bends right, via a gate, to accompany the clear cascading waters of **Langstrath Beck**, passing through a gate to a footbridge. Cross and bear left to meet up with Route **1**.

26 SERGEANT'S CRAG

Via Greenup Gill →*4km/2½ miles* ↑*480m/1575ft* ⊕*2hr 25min*

The eastern back-door approach

3 Alternatively, from the **Greenup Gill/Langstrath Beck confluence** (see Route **2**) continue with the popular bridleway ascending the Greenup Gill valley, in harmony with the Coast to Coast Walk. As the eastern slopes of **Eagle Crag** turn to grass break off the trail, ford the gill and make a pathless ascent of the steep slope to reach the ladder-stile in the ridge wall, following the clear path north to the summit.

Via Langstrath →*5.5km/3½ miles* ↑*500m/1640ft* ⊕*2hr 40min*

A pathless ascent from the west

4 Follow Route 2 to cross the **Langstrath Beck** footbridge, then follow the bridle path, right, to the gate at **Black Moss Pot**. Black Moss Pot is a tight rock-channel pool, deserving a moment's appreciative look, for the next 1.6km of bridle path to the footbridge at the foot of **Stake Beck** is quite uneventful, although there is no denying the magical feel of this deep mountain valley. Alternatively, follow the west-side footpath that climbs over the ladder-stile at Blackmoss, and at this point look up to the left to possibly spot climbers scaling Sergeant's Crag Slabs. Below and above Black Moss Pot the beck takes a wide, shingled, meandering course, with the craggy slopes of Rosthwaite Fell and Glaramara high to the right. Swan and Tray Dubs offer fine moments to draw close to the lively beck. Cross **Tray Dub** footbridge and ascend directly (pathless) to the summit.

The summit

The imposition of a wall, effectively isolating the upper dome of the fell, has served to restrict grazing and support a better flora than occurs in the poor acidic grassland beyond. A small cairn rests on a modest outcrop, with little hint of the impending precipice to the west to deflect attention from the fine view across and to the head of Langstrath. With a little time, you can investigate down the slope to the north, then west, where a grass ramp leads to the top of Sergeant's Crag Gully. You can also peer down the steep broken face towards the climbers' slabs and Blea Rock – impressive rock and valley scenery for the eagle-eyed.

Safe descent

In dubious weather, by far the best option is to cross the stile in the wall immediately S of the summit and head NE (**3**) to join the bridle path below Lining Crag that leads down Greenup Gill for Stonethwaite.

Ridge route

Eagle Crag →*0.8km/½ mile* ↓*60m/195ft* ↑*10m/35ft* ⏲*25min*
Navigation just could not be simpler. Head NNE from the summit on the one path, coming alongside the ridge wall, close right, then cross the step-up stile at the wall corner, which gives access to the neighbouring top.

Sergeant's Crag from Eagle Crag

27 ULLSCARF 726M/2382FT

Climb it from	Stonethwaite **14**, Watendlath **15**, Dob Gill **28** or Steel End **29**
Character	Centre-point of the Cumbrian mountain massif, remote and aloof, and a place of long strides and long vistas
Fell-friendly route	5
Summit grid ref	NY 291 121
Link it with	Bell Crags

Ullscarf's praises are seldom sung, yet for all the comparative tameness of the upper plateau, in harmony with High Raise, it really is a splendid place to stride. The summit and several lateral points including Low Saddle and Standing, Tarn and Nab Crags are all quite exceptional viewpoints in their own right.

The fell is defined to the south by damp Wythburn Dale and the altogether sunnier Greenup Gill, being divided from the natural northern extension of the range by an old bridle path which runs over a wet depression below Standing Crag. To the northwest, that part of the fell known to Watendlath folk as Coldbarrow Fell descends in an uncluttered fashion to Green Comb and Great Crag either side of Dock Tarn. The higher ground fails to live up to its brave front of crags, particularly those that form a stern defence to Wythburn Dale.

↑ *Ullscarf's summit cairn (photo: Maggie Allan)*

A cursory knowledge of the drainage of the fell is crucial to knowing where you are, as a wrong turn can leave you a long way from your intended valley base. Ullscarf is not a fell to toy with in misty conditions. The fell can be climbed from the west (1–4), from Stonethwaite; from the north (5), from Watendlath; and from the east (6–12), from Thirlmere (Dob Gill and Steel End).

Ascent from Stonethwaite 14

Via Greenhow Gill → 4.7km/3 miles ↑630m/2065ft ⏱2hr 30min

1 From the three-way signpost beside the telephone kiosk leave the hamlet by the lane on the left to 'Greenup Edge'. Cross Stonethwaite Bridge, momentarily pausing to gaze into the turquoise waters of **Stonethwaite Beck** and to look upstream to the shapely profile of Eagle Crag, which maintains a strong presence during this valley approach. After the gate meet the bridle path from Rosthwaite, turn right and, through the next gate, enter a lane on a rough track which continues via several further gates. Proceed beyond the footbridge above the **Langstrath Beck–Greenup Gill confluence**. Keep ahead up the Greenup Gill valley. At the hand-gate notice the overhanging crag high on the left along the rim of the valley, where peregrine falcons have been known to nest. The path receives periodic remedial repair to cope with the heavy boot traffic. There are two options: Routes **2** and **3**.

Gird your loins for a simple yet energetic pull up the steep fellside.

2 Having started out with Route **1**, after fording **Greenhow Gill** the path bears onto the right-hand side of the first tongue of moraine. Abandon the bridle path, bearing up onto this ridge to the left, and climb beside

27 Ullscarf

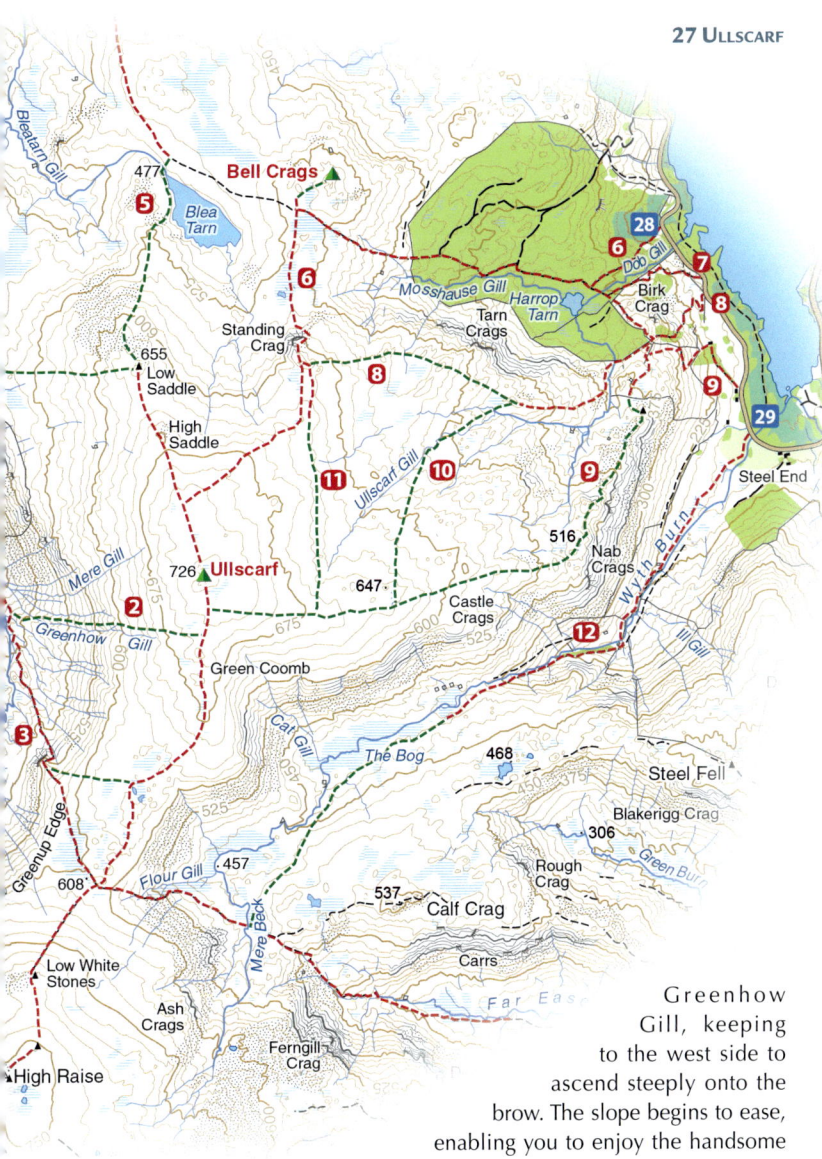

Greenhow Gill, keeping to the west side to ascend steeply onto the brow. The slope begins to ease, enabling you to enjoy the handsome

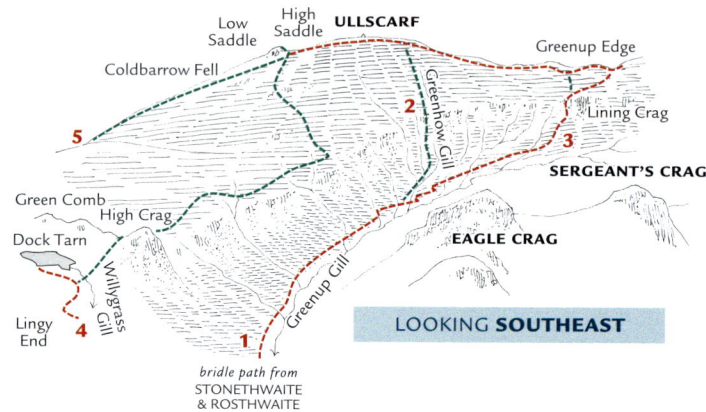

views back to Pounsey Crag. Keep beside the dwindling gill and come up by a line of quartz outcrops. Cross peaty exposures to join the ridge path, then go left, with little ascent remaining to the summit.

Via Lining Crag →5.2km/3¼ miles ↑630m/2065ft ⏱2hr 40min

3 Normal people choose moderate routes and, having started out on Route **1**, without a second thought will continue with the pony path through the moraine, crossing the dry-tarn site to ascend the gully to the left of Lining Crag. At the top the way ahead is in sore need of a sabbatical as the multitude of cross-ridge walkers have churned so much of the path down to bare peat. In order to help minimise the damage to Greenup Edge divert due east onto the ridge. There is little or no evidence of a path but the going is so much sweeter. The broad ridge is awash with pools – keep left to miss the worst of the spongy ground. Traverse to the ridge path and mount northward to the summit, with the occasional stake stump from the old metal estate fence as a guide.

Via Lingy End →4.7km/3 miles ↑635m/2085ft ⏱2hr 45min

This special route, ideal for anyone looking for an unusual ascent (possibly using the Greenup Gill path for a circular return), ventures onto the northern rim of the valley, bound for Low Saddle.

4 Park your car along the approach road, not in the hamlet. Entering the community, bear left at the kiosk, signed 'Greenup and Grasmere'. Cross Stonethwaite Bridge to reach a gate and join the main valley bridle path, coincident with Wainwright's Coast to Coast Walk. Go right, via the gate. After the sheepfold, which forms a delightful foreground to views of Eagle Crag, the lane dips. From the low wall opening, after some 50 metres bear half-left and rise up the pasture on a turf trod between swathes of bracken to a wall-stile. The path goes left, rising to a wall-stile. From here your route climbs purposefully through the deciduous woodland on a stony staircase, switching away from Willygrass Gill.

Emerging from the canopy, take an approving view south to Eagle Crag and Sergeant's Crag, dramatically seen at their very best. Rising onto the appropriately named **Lingy End**, climb by the heather banks and ruined shepherds' shelter. Skirt round the re-entrant of **Willygrass Gill**, with a view of the inaccessible High Crag above the eastern fork of the cascading gill.

After crossing the stile ascend until a wall is seen riding up to the right. Ford the gill, the outflow of **Dock Tarn**, and climb, with the wall to your right, over the shoulder of **High Crag**. Delight in the view of the meeting of the Greenup Gill and Langstrath valleys, with Eagle and Sergeant's Crags centre-stage, and the long view to Bowfell at the head of Langstrath quite unforgettable. The route traverses rough ground to come alongside the wall that protects the edge. Keep alongside the wall until a gill re-entrant breaks the steady progress, then angle up the rough slopes to the cairn on **Low Saddle** – a viewpoint which provides the best survey of the northern sector of the Central Fells. Follow the ridge up to **High Saddle**, join the fence, crossing a stile at the top, and head south to the summit.

Ascent From Watendlath 15 *off map N*

This is an efficient start-point.

Via Blea Tarn →*5.2km/3¼ miles* ↑*470m/1540ft* ⏲*2hr 15min*

5 Most walkers will start from the National Trust car park (pay and display). Exit either over the ladder-stile or by going right from the point of entry to a gate. The waymarked footpath fords Raise Beck and soon commences the zig-zag ascent of the steep bank, following centuries-old sled trails used for conveying peat from High Tove. The point of departure from the Armboth path is

Looking north from the acute fence corner

marked on a slate, 'to Wythburn', at the wall corner. The green path contours across the hillside, initially with an intake wall for company, though the wall is replaced by strategic cairns as guides on the long gradual rise southeast. The path clips the brow, missing the fence corner, and dips to the outflow of **Blea Tarn**, a wind-whipped sheet of water. Ford the beck precisely at the outflow of Blea Tarn and follow the western shore, nipping up onto the ridge at the first bay. There is nothing to impede – nor anything to encourage – speed! Climb steadily to crest **Low Saddle** and join Route **4**.

Ascent from Dob Gill 28

Via Harrop Tarn →*4km/2½ miles* ↑*550m/1805ft* ⏱*2hr 20min*

Eastern approaches are so different. When viewed across Thirlmere, the near eastern skyline is so craggy that it suggests great tidings for the explorer. The early stages of all approaches reinforce this perception, but Ullscarf is no alpine peak and the backing slopes soon falter into mediocre moorland. However, given sunshine and the right day, even these barren slopes have their beauty.

27 Ullscarf

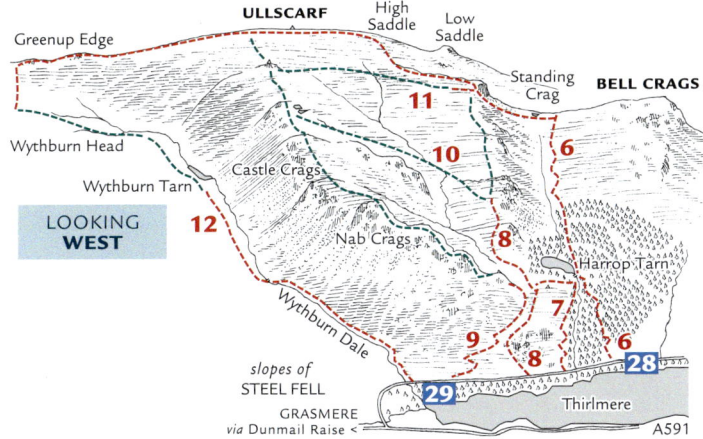

LOOKING WEST

6 From Dob Gill a made-path climbs directly to the outflow of **Harrop Tarn**.

The main forest track leads west; as it forks, on two occasions, keep up left (though on the latter occasion it is more straight on, rising as a path to the double kissing-gate exiting the conifers). The bridle path mounts the slope to the broad depression traversed by a fence. Do not go through the

Standing Crag

hand-gate but instead turn left, following the fence by a pool to reach the base of **Standing Crag**. Bear up left, via an easy gully, clambering to the top to rejoin the fence. Take the opportunity to stand at the brink of the cliff to gaze at the fine view north. Follow the fence up to the acute corner, walking free of the fence on the left to attain the summit cairn.

7 A further path begins from the road south of Dobgill Bridge, rising via hand-gates to cross the forest fence, via a ladder-stile and subsequent duck-boarding, to reach the footbridge below the outflow of **Harrop Tarn**, where you join Route **6**.

Via Tarn Crags →*4km/2½ miles* ↑*550m/1805ft* ⏱*2hr 20min*

8 Start from a roadside gate at NY 318 138, south of the glacially smoothed outcrop known as the Binka Stone. Angle diagonally left across the slope beneath **Birk Crag**; a groove leads through the juniper to a rising wall. At the top either venture to the cairn on top of the crag and a smart descent to **Harrop Tarn**, via a tall hand-gate, to join Route **6** or cross the adjacent stile and follow the plantation fence to ford **Ullscarf Gill**. Bear left on a green path, which curves up onto the ridge above a cluster of sheepfolds then becomes lost as a tangible path. Continue onto the rising ridge to gain the edge of **Tarn Crags**, a fine viewpoint for Bell Crags and over the plantations surrounding Harrop Tarn. Hold to the edge, stepping down a rock band or two and crossing marshy ground to reach the ridge fence above **Standing Crag**, where you can join Route **6**.

Ascent from Steel End 29

Via Nab Crags →*4.4km/2¾ miles* ↑*550m/1805ft* ⏱*2hr 30min*

An attractive ridge route

9 This route is best started from the Steel End car park. Follow the road, right, to go through the yard and gates at Stenkin (barn). Follow the wall to the site of the original West Head Farm – almost all trace of this farmstead has disappeared. Bear up left, by the fence, to a hand-gate in the fell-bounding wall. A continuing shepherds' path, of ancient purpose, winds up the rough fellside, coming close to the rising wall shielding **Birk Crag**; this path is more obscure on the damp ground. Continue to a wall-gap. The shepherds' path progresses

Old path above the former West Head Farm

to sheepfolds within Ullscarf Gill; however, as soon as you pass through the wall bear up left to the prominent wall cairn, known as the Beacon.

The continuing ridge, rising above Nab Crags, gives ample scope for the inventive fellwanderer. There is no path, which seems strange considering how bold the ridge appears when viewed from the Armboth road-end on the A591. Pass a curious ruin in the shelter of the first step of the ridge and thereafter make whatever progress appeals in order to reach a modest cairn directly overlooking the footbridge far below in the jaws of Wythburn Dale. The ridge now turns west, and it is less easy to keep to the scenic edge. The ridge rises progressively to a cluster of pools above Castle Crags. Head west to meet up with the ridge path then turn north to the summit.

Via Ullscarf Gill →*4.4km/2¾ miles* ↑*550m/1805ft* ⏲*2hr 30min*
10 The pools above Castle Crags (see Route **9**) can be reached (less impressively, it has to be said) from Route **8** by following Ullscarf Gill, via a slabby ravine, then curving south, without the benefit of a path, towards the brink.

The shepherds' traverse →*4km/2½ miles* ↑*560m/1835ft* ⏲*2hr 30min*
11 The old shepherds' traverse, formerly marked by a string of cairns making a beeline for Black Knott, can be best attempted via Standing Crag (see Routes **6** and **8**), though now only one cairn remains to guide you across the

Ridge-top pool (photo: Maggie Allan)

pretty torrid headstream terrain. Black Knott is a rocky oasis on the ridge, west of the clusters of pools. Here join Route **9**.

Via Wythburn Dale →*6.8km/4¼ miles* ↑*565m/1855ft* ⏲*3hr*

A soft route... underfoot!

12 From the Steel End car park go left to a kissing-gate or continue over the bridge a few strides further to reach a hand-gate and steps leading down into the meadow. The two paths advance in harmony on either side of the fenced **Wyth Burn**, via gates, ladder-stiles and stiles, to reunite at a wooden footbridge. Continue on the dale path, climbing above the southern bank of Wyth Burn. There are two fine waterslide cascades, which are all the more exciting when a strong wind surges spray back. Pass the twin portal moraines draining the former **Wythburn Tarn**, then the sinuous vestigal tarn itself, also known – not without cause – as **the Bog**. The old path dissolves underfoot and from here you progress pathless up the mossy dale to unite with the ancient east–west bridle path fording **Mere Beck**. Traverse **Wythburn Head**, climbing by **Flour Gill** onto the plateau pass of **Greenup Edge** to join the ridge path, which follows the line of fence-stake stumps north to the summit.

The summit

Walkers cross the summit and think little of the event, heaping greatest praise on Low Saddle as the panoramic climax of their visit. To the east there are broad acres of acidic grassland, declining into the peaty wastes of Ullscarf Gill. Coarser slopes spill quickly westward to Greenup and Bleatarn Gills. The stumps of the old estate fence may cause some visitors to stumble, but better the stumps than have the fell-top ruined by an actual fence. Sadly, from this point on, a stock-proof fence has been reinstated up the spine of the range to Bleaberry Fell and a little beyond.

Safe descents

The fence has one merit: in mist it is a sure guide. Follow it to the right, to the top of Standing Crag (**6**), and the path veers right to work down a gully to the crag's base then on beside the continuing fence to a hand-gate in the damp depression. From here join the old bridle path linking Watendlath, left (through the gate, **5**), and Thirlmere (Dob Gill). If caught in mist, with Borrowdale as your destination, cross the stile at the acute corner and go left, hugging the fence, to reach the wall that runs along the edge above the Greenup Gill valley. Follow this wall to the right (**4**) to reach Dock Tarn and the path down through the woods by Lingy End.

Ridge route

Bell Crags →*2.8km/1¾ miles* ↓*210m/690ft* ↑*30m/100ft* ⏱*45min*
Head N to the acute corner of the fence and go right, following the fence to the top of Standing Crag. Bear down, right, to the crag base, where the fence resumes. Follow this past the pools and ridge-top hand-gate, skirting marshy ground, to bear half-right onto the short summit ridge.

28 WALLA CRAG 379M/1243FT

Climb it from	Keswick **20**, Great Wood **19** or Ashness Bridge **17**
Character	Craggy scarp peering over Great Wood, with lovely approaches catering for all levels of fellwalking ambition
Fell-friendly route	1
Summit grid ref	NY 277 213
Link it with	Bleaberry Fell

There is no doubting the individualistic qualities of Walla Crag's imposing facade, so luxuriantly wreathed in trees. Through the decades the summit has been a prime objective for evening strolls from Keswick. Its views across to the Keswick vale are unrivalled and it is blessed with a lovely view over Derwentwater too.

Travellers venturing south from Keswick along the Borrowdale Road get their first taste of the rocky dramas ahead when they see, rising above the green canopy of Great Wood, the massive 'wall of crag'. Strictly speaking, the fell is the northwest shoulder of Bleaberry Fell, separated from the higher ground by a wide upland hollow drained by Brockle Beck. To the south the short incursion of Cat Gill separates Walla Crag from Falcon Crag, which has no pretensions to separate fell status even though it is a major two-tiered sporting venue for rock climbers.

↑ *Derwentwater from Walla Crag (photo: Maggie Allan)*

28 WALLA CRAG

Although the bold escarpment suggests a difficult climb, it can be out-flanked to give the gentlest of ascents (1, 6). However, steeper lines (3–5) need not be resisted, and these include a secretive under-cliff trod (5), which can be awkward in damp conditions, when tree roots are slick. At its centre, the outcrop is riven by Lady's Rake, a damp vegetated gully. Do not be tempted even to attempt to ascend this rotten cliff – even climbers give it a miss!

Ascent from Keswick 20

Via Springs Wood →*3.2km/2 miles* ↑*300m/985ft* ⏱*1hr 45min*

A straightforward ascent direct from the town centre

1 Start from the Moot Hall in Market Square in the centre of Keswick. Head southeast, following the pavement of **St John's Road**, which becomes the Old Ambleside Road after Castlehead Close, to turn right into **Springs Road** (note that there is no scope for car parking in this vicinity). Pass beyond Springs Farm, via a gate, into **Springs Wood** and ascend on a popular path, in close harmony with the beck, then switch right to run alongside pasture fencing.

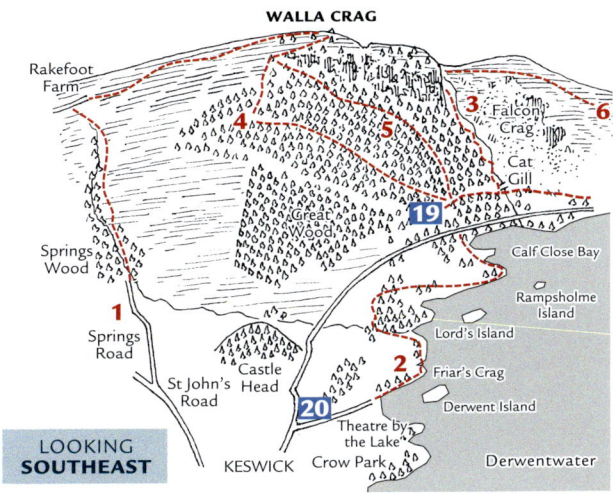

WALKING THE LAKE DISTRICT FELLS – BORROWDALE

250

After the Great Wood path merges from the right, pass through a kissing-gate and soon dip into the dell and cross a footbridge, then rise to meet the minor road at steps and a hand-gate. Go right. The road forks at **Rakefoot Farm**, where you go right, signed 'Wallacrag'. Cross the footbridge, rising, with a wall to your right, to a stile, and ascend with the wall to your right. Either go through the first hand-gate and wind up within the scarp-edge enclosure or continue to the top and cross a stile to reach the summit cairn.

Via Friar's Crag and Calf Close Bay →*3.5km/2¼ miles* ⏲*1hr*
2 A lovely lakeside approach from the Lake Road car park, via **Friar's Crag**, **the Ings** and **Calf Close Bay**, makes an ideal start to the climb.

Ascent from Great Wood 19

Three contrasting and delightfully sylvan routes lead to the top from the National Trust car park.

Via Cat Gill →*0.8km/½ mile* ↑*300m/985ft* ⏲*1hr 15min*
3 To go via Cat Gill head south, passing above the former car park area. Ignore the forest track that swings left and keep forward on the footpath, which leads to the footbridge spanning **Cat Gill**. Do not cross but instead

The lower and upper tiers of Falcon Crag

ascend the cobbled path, which rises steeply beside the cacophony of the ravine, via two hand-gates. Pass through a kissing-gate then proceed, via a zig-zag stepped section, to another kissing-gate. The slope eases as you mount the steps by the wall. Either continue, with the wall to your left, or cross the stile to complete the ascent within the tree-fringed scarp enclosure. Take one notable early 'spur opportunity' to wander left, for a special view over Derwentwater. Continue to reach and cross a stile in the wall – you are now above the inaccessible gully of Lady's Rake – and advance on a popular path to the open summit.

Via forest tracks or the under-cliff path → *1.6km/1 mile* ↑*340m/1115ft* ⏱*50min*

The undoubted beauty of Great Wood fully merits a more leisurely line along the forest tracks.

4 You have a choice here. The first option is to head north, switching right as the gate to the valley road comes into view. As you gently rise ignore the track to the left into the Watson's Park section of the wood. The track swings right and merges with the footpath from Springs Wood then promptly bears off up the bank, with a small gill to the right. Alternatively, this point can be reached more directly by advancing south from the car park, and this time swinging left to climb steadily with the forest track. Where the track levels and shapes to descend, cross a small gill.

Bear up the slope. Ford the gill below the enclosure-fence corner and continue, now on the right bank. Emerge from the woodland and keep the fence to your right until the slope eases, coming onto heathery ground, with superb views of Skiddaw and Blencathra the rich reward. Either go through the hand-gate in the wall to complete the ascent, principally within the pasture, or continue up the escarpment edge, which is attractively garnished with heather. A matter of metres beyond the hand-gate notice the small balcony viewpoint. This is not only a fine moment to pause and survey a sumptuous prospect towards Keswick, it also marks the top of the sub-edge or under-cliff path (see Route **5**).

The under-cliff path, very much the third way, requires a degree of confidence as there is some awkward footing.

5 At the point on the second option of Route **4** where the forestry track sweeps left, spot an unwaymarked narrow path rising directly up through the conifers. This climbs and winds assiduously towards the foot of the crag, directly beneath Lady's Rake. It duly drifts left, seeking ledges and tight passages between trees. The path remains consistent but is never more than a thin trod. Stay directly below the escarpment outcrop. Towards the end of the traverse, after a gill, one particular ledge at a dry gully may be troublesome in damp conditions. On emerging at the aforementioned balcony (see Route **4**) go right to climb the attractive escarpment edge to the summit.

Ascent from Ashness Bridge 17

Few visitors miss the opportunity to admire and photograph the famous view from above the bridge. What the majority fail to realise is that this is but one component of a suite of four stunning viewpoints for this prospect of Skiddaw. To draw the composition together, embark on a circular expedition, best commenced from this, the first formal car park on the Watendlath road.

Via Falcon Crag → *1.5km/1 mile* ↑ *160m/525ft* ⏱ *50min*

6 Advance north, crossing **Ashness Bridge**. You can follow the footpath that contours ahead to a hand-gate in the down-wall and subsequently fork

Walla Crag from Falcon Crag

half-right, up the bracken slope. The path climbs, less than comfortably in places, up to a stile in a modern fence, to join the higher path in a wet patch devoid of bracken. Alternatively, bear up directly from the bridge, cross the fence-stile beside the old fold and ascend to where a path bears off to the left up the bracken slope, then continue to a hand-gate in the wall.

Watch for a side path, half-left, which can be followed down the grassy spur to the cairn at the top of **Falcon Crag**. This is the second notable viewpoint of the tour (Ashness Bridge being the first), providing a superb prospect over Great Wood, framed by Walla Crag and Derwentwater.

Climb back up to the path to traverse above the steep re-entrant of **Cat Gill** and ford the gill, en route to the stile into the Walla Crag escarpment enclosure. The summit of Walla Crag provides the third viewpoint.

To reach the fourth continue down the northern scarp, through the heather, to the small balcony at the top of the under-cliff path. This provides the most pleasing view of Skiddaw and Blencathra. Head on down the edge-path to reach the forest track and turn left, following Route **5**, to meet the lower footpath. Bear left to cross the **Cat Gill** footbridge and traverse the undulating path below **Falcon Crag,** at one point slipping through a gorse tunnel. The crag is famed for its climbs and – appropriately – resident peregrines. The path brings you back to **Ashness Bridge** and your start point.

The summit

Nature has provided the fell with a bald crown of naked rock, and to the west the ground falls precipitously. Heather enlivens the near ground, interlaced with native trees which line the edge to north and south. This is a momentous belvedere from which to admire the perennially attractive fell-surround of Derwentwater. All visitors are drawn to the rocky western edge for the best views. Standing on the fell, witness the stark division between the sleeker lines of the Skiddaw slates, as represented by the Northwestern Fells across the lake, and the igneous rocks of the Borrowdale volcanic group, gathering in force to the south and culminating on Scafell Pike.

The summit cairn is set back from this brink. In recent years the fell's height has been reassessed and an additional 3m added. Beyond the wall the fell merges into sheep pasture.

Looking east from the summit

Safe descents

For Great Wood car park Cat Gill (**3**) and the paths that swing down from the N (**4**) are fine, but avoid the under-cliff path. The easiest option of all is to head for Rakefoot Farm (**1**) on the green tracks across the open pasture to the NE and to descend the sheltered Springs Wood path.

Ridge route

Bleaberry Fell →2km/1¼ miles ↓45m/150ft ↑255m/835ft ⊕1hr 15min
Head S and cross the wall-stile, following the Ashness Bridge path. After some 200 metres bear half-left (SSE) at a cairn and join the path crossing the upper Cat Gill ford. The line becomes clearer after you traverse the damp ground. Rise to glance by a sheepfold, to the E of a knoll, and skirt the peaty hollow, before climbing the steep NW prow, on the smart new path, to reach a viewpoint cairn. Continue, via a further large cairn, to the summit wind-shelter cairn.

1 THE HIGH SPY RIDGE

Start/Finish	Chapel Bridge/Little Town **7**
Distance	13km/8 miles
Ascent/Descent	745m/2445ft
Time	6hr
Terrain	After the steep bracken slope onto Catbells, the ridge-top route is unimpeded and encourages generous strides until the narrower path cutting back from the headstream of Newlands Beck brings some loose gravel underfoot. The main part of the valley route is secure, switching to firm track midway.
Summits	Catbells, Maiden Moor and High Spy

Join the throng en route to Catbells to share their delight, then flee the crowds, glorying in fine fell terrain, following the edge by Maiden Moor to High Spy. The return route through the wild valley of Newlands Beck is a wonderful contrast.

Start from the Chapel Bridge parking area and follow the road north to **Little Town**. After the first house on the right cut back with its access track and go through the gate (signed 'Hause Gate leading to Catbells'). At the first junction, with a green path ahead, switch left with the track. Stay beside the wall to cross

↑ *Derwentwater from Maiden Moor*

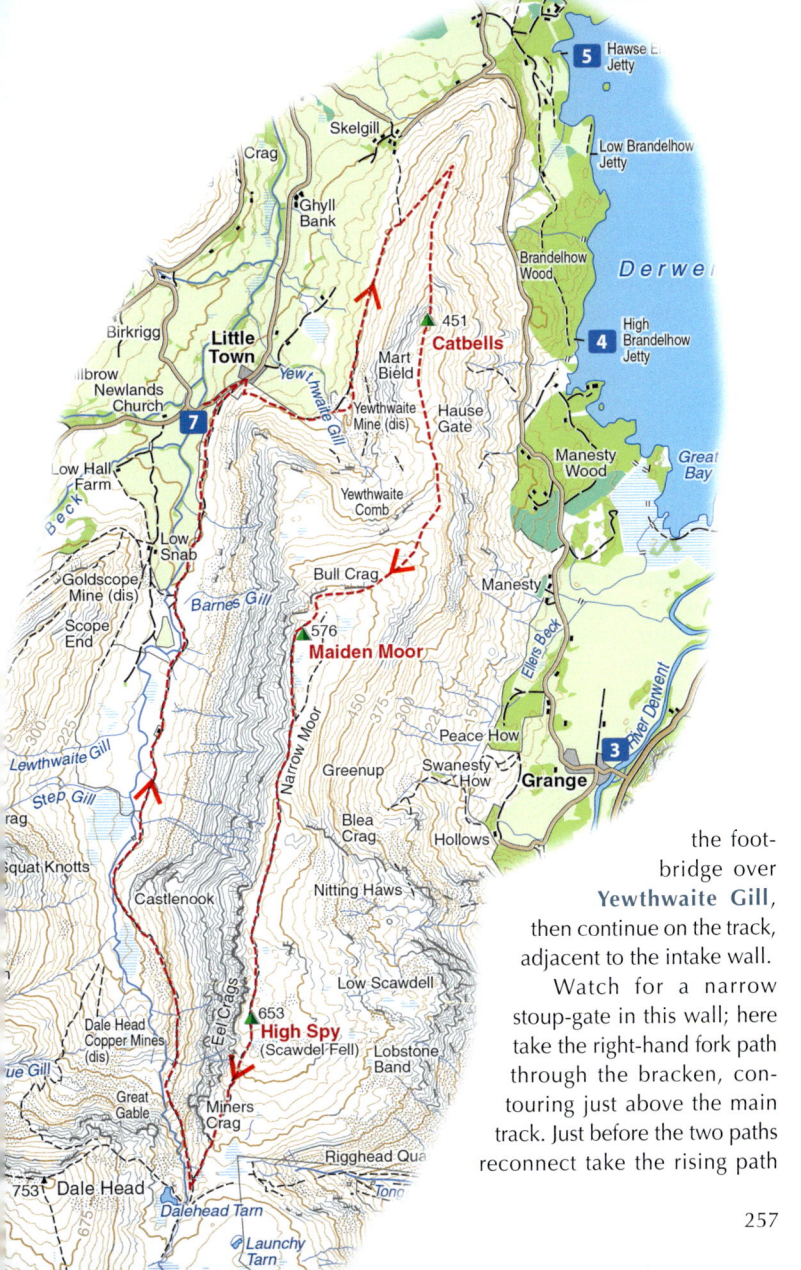

the footbridge over **YEWTHWAITE GILL**, then continue on the track, adjacent to the intake wall. Watch for a narrow stoup-gate in this wall; here take the right-hand fork path through the bracken, contouring just above the main track. Just before the two paths reconnect take the rising path climbing the fell, its modest popularity enabling it to beat back the bracken. Ignore the right-hand shortcut higher up, created by over-hasty walkers. The green path reaches the ridge-top saddle on Skelgill Bank; here turn right to follow the spine of the ridge – the way of many.

Catbells rises impressively ahead and is climbed via small rocky sections, which occasionally call for the use of hands. The fun ends on the bare rock crest, where a small topograph offers information about the inspirational view.

The ridge path gently declines to **Hause Gate** (no actual gate!) and embarks on the easy climb onto **Maiden Moor**, curving southwest. Where the path forks keep right to reach the cairn on **Bull Crag**, with its handsome northern prospect. Continue along the edge, with great views into the Newlands valley, passing the tiny summit cairn, to reconnect with the popular ridge path, which now rises by **Blea Crag**; divert left to visit the cairn on this crest for its view into the Jaws of Borrowdale. Rejoin the ridge path to reach the sturdy summit cairn of **High Spy**. Just short of the cairn you can revel in the craggy view into the head of Newlands Beck valley.

The ridge path descends, with various strands all coalescing just short of the ford of the headstream of Newlands Beck. At once cut back right, descending on a narrow path which offers amazing views of Miners Crag, followed by the fierce line of cliffs that defend the western face of High Spy. Close at hand, peer at the long water-shoot and, lower, the impressive, exuberant vertical waterfall. The path passes the old sheep-wash fold, with the spoil of a mine across the beck. Coming by a wall, the path becomes a track and passes the Carlisle Mountaineering Club Hut, heading towards Little Town. Watch for the car park below; a cobbled path provides a shortcut down to a stile off the track to bring the route sweetly onto the road.

Ridge path to Blea Crag

2 AROUND THE JAWS OF BORROWDALE

Start/Finish	Rosthwaite **1**
Distance	15km/9¼ miles
Ascent/Descent	880m/2885ft
Time	6hr 30min
Terrain	A loose slate trail on the final clamber onto Castle Crag and a cobbled track down towards the Derwent gorge; simple walking into Troutdale, the subsequent ascent a stone-pitched woodland way – though this concludes roughly on King's How. The ridge to Brund Fell and over Puddingstone Back has some marshy ground. Perhaps more testing is the tangled heathery terrain on Great Crag, a traverse that ends with a steeply pitched woodland path.
Summits	Castle Crag, Grange Fell (Kings How and Brund Fell) and Great Crag

This is where Borrowdale begins, a landscape of heights and delights. The walk reaches up onto the rocky heads peering above richly wooded slopes, a wonderful blend of the natural and the landscaped, worthily contrived for magnificent scenic effect.

↑ *Heather in full bloom on Great Crag (photo: Maggie Allan)*

WALKING THE LAKE DISTRICT FELLS – BORROWDALE

From the car park close to Rosthwaite village hall pass on by Yew Tree Farm and 'Flock In' café along the walled lane, which bears right on meeting the **Derwent** to cross the cobbled New Bridge spanning the stony riverbed of the youthful river. Turn right and take the right-hand gate of the facing pair with the meadow way. The path duly moves away from the

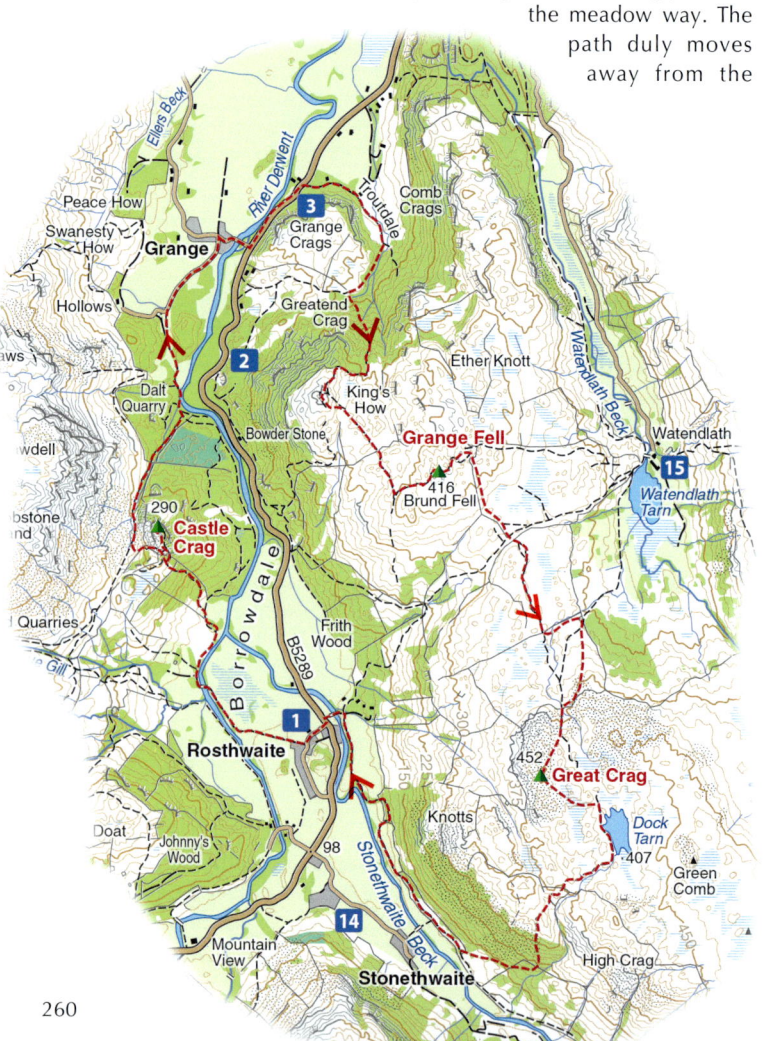

King's How from Castle Crag

river. Where it swings right go forwards via a gate/stile and ascend the bank on a clear if loose path, passing through a gateway, to come up the slope to a ladder-stile. Ahead a zig-zag path climbs the slate tip to a quarry; keep right to complete the ascent of Castle Crag. The view north to Derwentwater and, near right, to your next objective, King's How, is spellbinding.

Carefully retrace your climb. At the foot of the slate tip keep right to come beside a fence to reach a hand-gate and steps, with fine craggy views on either side. Descending via a wall gap, reach the cobbled bridle-track (the Cumbria Way) in the hidden valley, heading down, via a gate, into woodland. The track comes to a broad shingled bend in the river, beautifully shrouded in woodland; take a moment to appreciate the lovely setting.

Cross a footbridge and then join the track, which becomes a roadway leading into Grange-in-Borrowdale, where the café might tempt you to take a short break. Go right to cross the double-arched Grange Bridge. At the road junction turn left and slip over the low wall to hug the river on a path which avoids the discomforts of the oft-busy valley road. At a trio of gauges the path swings up to run on beside the road.

Cross the road opposite Riverside, following the access lane to Troutdale, passing to the rear of Leathes Hotel, to reach a gate after Troutdale Lodge, from where you enter the bracken-floored valley, encircled by rich woodland, with Black Crag looming ahead. Don't ford Troutdale Beck. The path, entering woodland, climbs close to its tumbling waters, becoming stone-stepped and climbing to a stile. The narrow-stepped way eventually emerges onto a marshy hollow. Keep right, climbing the northern slope to the bare summit of **King's How**. The position and elevation gives a peerless perspective over the head of Borrowdale, the Jaws of Borrowdale and Derwentwater.

Descend north but watch to cut back left into the aforementioned damp hollow, heading east to cross a ladder-stile. The obvious path winds up through the heather and outcropping to reach a rock 'door', with the true summit, **Brund Fell**, that to the left.

Descend east with the ridge trail to a ladder-stile, left of the wall-step. Cross and descend the damp moor south. Go straight over the popular bridleway at the top of Puddingstone Bank, via the facing hand-gate. Continue on a moorland path, which comes to a further hand-gate, where you bear left, guided by green-topped posts (avoiding the bog-myrtle mire ahead). This path joins the path rising from Watendlath, swinging right, skirting the marshy moorland, with the benefit of the odd set of stepping-stones. The route draws up by a gill to a hand-gate then mounts a flight of pitched steps, of great assistance in reaching the summit of **Great Crag**. Watch for the right-hand turn to reach the top – there are two cairned tops actually.

From the south top cut back east and follow the path, skirting to the left-hand side of a marshy hollow, to rejoin the ridge path coming along the rough heather-decked fringe of **Dock Tarn**. It is all too easy to find yourself in heather-tangled, pathless terrain; finding the tarn is key. The ridge path beyond the tarn angles southwest, descending to a stile, with a superb view of Eagle Crag and Langstrath ahead. The path passes a ruin on Lingy End and then sets to work descending the steep stone steps into the native woodland; don't rush.

Lower down, on passing through a hand-gate the slope eases; your route angles west, coming upon the valley bridleway (the Coast to Coast Walk). After a gate continue with the stony path, which alternates as a walled lane with gates, leading by the bank of **Stonethwaite Beck**, to arrive at the entrance to Hazel Bank at the foot of the Puddingstone Bank path. Here cross the **Derwent** bridge to return to the start in Rosthwaite, beside the bus stop.

3 THE GILLERCOMB SKYLINE

Start/Finish	Seathwaite **12**
Distance	8.5km/5¼ miles
Ascent/Descent	790m/2590ft
Time	5hr
Terrain	Pitching by Sour Milk Gill gives way to uncertain boulders as you search for the thin path below the Hanging Stone to gain the simple ridge to Base Brown. Thereafter there is no hindrance on the ridge connections. A pathless stretch ensues down Seatoller Common to the wad mines then a steep zig-zag into thorn and bracken on the final descent towards the river.
Summits	Base Brown, Green Gable, Brandreth and Grey Knotts

A rounded fell expedition, part heavily trodden, part seldom trodden, consistently rewarding. The circuit exalts Base Brown, Green Gable and Grey Knotts as viewpoints and cautiously introduces the seldom-visited wad mines.

Park either beside the road leading to Seathwaite farm or in the allocated field to the right of the farmyard entrance. Walk through the cobbled farmyard

↑ *Green Gable from Brandreth*

WALKING THE LAKE DISTRICT FELLS – BORROWDALE

between the white-washed house and barns, seeking the gate, right, midway, which gives access to a footpath in the walled lane, leading to a gated footbridge over the Derwent. Stride forward, ascending to a shallow-angled ladder-stile. The pitched path winds up the steep rough slope, coming close to an eye-catching cascade in Sour Milk Gill, then tackles a grooved slab to duly arrive at the intake wall; go left, over a glacially rounded outcrop, to a hand-gate. Keep to the pitched path as Gillercomb opens; ahead the impressive cliff of Raven Crag (Gillercomb Buttress) holds attention.

As the trail curves left break away, with no apparent path, targeting a very large boulder, clambering over slightly awkward rocks. Keeping to the right of the boulder, you will soon

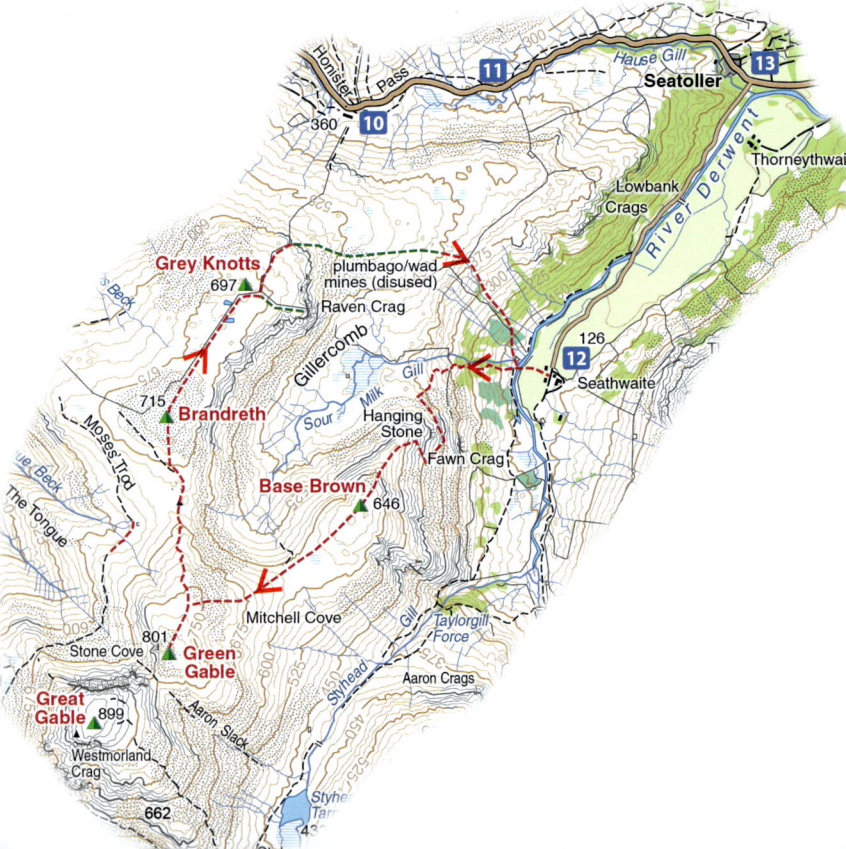

Haystacks from Green Gable

discover the faint trace of a path. This takes you left to completely avoid the cliff, passing under the perilously perched **Hanging Stone**. The path dips then cuts back, clambering up the grassy steps onto the ridge. The simple ridge pitches up once more to reach the summit cairn of **Base Brown**.

Maintaining a southwesterly course, walk easily down to where the main path out of Gillercomb – the path you were on lower down, in fact – gains the ridge at a stone gutter. The loose stones and cairns are indicative of the path's popularity. Push on up to reach the summit of **Green Gable**.

From here backtrack, using the line of old metal boundary stakes as your clue to the way down to the pools in the saddle of Gillercomb Head. Skirt to the right, proceeding up the rocky ramble north to the summit of **Brandreth**, identified by the metal stakes.

Follow the ridge-top fence, on the right-hand side (ignore the kissing-gate), past the lovely pools to the outcrop marking the top of **Grey Knotts**. Go east off the rocky crown to where the fence forks. Cautious walkers might be tempted to follow the fence further east to peer into the huge hanging valley of Gillercomb from the perilous brink (which forms the top stance of the famous Gillercomb Buttress climb). From the fence fork, cross the paling; the path descends on the left side of the broken fence until a stile sets it on the right (east) side. Continue down, passing a cairn, via two minor rock-steps. As the slope eases veer away east, onto the pathless moor; what appears to be a sheep path materialises, dipping down. The slope eases once more. Cross damp patches to find the topmost excavation evidence of the **wad mines**.

Cross the ladder-stile spanning the common-bounding wall then keep to the right-hand path, descending in a series of rather vague zig-zags, with opportunities to view the mine adits. **Do not enter the mines; there are vertical shafts near the entrances!** The slope is covered with anthills and, lower down, thorn and bracken make life less comfortable. Stick close to – though not in – the descending gill until forced to ford, then slip through the gap in the descending wall to reach the footbridge spanning **Sour Milk Gill**, by an old fold. Continue to reach and cross the **Derwent** footbridge once again, retracing your earlier route back to Seathwaite farm.

Base Brown from the brink of Raven Crag

4 GLARAMARA RIDGE WALK

Start/Finish	Seatoller **13**
Distance	14km/8¾ miles
Ascent/Descent	995m/3265ft
Time	6hr 30min
Terrain	Just one predictable obstacle, the summit of Glaramara: the main path confronts a long rock-step, invariably wet and slick, but this can be circumnavigated by steering right as you approach the cairn at the base.
Summits	Glaramara and Allen Crags

A much-loved fellwalking trip in the heart of the Cumbrian mountains, with fine views to east and west from the ridge-top and intimate valley scenes on the return.

Leave the car park by the Rosthwaite footpath, diagonally opposite the entrance; this leads to a gate/stile, after which keep the wall close right, passing above and behind the Glaramara Centre. Go through a hand-gate and enter an open oakwood. At the third wall-gap steer right, down to a stone bridge spanning the Derwent, then pass through the gate into the valley

↑ *Borrowdale from Thorneythwaite Fell*

Great Gable from the ridge south of Glaramara

pasture and continue to a gate into a short lane, beside the handsome twin terrace of **Mountain View**. Cross straight over the valley road, following the **Thorneythwaite farm** lane.

Soon come upon a footpath sign 'Glaramara 2 miles' at a gate on the left. Join the rising track, passing through open woodland and up by a gate. Soon the trees recede. After the second gate admire the Combe Gill cascades close left. You might also notice that the track is disturbed, secreting the hydro-scheme pipe. The path, with some pitching, winds attractively up the **Thorneythwaite Fell** ridge, giving fine views east towards Bessyboot, Rosthwaite Cam, Dovenest Crag and the wild mountain hollow set deep beneath Combe Head. The trail takes a right turn near the traces of an ancient wall and skirts round the right-hand side of a rock bluff, with further pitching, past a cairn which boasts a lovely view north through the Jaws of Borrowdale.

You might be tempted to visit the cairn atop Combe Head – though the hollow immediately to its south is excessively marshy, the strict ridge route using stones to cope with the wet ground. The ultimate bastion of **Glaramara** is an obstacle; the path is confronted with a genuine scramble. Being north-facing, it is always wet and is dicey when icy. It can be avoided by skirting round to the right, accessing the crowning cairn from the south. This is a great spot, a worthy ambition with a fine prospect.

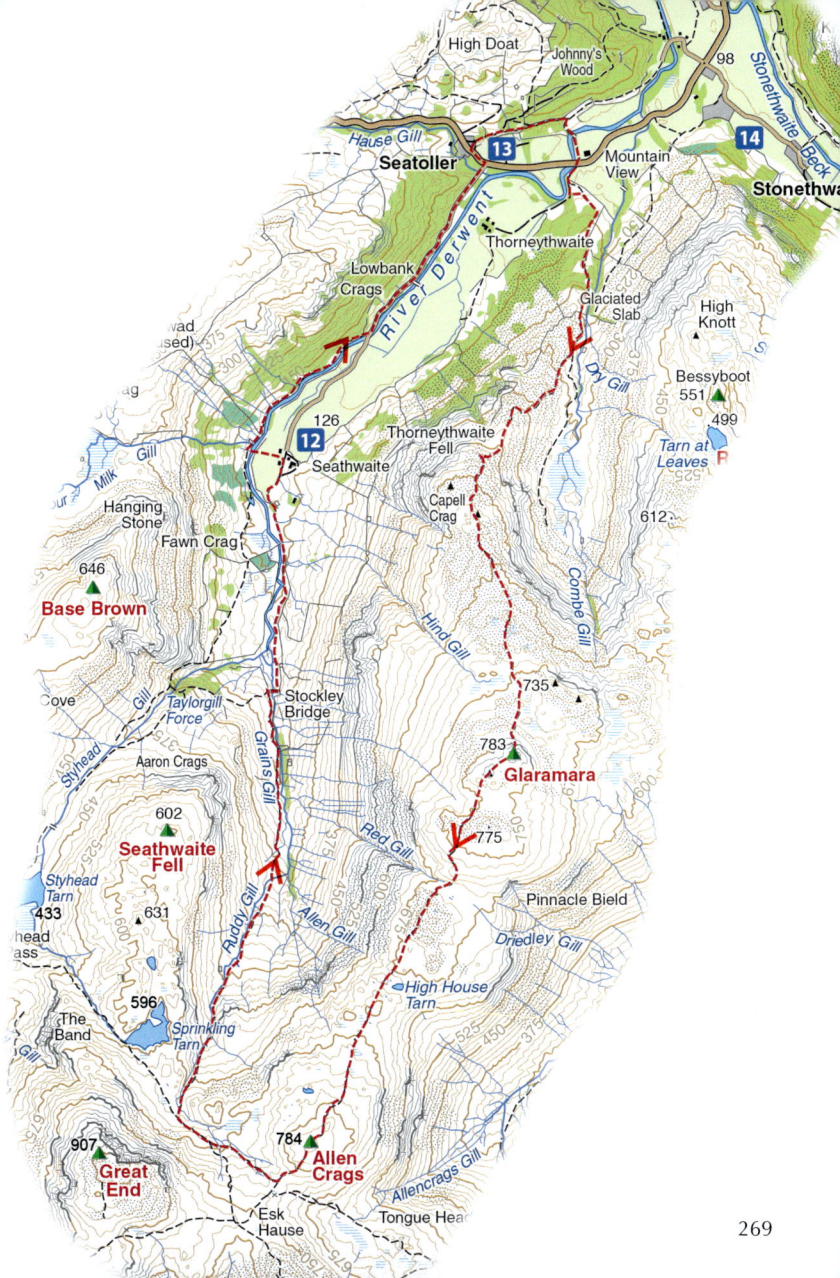

The ridge path leads on south-southwest, dipping and rising; it contrives to seem longer than you might imagine but is never dull. Be sure to make time to admire the various pools and tarns set among the rocky terrain; they all have charm. The summit cairn of **Allen Crags** is a fine place to pause before the quick descent to the saddle, the high point of the ancient bridleway from Sty Head to Great Langdale.

Short of the cross-wall shelter, turn right. Soon the headstream of **Ruddy Gill** appears, close right, and after a path (descending from Esk Hause) merges from the left the ravine becomes deeper. But there is respite where you take leave of the Sty Head path, forking right to cross stepping-stones over Ruddy Gill. The journey is now down-dale, frequent pitching reflecting its popularity, clear every step of the way. Two minor fords lead to a footbridge where you can admire the jubilant waters-meet of Allen Gill. Hereon the valley stream is known as **Grains Gill**. Later, coming by a wall, pass through a gate to cross the exquisitely picturesque **Stockley Bridge**.

The cobbled way leads on, via gates, to enter the farmyard of **Seathwaite farm**. You can simply follow the road; however, the more charming option is to pass under the barn canopy and follow the walled lane to a footbridge over the **Derwent**, turn right and cross a second, smaller footbridge, then follow the riverside trail to Seathwaite Bridge, where you join the valley road to Seatoller and your start point.

Rock pool near High House Tarn

Looking down on Wasdale from Westmorland Cairn, Great Gable

MORE TO EXPLORE

Circular
- from Seatoller **13** or Stonethwaite **14**: Bessyboot (Rosthwaite Fell) – Rosthwaite Cam (Rosthwaite Fell) – Glaramara – Thornythwaite Fell (Glaramara)
- from Great Wood **19**: Walla Crag – Bleaberry Fell – High Seat
- from Stonethwaite **14**: Eagle Crag – Sergeant's Crag – High Raise – Ullscarf

USEFUL CONTACTS

Tourist information
The Moot Hall in Keswick is the focal tourist information centre for this guide. There is also an information point in Borrowdale, at Seatoller.

Keswick
keswicktic@lake-district.gov.uk
tel 0845 901 0845

Seatoller Barn
tel 017687 77294

Accommodation
In addition to the tourist information centres and search engines, the Visit Cumbria website has a good database of local accommodation options:
www.visitcumbria.com.

Weather
It is well worth consulting either of these forecasts to gauge the best times to be on the tops.

Lake District Weatherline
tel 0844 846 2444
www.lakedistrictweatherline.co.uk

Mountain Weather Information Service
Full mountain forecasts for 3 days at a time
www.mwis.org.uk (choose English and Welsh Forecast/Lake District)
App: Mountain Forecast Viewer

Transport
Traveline
Information on buses, trains and coaches – such as they are
www.traveline.info

Stagecoach
Bus information
www.stagecoachbus.com
App: Stagecoach Bus

Organisations

The National Trust
The National Trust owns 90% of the farms in the national park, as well as historic sites and properties, camp sites and car parks.
www.nationaltrust.org.uk
App: National Trust – Days Out

Fix the Fells
Fix the Fells repairs and maintains 351 upland paths in the national park. Read about their work, volunteer or donate on this website.
www.fixthefells.co.uk

Mountain Rescue
The Lake District Search and Mountain Rescue Association manages 12 teams of volunteers across the national park. The site has useful safety information. Downloading the free OS Locate app will enable you to tell the team your grid ref, whether you have phone signal or not, should you need to call them.
www.ldsamra.org.uk

A FELLRANGER'S GLOSSARY

Navigational features

Word	Explanation
arête	knife-edge ridge
band	binding strip of land
bank-barn	barn accessible on two levels (often built on a slope or bank)
beck	main stream flowing into and through valleys to lakes and rivers
boiler-plates	non-technical term for exposed broad slabs of rock
cairn/man	small pile of loose stones indicating a path or path junction
clint	block forming part of a natural limestone pavement
combe/cove	hanging valley high in the fells
common	undivided land grazed by several farmers
cop	viewpoint
crag	substantial outcrop of rock
dale	valley
dodd	rounded hilltop
drumlin	large mound that accumulated beneath a melting glacier
dub	dark pool
fell	mountain pasture – frequently attributed to the whole hill
force	waterfall
garth	small enclosure close to farm buildings
gate	dialect term for a track
ghyll/gill	steeply sloping watercourse
glen	from British term 'glyn' meaning valley
grain	lesser watercourse above a confluence
hag	eroded section of peat moor
hause, saddle, col, dore, scarth	high gap between fells
holm	dry riverside meadow
hope	secluded valley
howe	hill or mound
ill	treacherous
intake	upper limit of valley enclosure
keld	spring
knott	compact or rugged hilltop
laithe	barn in the field or on the fell (rather than next to the farmstead)
ling	heather

A FELLRANGER'S GLOSSARY *continued*

lonnin	quiet lane
man	from Celtic term 'maen' meaning stone marker
mell	bald hill
mere	pool or lake
mire	marshy ground
moraine	residual valley-head pillow-mound debris left after a glacier melts away
nab, naze	hill-spur or nose
ness	promontory
nether	lower
nook	secluded corner
outcrop	crag or obvious collection of rocks
out-gang	shepherds' drove lane to a particular fell pasture
park	enclosed hunting ground
pike	sharp or rocky summit
place	plot of ground
raise	heap of stones
rake	grooved track
ridding	(the action of) clearing
rigg	ridge
roche moutonnée	a 'sheep-back' rock formation created by the passing of a glacier
scale	summer-pasture shieling (hut)
scarp/scar	steep hillside
scree	weathered rock debris beneath a crag
seat	summer pasture/high place
shaw	small wood
sheep-creep	small field-to-field access-hole/gap for sheep
shelter-cairn	circular wind-break wall
shieling	hut built for use while pasturing
sike	small stream
slack	small, shallow or stony valley
sled-gate	track for pony-drawn sledges
slump	sedimentary rock that has slipped, creating dykes (intrusions), fractures or ridges
stang	pole
stead	site of a farm

sty	steep path
swine	pigs
tarn	small mountain pool, from the Norse 'tjorn' meaning tear
thwaite	clearing
tongue	'a low jutting ridge'
traverse	walking route across the fells
trig point	Ordnance Survey triangulation column
trod	path created by animals
wash-fold	sheepfold where sheep were once gathered for washing in the beck
water	feeder lake to a river
wath	ford
whin	gorse
wick	inlet or bay or subsidiary farm
wray	secluded corner
yeat	gate

Place names

Name	Explanation
Bessyboot	refers to a 'lost' sheepfold, apparently once known as Elizabeth's bothy – in local vernacular, Bessyboot
Binka Stone	'bink' = a doorstep
Blea (Tarn)	'coarse or rough ground'
Brockle Beck	'stream associated with badgers'
Caffel Side	'red deer calf's fellside'
Cockrigg Crags	'the courtship ground of black cock'
Derwent	'the oak-fringed river'
Dock (Tarn)	from the Old English 'docce' meaning 'water lily'
Gillercomb	'the hanging valley with a striking outflow ravine' (Sour Milk Gill)
Grange (-in-Borrowdale)	'home (granary store) farm' (established by the monks of Furness Abbey)
Hogg's Earth	'the shelter of over-wintering hoggets' (yearling sheep)
Langstrath	originally 'Langstrode' ('the long marsh overgrown with brushwood'), later corrupted to Langstrath ('strath' meaning 'valley')
Launchy (Ghyll)	from the Old Norse 'laun' meaning 'secret'
Lincomb (Tarn)	'upland hollow with deep pools'

A FELLRANGER'S GLOSSARY *continued*

Low Scawdel	'bald head'
Man	'the stones'
Mart Bield	'the shelter of pine marten'
Rosthwaite	'the enclosure surrounding a cairn'
Rosthwaite Cam	from its likeness to the crookedly set stones used to cap drystone walls, known as cams
Ruddy Gill	'red-banked ravine'
Seatoller	'summer dwelling in the alders'
Seathwaite	'summer dwelling in a clearing'
Shoulthwaite	thought to mean 'circular enclosure' – suggesting, perhaps, a lost round-house?
Sty Head	'top of the steep path' (from Wasdale)
The Pewits	'pewit' is another name for the green plover or lapwing, reflecting its 'pee-wit' call
Sprinkling Tarn	from the same root as the River Sprint, 'to spurt'
Stockley (Bridge)	'clearing with tree trunks'
Thirlmere	'lake of the giant'
Watendlath	'water-end laithe (barn)'

Fell names
Just the more intriguing ones…

Name	**Explanation**
Base Brown	'Bruni's cowshed'
Brandreth	'the beacon place' (a 'brandreth' being a three-footed metal fire-stand)
Catbells	'bell-shaped summit of wild-cats'
Glaramara	originally 'Houedgleuermerhe', meaning 'headland of the shieling by the chasms'; the 'Houed' was dropped when the summer-farmstead was lost
High Spy	'lookout hill'
High Tove	'tove' = a variant of 'tuft', descriptive of the clumps of rushes
Sergeant's Crag	seemingly named after a William Sargyante, referred to in 1602; the surname is derived from Land Sargeant, someone responsible for defining and enforcing manorial estate boundaries
Ullscarf	'wolf gap'

THE LAKE DISTRICT FELLS

Fell name	Height	Volume
Allen Crags	784m/2572ft	Borrowdale
Angletarn Pikes	567m/1860ft	Mardale and the Far East
Ard Crags	581m/1906ft	Buttermere
Armboth Fell	479m/1572ft	Borrowdale
Arnison Crag	434m/1424ft	Patterdale
Arthur's Pike	533m/1749ft	Mardale and the Far East
Bakestall	673m/2208ft	Keswick
Bannerdale Crags	683m/2241ft	Keswick
Barf	468m/1535ft	Keswick
Barrow	456m/1496ft	Buttermere
Base Brown	646m/2119ft	Borrowdale
Beda Fell	509m/1670ft	Mardale and the Far East
Bell Crags	558m/1831ft	Borrowdale
Binsey	447m/1467ft	Keswick
Birkhouse Moor	718m/2356ft	Patterdale
Birks	622m/2241ft	Patterdale
Black Combe	600m/1969ft	Coniston
Black Fell	322m/1056ft	Coniston
Blake Fell	573m/1880ft	Buttermere
Bleaberry Fell	589m/1932ft	Borrowdale
Blea Rigg	556m/1824ft	Langdale
Blencathra	868m/2848ft	Keswick
Bonscale Pike	529m/1736ft	Mardale and the Far East
Bowfell	903m/2963ft	Langdale
Bowscale Fell	702m/2303ft	Keswick
Brae Fell	586m/1923ft	Keswick
Brandreth	715m/2346ft	Borrowdale
Branstree	713m/2339ft	Mardale and the Far East
Brim Fell	795m/2608ft	Coniston
Brock Crags	561m/1841ft	Mardale and the Far East

THE LAKE DISTRICT FELLS *continued*

Fell name	Height	Volume
Broom Fell	511m/1676ft	Keswick
Buckbarrow (Corney Fell)	549m/1801ft	Coniston
Buckbarrow (Wast Water)	430m/1411ft	Wasdale
Calf Crag	537m/1762ft	Langdale
Carl Side	746m/2448ft	Keswick
Carrock Fell	662m/2172ft	Keswick
Castle Crag	290m/951ft	Borrowdale
Catbells	451m/1480ft	Borrowdale
Catstycam	890m/2920ft	Patterdale
Caudale Moor	764m/2507ft	Mardale and the Far East
Causey Pike	637m/2090ft	Buttermere
Caw	529m/1736ft	Coniston
Caw Fell	697m/2287ft	Wasdale
Clough Head	726m/2386ft	Patterdale
Cold Pike	701m/2300ft	Langdale
Coniston Old Man	803m/2635ft	Coniston
Crag Fell	523m/1716ft	Wasdale
Crag Hill	839m/2753ft	Buttermere
Crinkle Crags	860m/2822ft	Langdale
Dale Head	753m/2470ft	Buttermere
Dodd	502m/1647ft	Keswick
Dollywaggon Pike	858m/2815ft	Patterdale
Dove Crag	792m/2599ft	Patterdale
Dow Crag	778m/2552ft	Coniston
Eagle Crag	520m/1706ft	Borrowdale
Eskdale Moor	337m/1105ft	Wasdale
Esk Pike	885m/2904ft	Langdale
Fairfield	873m/2864ft	Patterdale
Fellbarrow	416m/1365ft	Buttermere
Fleetwith Pike	648m/2126ft	Buttermere

Fell name	Height	Volume
Froswick	720m/2362ft	Mardale and the Far East
Gavel Fell	526m/1726ft	Buttermere
Gibson Knott	421m/1381ft	Langdale
Glaramara	783m/2569ft	Borrowdale
Glenridding Dodd	442m/1450ft	Patterdale
Gowbarrow Fell	481m/1578ft	Patterdale
Grange Fell	416m/1365ft	Borrowdale
Grasmoor	852m/2795ft	Buttermere
Gray Crag	697m/2287ft	Mardale and the Far East
Grayrigg Forest	494m/1621ft	Mardale and the Far East
Graystones	456m/1496ft	Keswick
Great Borne	616m/2021ft	Buttermere
Great Calva	690m/2264ft	Keswick
Great Carrs	788m/2585ft	Coniston
Great Cockup	526m/1726ft	Keswick
Great Crag	452m/1483ft	Borrowdale
Great Dodd	857m/2812ft	Patterdale
Great End	907m/2976ft	Borrowdale, Langdale, Wasdale
Great Gable	899m/2949ft	Borrowdale, Wasdale
Great How	523m/1716ft	Wasdale
Great Mell Fell	537m/1762ft	Patterdale
Great Rigg	767m/2516ft	Patterdale
Great Sca Fell	651m/2136ft	Keswick
Great Worm Crag	427m/1401ft	Coniston
Green Crag	489m/1604ft	Coniston
Green Gable	801m/2628ft	Borrowdale
Grey Crag	638m/2093ft	Mardale and the Far East
Grey Friar	772m/2533ft	Coniston
Grey Knotts	697m/2287ft	Borrowdale

THE LAKE DISTRICT FELLS *continued*

Fell name	Height	Volume
Grike	488m/1601ft	Wasdale
Grisedale Pike	791m/2595ft	Buttermere
Hallin Fell	388m/1273ft	Mardale and the Far East
Hard Knott	552m/1811ft	Coniston
Harrison Stickle	736m/2415ft	Langdale
Hart Crag	822m/2697ft	Patterdale
Harter Fell (Eskdale)	653m/2142ft	Coniston
Harter Fell (Mardale)	778m/2553ft	Mardale and the Far East
Hart Side	758m/2487ft	Patterdale
Hartsop above How	586m/1923ft	Patterdale
Hartsop Dodd	618m/2028ft	Mardale and the Far East
Haycock	798m/2618ft	Wasdale
Haystacks	598m/1962ft	Buttermere
Helm Crag	405m/1329ft	Langdale
Helvellyn	950m/3116ft	Patterdale
Hen Comb	509m/1670ft	Buttermere
Heron Pike	621m/2037ft	Patterdale
Hesk Fell	476m/1562ft	Coniston
High Crag	744m/2441ft	Buttermere
High Hartsop Dodd	519m/1703ft	Patterdale
High Pike (Caldbeck)	658m/2159ft	Keswick
High Pike (Scandale Fell)	656m/2152ft	Patterdale
High Raise (Central Fells)	762m/2500ft	Langdale
High Raise (Haweswater)	802m/2631ft	Mardale and the Far East
High Rigg	355m/1165ft	Borrowdale
High Seat	608m/1995ft	Borrowdale
High Spy	653m/2142ft	Borrowdale
High Stile	807m/2648ft	Buttermere
High Street	828m/2717ft	Mardale and the Far East
High Tove	515m/1690ft	Borrowdale

Fell name	Height	Volume
Hindscarth	727m/2385ft	Buttermere
Holme Fell	317m/1040ft	Coniston
Hopegill Head	770m/2526ft	Buttermere
Ill Bell	757m/2484ft	Mardale and the Far East
Illgill Head	609m/1998ft	Wasdale
Iron Crag	640m/2100ft	Wasdale
Kentmere Pike	730m/2395ft	Mardale and the Far East
Kidsty Pike	780m/2559ft	Mardale and the Far East
Kirk Fell	802m/2631ft	Wasdale
Knock Murton	447m/1467ft	Buttermere
Knott	710m/2329ft	Keswick
Knott Rigg	556m/1824ft	Buttermere
Lank Rigg	541m/1775ft	Wasdale
Latrigg	368m/1207ft	Keswick
Ling Fell	373m/1224ft	Keswick
Lingmell	807m/2649ft	Wasdale
Lingmoor Fell	470m/1542ft	Langdale
Little Hart Crag	637m/2090ft	Patterdale
Little Mell Fell	505m/1657ft	Patterdale
Little Stand	739m/2426ft	Langdale
Loadpot Hill	671m/2201ft	Mardale and the Far East
Loft Crag	682m/2237ft	Langdale
Longlands Fell	483m/1585ft	Keswick
Long Side	734m/2408ft	Keswick
Lonscale Fell	715m/2346ft	Keswick
Lord's Seat	552m/1811ft	Keswick
Loughrigg Fell	335m/1099ft	Langdale
Low Fell	423m/1388ft	Buttermere
Low Pike	507m/1663ft	Patterdale
Maiden Moor	576m/1890ft	Borrowdale

THE LAKE DISTRICT FELLS *continued*

Fell name	Height	Volume
Mardale Ill Bell	761m/2497ft	Mardale and the Far East
Meal Fell	550m/1804ft	Keswick
Mellbreak	512m/1680ft	Buttermere
Middle Dodd	653m/2143ft	Patterdale
Middle Fell	585m/1919ft	Wasdale
Muncaster Fell	231m/758ft	Coniston
Nab Scar	450m/1476ft	Patterdale
Nethermost Pike	891m/2923ft	Patterdale
Outerside	568m/1863ft	Buttermere
Pavey Ark	697m/2287ft	Langdale
Pike o'Blisco	705m/2313ft	Langdale
Pike o'Stickle	708m/2323ft	Langdale
Pillar	892m/2926ft	Wasdale
Place Fell	657m/2155ft	Mardale and the Far East
Raise	884m/2900ft	Patterdale
Rampsgill Head	792m/2598ft	Mardale and the Far East
Rannerdale Knotts	355m/1165ft	Buttermere
Raven Crag	463m/1519ft	Borrowdale
Red Pike (Buttermere)	755m/2477ft	Buttermere
Red Pike (Wasdale)	828m/2717ft	Wasdale
Red Screes	777m/2549ft	Patterdale
Rest Dodd	697m/2287ft	Mardale and the Far East
Robinson	737m/2418ft	Buttermere
Rossett Pike	651m/2136ft	Langdale
Rosthwaite Fell	551m/1808ft	Borrowdale
Sail	771m/2529ft	Buttermere
Sale Fell	359m/1178ft	Keswick
Sallows	516m/1693ft	Mardale and the Far East
Scafell	964m/3163ft	Wasdale

Fell name	Height	Volume
Scafell Pike	977m/3206ft	Borrowdale, Langdale, Wasdale
Scar Crags	672m/2205ft	Buttermere
Scoat Fell	843m/2766ft	Wasdale
Seatallan	693m/2274ft	Wasdale
Seathwaite Fell	631m/2070ft	Borrowdale
Seat Sandal	736m/2415ft	Patterdale
Selside Pike	655m/2149ft	Mardale and the Far East
Sergeant Man	736m/2414ft	Langdale
Sergeant's Crag	574m/1883ft	Borrowdale
Sheffield Pike	675m/2215ft	Patterdale
Shipman Knotts	587m/1926ft	Mardale and the Far East
Silver How	395m/1296ft	Langdale
Skiddaw	931m/3054ft	Keswick
Skiddaw Little Man	865m/2838ft	Keswick
Slight Side	762m/2500ft	Wasdale
Souther Fell	522m/1713ft	Keswick
Stainton Pike	498m/1634ft	Coniston
Starling Dodd	635m/2083ft	Buttermere
Steel Fell	553m/1814ft	Langdale
Steel Knotts	433m/1421ft	Mardale and the Far East
Steeple	819m/2687ft	Wasdale
Stickle Pike	376m/1234ft	Coniston
Stone Arthur	503m/1650ft	Patterdale
St Sunday Crag	841m/2759ft	Patterdale
Stybarrow Dodd	846m/2776ft	Patterdale
Swirl How	804m/2638ft	Coniston
Tarn Crag (Easedale)	485m/1591ft	Langdale
Tarn Crag (Longsleddale)	664m/2179ft	Mardale and the Far East
Thornthwaite Crag	784m/2572ft	Mardale and the Far East

THE LAKE DISTRICT FELLS *continued*

Fell name	Height	Volume
Thunacar Knott	723m/2372ft	Langdale
Troutbeck Tongue	363m/1191ft	Mardale and the Far East
Ullock Pike	690m/2264ft	Keswick
Ullscarf	726m/2382ft	Borrowdale
Walla Crag	379m/1243ft	Borrowdale
Wallowbarrow Crag	292m/958ft	Coniston
Walna Scar	621m/2037ft	Coniston
Wandope	772m/2533ft	Buttermere
Wansfell	489m/1604ft	Mardale and the Far East
Watson's Dodd	789m/2589ft	Patterdale
Wether Hill	673m/2208ft	Mardale and the Far East
Wetherlam	762m/2500ft	Coniston
Whinfell Beacon	472m/1549ft	Mardale and the Far East
Whinlatter	517m/1696ft	Keswick
Whin Rigg	536m/1759ft	Wasdale
Whiteless Pike	660m/2165ft	Buttermere
Whiteside	707m/2320ft	Buttermere
White Side	863m/2831ft	Patterdale
Whitfell	573m/1880ft	Coniston
Winterscleugh	464m/1522ft	Mardale and the Far East
Yewbarrow	628m/2060ft	Wasdale
Yoadcastle	494m/1621ft	Coniston
Yoke	706m/2316ft	Mardale and the Far East

LISTING OF CICERONE GUIDES

BRITISH ISLES CHALLENGES, COLLECTIONS AND ACTIVITIES

Great Walks on the England Coast Path
Map and Compass
The Big Rounds
The Book of the Bivvy
The Book of the Bothy
The Mountains of England and Wales
  Vol 1 — Wales
  Vol 2 — England
The National Trails
Walking the End to End Trail
Cycling Land's End to John o' Groats

LAKE DISTRICT

Bikepacking in the Lake District
Cycling in the Lake District
Joss Naylor's Lakes, Meres and Waters of the Lake District
Lake District Winter Climbs
Lake District: High Level and Fell Walks
Lake District: Low Level and Lake Walks
Mountain Biking in the Lake District
Outdoor Adventures with Children — Lake District
Scrambles in the Lake District — North
Scrambles in the Lake District — South
Trail and Fell Running in the Lake District
Walking The Cumbria Way
Walking the Lake District Fells
  — Borrowdale
  — Buttermere
  — Coniston
  — Keswick
  — Langdale
  — Mardale and the Far East
  — Patterdale
  — Wasdale
Walking the Tour of the Lake District

NORTH-WEST ENGLAND AND THE ISLE OF MAN

Walking the King Charles III England Coast Path: North West
Walking the King Charles III England Coast Path: North West
  — Cumbria Map Booklet
  — Lancashire and Merseyside Map Booklet
Cycling the Pennine Bridleway
Walking the Pennine Way
Walking the Pennine Way Map Booklet
Isle of Man Coastal Path
The Lune Valley and Howgills
Walking in Cumbria's Eden Valley
Walking in Lancashire
Walking in the Forest of Bowland and Pendle
Walking on the Isle of Man
Walking on the West Pennine Moors
Walking the Ribble Way
Hadrian's Wall Path
Hadrian's Wall Path Map Booklet
The Coast to Coast Cycle Route
The Coast to Coast Map Booklet
The Coast to Coast Walk

NORTH-EAST ENGLAND, YORKSHIRE DALES AND PENNINES

Walking the Dales Way
The Dales Way Map Booklet
Cycling the Reivers Route
Cycling the Way of the Roses
Cycling in the Yorkshire Dales
Great Mountain Days in the Pennines
Mountain Biking in the Yorkshire Dales
The Cleveland Way and the Yorkshire Wolds Way
The Cleveland Way Map Booklet
The North York Moors
Trail and Fell Running in the Yorkshire Dales
Walking in County Durham
Walking in Northumberland
Walking in Northumberland
Walking in the North Pennines
Walking in the Yorkshire Dales
  — North and East
  — South and West
Walking St Cuthbert's Way
Walking St Oswald's Way and Northumberland Coast Path

DERBYSHIRE, PEAK DISTRICT AND MIDLANDS

Cycling in the Peak District
Dark Peak Walks
Scrambles in the Dark Peak
Walking in Derbyshire
Walking in the Peak District
  — White Peak East
  — White Peak West

SOUTHERN ENGLAND

20 Classic Sportive Rides in South East England
20 Classic Sportive Rides in South West England
Bikepacking — South East Gravel
Cycling in the Cotswolds
Mountain Biking on the North Downs
South West Coast Path Map Booklet
  — Vol 1: Minehead to St Ives
  — Vol 2: St Ives to Plymouth
  — Vol 3: Plymouth to Poole
Suffolk Coast and Heath Walks
The Cotswold Way
The Cotswold Way Map Booklet
The Kennet and Avon Canal
The Lea Valley Walk
The Lea Valley Walk
The North Downs Way
North Downs Way Map Booklet
The Peddars Way and Norfolk Coast Path
The Pilgrims' Way
The Ridgeway National Trail
The Ridgeway Map Booklet
The South Downs Way
The South Downs Way Map Booklet
The Thames Path
The Thames Path Map Booklet
The Two Moors Way
Two Moors Way Map Booklet
Walking Hampshire's Test Way
Walking in Essex
Walking in Kent
Walking in London
Walking in Norfolk
Walking in the Chilterns
Walking in the Cotswolds
Walking in the Isles of Scilly
Walking in the New Forest
Walking in the North Wessex Downs
Walking on Dartmoor
Walking on Guernsey
Walking on Jersey
Walking on the Isle of Wight
Walking the Dartmoor Way
Walking the Jurassic Coast
Walking the Sarsen Way
Walking the South West Coast Path
Walks in the South Downs National Park

WALES AND WELSH BORDERS

Cycle Touring in Wales
Cycling Lon Las Cymru
Great Mountain Days in Snowdonia
Hillwalking in Shropshire
Mountain Walking in Snowdonia
Offa's Dyke Path
Offa's Dyke Map Booklet
Scrambles in Snowdonia
Snowdonia: 30 Low-level and Easy Walks
  — North
  — South
The Cambrian Way
The Pembrokeshire Coast Path
Pembrokeshire Coast Path Map Booklet
The Snowdonia Way
The Wye Valley Walk
Walking Glyndwr's Way
Walking in Carmarthenshire
Walking in Gower
Walking in Pembrokeshire
Walking in the Brecon Beacons
Walking on Gower
Walking the Severn Way
Walking the Shropshire Way
Walking the Wales Coast Path

SHORT WALKS SERIES

15 Short Walks in Dumfries and Galloway
15 Short Walks in Perthshire North — Pitlochry, Aberfeldy and Dunkeld
15 Short Walks in the Scottish Borders
15 Short Walks in the Trossachs — Callander and Aberfoyle
15 Short Walks on the Isle of Mull
15 Short Walks on the Isle of Skye

15 Short Walks on the Orkney Islands
15 Short Walks on the Shetland Islands
15 Short Walks Hadrian's Wall
15 Short Walks in the Lake District
— Keswick, Borrowdale and Buttermere
— Windermere Ambleside and Grasmere
— Coniston and Langdale
15 Short Walks in Arnside and Silverdale
15 Short Walks in the Ribble Valley
15 Short Walks in Nidderdale
15 Short Walks in Northumberland — Wooler, Rothbury, Alnwick and the coast
15 Short Walks in the Yorkshire Dales
— Grassington, Skipton, Malham and Ilkley
— Sedbergh, Kirkby Lonsdale and Ingleton
15 Short Walks in the Peak District — Bakewell and the White Peak
15 Short Walks in the Peak District — Edale and the Hope Valley
15 Short Walks on the Malvern Hills
15 Short Walks Cheddar and the Mendips
15 Short Walks in Cornwall
— Newquay and the North Coast
— Falmouth and the Lizard
— Land's End and Penzance
15 Short Walks in Norfolk — Broads and Coast
15 Short Walks in South Devon — Salcombe, Brixham and the coast
15 Short Walks in the South Downs — Brighton, Eastbourne and Arundel
15 Short Walks in the Surrey Hills
15 Short Walks on Dartmoor North — Okehampton and Chagford
15 Short Walks on Dartmoor South — Ivybridge and Princetown
15 Short Walks on Exmoor
15 Short Walks on the Isle of Wight
15 Short Walks Winchester
15 Short Walks in Bannau Brycheiniog — Brecon Beacons
15 Short Walks in Pembrokeshire — Tenby and the south
15 Short Walks in the Forest of Dean

SCOTLAND

Ben Nevis and Glen Coe
Cycling in the Hebrides
Cycling in the Hebrides
Cycling the North Coast 500
Great Mountain Days in Scotland
Mountain Biking in Southern and Central Scotland
Mountain Biking in West and North West Scotland
Not the West Highland Way: A Mountain High Way
Scotland
Scotland's Best Small Mountains
Scottish Wild Country Backpacking
Skye Munros
Skye's Cuillin Ridge Traverse
The Borders Abbeys Way
The Hebridean Way
The Hebrides
The Isle of Skye
The Skye Trail
The Southern Upland Way
The West Highland Way
West Highland Way Map Booklet
Walking Ben Lawers, Rannoch and Atholl
Walking in the Cairngorms
Walking in the Pentland Hills
Walking in the Scottish Borders
Walking in the Southern Uplands
Walking in Torridon, Fisherfield, Fannichs and An Teallach
Walking Loch Lomond and the Trossachs
Walking on Arran
Walking on Harris and Lewis
Walking on Jura, Islay and Colonsay
Walking on Mull, Coll and Tiree
Walking on Rum and the Small Isles
Walking on the Orkney and Shetland Isles
Walking on Uist and Barra
Walking Rum and the Small Isles
Walking the Cape Wrath Trail
Walking the Corbetts
Vol 1 — South of the Great Glen
Vol 2 — North of the Great Glen
Walking the Fife Pilgrim Way
Walking the Galloway Hills
Walking the Great Glen Way
Walking the Great Glen Way Map Booklet
Walking the John o' Groats Trail
Walking the Munros
Vol 1 — Southern, Central and Western Highlands
Vol 2 — Northern Highlands and the Cairngorms
Winter Climbs in the Cairngorms
Winter Climbs: Ben Nevis and Glen Coe

ALPS CROSS-BORDER ROUTES

100 Hut Walks in the Alps
Alpine Ski Mountaineering Vol 1 — Western Alps
Hiking the Tour of Monte Rosa
The Karnischer Hohenweg
The Tour of the Bernina
Trail Running — Chamonix and the Mont Blanc region
Trekking Chamonix to Zermatt
Trekking in the Alps
Trekking in the Silvretta and Ratikon Alps
Trekking Munich to Venice
Trekking the Tour du Mont Blanc
Tour du Mont Blanc Map Booklet
Walking in the Alps

FRANCE, BELGIUM AND LUXEMBOURG

Camino de Santiago — Via Podiensis
Chamonix Mountain Adventures
Cycling London to Paris
Cycling the Canal de la Garonne
Cycling the Canal du Midi
Mont Blanc Walks
Mountain Adventures in the Maurienne
Short Treks on Corsica
The GR5 Trail — Through the French Alps
The GR5 Trail — Vosges and Jura
The Moselle Cycle Route
Trekking in the Vanoise
Trekking the Cathar Way
Trekking the GR10
Trekking the GR20 Corsica
Trekking the Robert Louis Stevenson Trail
Via Ferratas of the French Alps
Walking in Provence — East
Walking in Provence — West
Walking in the Auvergne
Walking in the Briançonnais
Walking in the Dordogne
Walking in the Haute Savoie: North
Walking in the Haute Savoie: South
Walking on Corsica
Walking the Brittany Coast Path
The GR5 Trail — Benelux and Lorraine
Walking in the Ardennes
The River Loire Cycle Route
The River Rhone Cycle Route
Cycling the Route des Grandes Alpes

PYRENEES AND FRANCE/SPAIN CROSS-BORDER ROUTES

Shorter Treks in the Pyrenees
The Pyrenean Haute Route
The Pyrenees
Trekking the Cami dels Bons Homes
Trekking the GR11 Trail
Walks and Climbs in the Pyrenees

SPAIN AND PORTUGAL

Camino de Santiago: Camino Frances
Coastal Walks in Andalucia
Costa Blanca Mountain Adventures
Cycling the Camino de Santiago
Mountain Walking in Mallorca
Mountain Walking in Southern Catalunya
Spain's Sendero Historico: The GR1
The Andalucian Coast to Coast Walk
The Camino del Norte and Camino Primitivo
The Camino Ingles and Ruta do Mar
The Mountains Around Nerja
The Mountains of Ronda and Grazalema
The Sierras of Extremadura
Trekking in Mallorca
Trekking in the Canary Islands
Trekking the GR7 in Andalucia
Walking and Trekking in the Sierra Nevada
Walking in Andalucia
Walking in Catalunya — Barcelona
Walking in Catalunya — Girona Pyrenees
Walking in the Picos de Europa
Walking La Via de la Plata and Camino Sanabres
Walking on Gran Canaria
Walking on La Gomera and El Hierro
Walking on La Palma
Walking on Lanzarote and Fuerteventura

Walking on Tenerife
Walking on the Costa Blanca
Walking the Camino dos Faros
Portugal's Rota Vicentina
The Camino Portugues
Walking in Portugal
Walking in the Algarve
Walking in the Algarve
Walking on Madeira
Walking on the Azores
Cycling the Ruta Via de la Plata

SWITZERLAND

Switzerland's Jura Crest Trail
The Swiss Alps
Tour of the Jungfrau Region
Trekking the Swiss Via Alpina
Walking in Arolla and Zinal
Walking in the Bernese Oberland — Jungfrau region
Walking in the Engadine — Switzerland
Walking in Ticino
Walking in Zermatt and Saas-Fee

GERMANY

Hiking and Cycling in the Black Forest
The Danube Cycleway Vol 1
The Rhine Cycle Route
The Westweg
Walking in the Bavarian Alps
The Elbe Cycle Route

POLAND, SLOVAKIA, ROMANIA, HUNGARY AND BULGARIA

The Danube Cycleway Vol 2
The High Tatras
The Mountains of Romania

SCANDINAVIA, ICELAND AND GREENLAND

Hiking in Norway
— North
— South
Trekking the Kungsleden
Trekking in Greenland — The Arctic Circle Trail
Walking and Trekking in Iceland

SLOVENIA, CROATIA, SERBIA, MONTENEGRO AND ALBANIA

Hiking Slovenia's Juliana Trail
Mountain Biking in Slovenia
The Islands of Croatia
The Julian Alps of Slovenia
The Mountains of Montenegro
The Peaks of the Balkans Trail
The Slovene Mountain Trail
Walking in Slovenia: The Karavanke
Walking the Julian Alps of Slovenia
Walks and Treks in Croatia

ITALY

Alta Via 1 — Trekking in the Dolomites
Alta Via 2 — Trekking in the Dolomites
Day Walks in the Dolomites
Italy's Grande Traversata delle Alpi
Ski Touring and Snowshoeing in the Dolomites
The Way of St Francis: Via di Francesco
Trekking Gran Paradiso: Alta Via 2
Trekking in the Apennines
Trekking the Giants' Trail: Alta Via 1 through the Italian Pennine Alps
Via Ferratas of the Italian Dolomites
— Vol 1
— Vol 2
Walking Gran Paradiso National Park
Walking in Abruzzo
Walking in Italy's Cinque Terre
Walking in Italy's Stelvio National Park
Walking in Sicily
Walking in the Aosta Valley
Walking in the Dolomites
Walking in Tuscany
Walking in Umbria
Walking Lake Como and Maggiore
Walking Lake Garda and Iseo
Walking on the Amalfi Coast
Walking the Cammino Materano
Walking the Via Francigena Pilgrim Route
— Part 1
— Part 2
— Part 3
— Part 4
Walks and Treks in the Maritime Alps

IRELAND

The Wild Atlantic Way and Western Ireland
Walking the Kerry Way
Walking the Wicklow Way

INTERNATIONAL CHALLENGES, COLLECTIONS AND ACTIVITIES

Europe's High Points
Pocket First Aid and Wilderness Medicine

AUSTRIA

Innsbruck Mountain Adventures
Trekking Austria's Adlerweg
Trekking in Austria's Hohe Tauern
Trekking in Austria's Stubai Alps
Trekking in Austria's Zillertal Alps
Walking in Austria
Walking in the Salzkammergut: the Austrian Lake District

MEDITERRANEAN

Trekking in Greece
Walking and Trekking in Zagori
Walking and Trekking on Corfu
Walking on the Greek Islands — the Cyclades
Walking in Cyprus
Walking on Malta

HIMALAYA

8000 metres
Annapurna
Everest: A Trekker's Guide
Trekking in the Indian Himalayas
Trekking in the Karakoram

NORTH AMERICA

Hiking and Cycling the California Missions Trail
Hiking the Pacific Crest Trail
The John Muir Trail

SOUTH AMERICA

Aconcagua and the Southern Andes
Hiking and Biking Peru's Inca Trails
Trekking in Torres del Paine

AFRICA

Climbing Toubkal
Kilimanjaro
Walking in the Drakensberg
Walks and Scrambles in the Moroccan Anti-Atlas

NEW ZEALAND AND AUSTRALIA

Hiking the Overland Track

CHINA, JAPAN AND ASIA

Hiking and Trekking in the Japan Alps and Mount Fuji
Hiking in Hong Kong
Japan's Kumano Kodo Pilgrimage
Trekking in Bhutan
Trekking in Ladakh
Trekking in Tajikistan
Trekking in the Himalaya

TECHNIQUES

Fastpacking
The Mountain Hut Book

MINI GUIDES

Alpine Flowers
Navigation

MOUNTAIN LITERATURE

A Walk in the Clouds
Abode of the Gods
Fifty Years of Adventure
The Pennine Way — the Path, the People, the Journey
Unjustifiable Risk?

For full information on all our guides, books and eBooks,
visit our website:
www.cicerone.co.uk

CICERONE

Trust Cicerone to guide your next adventure, wherever it may be around the world...

Discover guides for hiking, mountain walking, backpacking, trekking, trail running, cycling and mountain biking, ski touring, climbing and scrambling in Britain, Europe and worldwide.

Connect with Cicerone online and find inspiration.

- buy books and ebooks
- articles, advice and trip reports
- GPX files and updates
- regular newsletter

cicerone.co.uk